IT WAS
THE FACE OF
DEATH

Terrifyingly they loomed right upon us, until the line of Japanese soldiers resolved itself into just one Japanese who with each pounding stride toward me assumed increasingly fearful proportions. I could see his bloodshot eyes bulging as he stared at me, the look of the killer glaring from them . . . The muzzle of his rifle dropped to become a completely round, black hole pointing at me.

THE BANTAM WAR BOOK SERIES

This is a series of books about a world on fire.

These carefully chosen volumes cover the full dramatic sweep of World War II. Many are eyewitness accounts by the men who fought in this global conflict in which the future of the civilized world hung in balance. Fighter pilots, tank commanders and infantry commanders, among others, recount exploits of individual courage in the midst of the large-scale terrors of war. They present portraits of brave men and true stories of gallantry and cowardice in action, moving sagas of survival and tragedies of untimely death. Some of the stories are told from the enemy viewpoint to give the reader an immediate sense of the incredible life and death struggle of both sides of the battle.

Through these books we begin to discover what it was like to be there, a participant in an epic war for freedom.

Each of the books in the Bantam War Book series contains a dramatic color painting and illustrations specially commissioned for each title to give the reader a deeper understanding of the roles played by the men and machines of World War II.

THE HUNDRED DAYS OF LT. MACHORTON

IAN MACHORTON

in collaboration with Henry Maule

BANTAM BOOKS · TORONTO · NEW YORK · LONDON

*This low-priced Bantam Book
has been completely reset in a type face
designed for easy reading, and was printed
from new plates. It contains the complete
text of the original hard-cover edition.*
NOT ONE WORD HAS BEEN OMITTED.

THE HUNDRED DAYS OF LT. MACHORTON
*A Bantam Book | published by arrangement with
the author and Henry Maule*

PRINTING HISTORY
Published 1958 in Great Britain under the title,
Safer Than A Known Way
Bantam edition | March 1979
2nd printing

CONTENTS

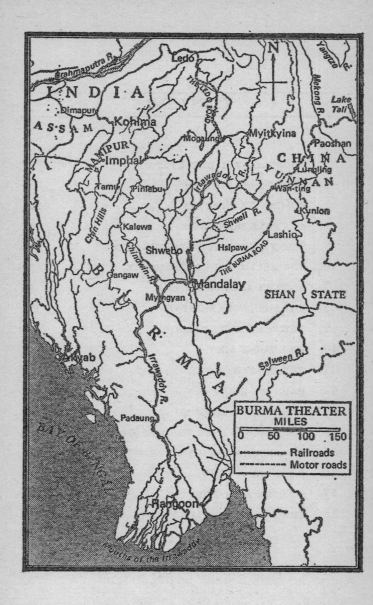

"I said to the man who stood at the gate of the year: 'Give me a light that I may tread safely into the unknown.' And he replied: 'Go out into the darkness and put your hand into the hand of God. That shall be to you better than a light and safer than a known way!'"

Lt. Ian MacHorton

THE HUNDRED DAYS OF
LT. MACHORTON

Orde Wingate

1

CHOICE OF THE BULLET

As though to make my mind up for me, the great white moon that gleamed and gloomed through the restless jungle's roof abruptly illumined the cold barrel of my revolver. Glinting in the shadowy undergrowth beside my wounded leg, the .38 Colt seemed to offer the answer to my unspoken question. Should I shoot myself, or wait until the Japs came to take me?

I gazed at it lying at the foot of the little grassy bank against which I was propped. It would all be so easy. I only had to cock it, hold it with hand on my chest so that the black-rimmed snout was between my teeth; count "one, two, three," and that was all. Just like that. Just like the Gurkha Naik Premsingh Gurung had done when we had left him behind, too badly wounded to walk, after the Kyaikthin ambush . . . Then the growing strength of my resolve drained away all in one sudden outrush. I imagined myself with the whole of the back and top of my skull blown out in a blood-bespattered ragged hole. No! That I could never do! For that I did not have the courage.

The picture of my home, my mother, my father, too startingly clear for my recent resolve to survive, flooded my mind. No! death by my own hand was not what I wanted. I wanted to live—even if it meant the vilest sort of imprisonment in Jap hands. I must live! With a peculiar detachment, as though it had been my right hand's idea all the time and not mine, I watched my fingers withdraw from the revolver's butt. After all, while there was life there really was hope. I was still alive, even if I could not walk.

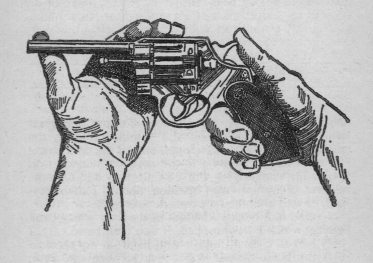

But Premsingh had been alive and strong, and all that was wrong with him was that he could not walk. He, like I, would have been carried back out of the firing line in any normal battlefield, and transported to base hospital for nursing back to health and strength. In any battlefield other than this fantastic intangible one that Wingate had chosen for his Chindits in North Burma, three hundred miles behind the Jap lines! Our rules said "Leave all wounded who can't walk." And that was why Premsingh had chosen the bullet. No emotional mental pictures had stayed his hand.

To escape from the utter aloneness that was now mine in the palpitating vastness of the jungle night I forced my mind to go back over the past twelve hours. Back over the terrifying events which had brought me to my present desperate plight. It had been at the fight on the hillside at Mong Mit, where the Japs had caught up with our party of survivors from the battered and scattered No. 2 Column of Orde Wingate's First Chindit Expedition. I had been hurled from the cover of a boulder by a great blast of air as a mortar bomb burst shatteringly behind me. With sickening force I thudded down behind another boulder six feet outside the perimeter of the defensive position where we were making our desperate stand.

Frantically I had tried to scramble back. But I could not move. I twisted around sick with apprehension to see what was trapping my leg to hold it, numbed and helpless, as though a huge tree trunk had rolled upon me. Then I saw that the faded khaki drill covering my left hip was jaggedly ripped, and around the rent there was already an ominously darkening blood-stain. I felt the sticky blood trickle down the back of my leg in a little hot eager run. Panic overwhelmed me! I could not walk! I could not move my leg! A vision of Naik Premsingh, who had been left behind in the jungle on my orders, flooded my mind.

I knew the drill all right! Lieut.-Colonel Alexander, Commander of the Gurkha group in the Expedition, had called all his officers together and made Wingate's orders patently clear before we had set out from Imphal. It had seemed to worry some of the older officers but to a brand new second lieutenant it seemed a thing which could safely be put into the back of one's mind and forgotten.

After all, I had consoled my conscience with effective ease, anyone unlucky enough to get wounded could hardly expect the whole expedition to be jeopardized just for his sake. In any case, we had all been taught the rudiments of first aid and each one had an issue of morphia with instructions how to use it. If the worst came to the worst, there was sufficient morphia to give oneself a lethal shot in the arm. Just as easy as that!

No, to me the likelihood of having to leave wounded behind to the tender mercies of the jungle and the Japs was something that it was very easy to dismiss as "just one of those things which most likely won't happen

—and almost certainly not to me!" Now it had happened!

Awful fears clamoured through my mind as I lay there in immobile agony. What would Colonel Alexander do with me? Could he be so heartless as to leave me to the tender mercies of the Japs? I, his youngest officer and still only a boy, who but yesterday had been a happy carefree schoolboy; who only a few moments ago had been a desperate but 100-per-cent physically capable, fighting man. Surely neither Colonel Alexander, nor any other of those who were my senior officers—prone off duty to be so kind and fatherly to me as the boy of the outfit—could deliberately speak the words that would sentence me to death?

Frustration, then stark terror, overwhelmed me. Frustration at being held down physically although my mind shouted to me to scramble back to safety. Terror at the prospect of being left alone in the vast and brooding twilight of the jungle until the Japs came, bringing torture and death.

Into my shocked mind there swelled a vision of a dog I had as a boy seen run over by a lorry and left, its spine broken, bewildered and frantic because its body would not respond to the messages its brain was sending for it to jump up and run away and lick its wounds. Now I was just like that. My body would not move although my whole being urged me to get back under cover. Soaked with sweat at the agony of my effort, my left leg hanging useless, I tried to pull myself up over the smooth surface of the great boulder above me. But my desperate fingers slipped so that I slithered back helpless and in despair.

The bitter battle which had burst upon us from the black depths of the jungle below our scorched hill-top, rose to a new crescendo of noise. Then, through the red mist of my pain I was aware of a face peering at me from over the top of the rock. It was Kulbahadur, my Gurkha orderly. Completely disregarding the bullets which whipped and ricocheted among the boulders like furious bees, Kulbahadur paused only to shout to someone under cover behind him before he wriggled over the boulder and dropped down to lie at my side. Next Havildar Lalbahadur, the Gurkha sergeant who was my second in command, also risked the hail of Jap bullets by slithering over the top of the boulder to reach down towards me. Kulbahadur, stocky but very strong, got his shoulder under me and pushed me up the face of the rock. Then he and Lalbahadur with tremendous exertion pushed and pulled me over the top until I dropped down behind to be with them in temporary safety once more.

Jap bullets still whined and buzzed. Mortar bombs crashed beyond and around the rocks behind us. But behind the big boulder where we lay was a haven indeed. Still gasping for breath, Kulbahadur unfastened my belt and tugged my trousers down to expose my hip and thigh, which were now a mass of blood. It was pulsing out from an ugly wound where a long thin mortar splinter had cut into flesh and muscle a few inches below the hip joint.

Havildar Lalbahadur, seeing that I was now safe from immediate danger and that Kulbahadur was treating my wound, hurled himself out bent double from the shelter of the boulder to take over my place in command of the platoon. A yard short of the boulder to which he was running to carry on controlling the fight he suddenly straightened out like a puppet on violently tugged strings. Without a cry he plunged forward, bounced when he hit the ground, jerked spasmodically, and lay still.

I closed my eyes, not only because of the sudden onrush of pain from my wound. Tough, always smiling, Havildar Lalbahadur had been one of the sure things in life. He had strength and skill-at-arms and ardent courage. He was also a faithful friend.

Across the boulder strewn hillside Captain Stocks, R.A.M.C., our Column M.O., leaped into sight ducking and weaving through the no-man's-land of grenade bursts and zipping bullets. His red cross haversack was bouncing on his hip as he ran. How he managed to get through that hail of fire unscathed, I never knew. Next moment he had reached my boulder and flung himself down beside me. He was feeling my thigh bone with one hand and my hip joint with the other.

"It's a mortar splinter," he gasped, breathless from his dash. "It's still in there. Can you move your leg?"

I tried. Pain in a searing fire swept through me and a cold sweat stood out on my brow.

"I can't, Doc, I can't," I groaned.

"Where's your morphia?" he bellowed. This I heard.

In my shocked weakness I could not even reply. But Kulbahadur rummaged in my pack and withdrew a phial. Captain Stocks ripped off the top, exposing the sterilized needle. He jabbed it into my arm and squeezed.

The pulsing of blood in my ears increased to a roaring that overwhelmed even the noise of battle. I was swallowed up in a red-black cloud of unconsciousness.

2

LEFT TO MY FATE

When I became conscious again it was quite dark. I could not think where I was. There was a vile taste in my mouth and I knew that I had been sick. Then Kulbahadur leaned over me with a water bottle. "Drink some of this, Sahib," he said with a reassuring smile. Although the water must have been warm and brackish from the torrid heat of the day in which we had fought our battle on the bald mountain top, it tasted to me now as cool and sweet as nectar.

From behind a rock another figure arose. It was Lieut. Arthur Best. "Hallo old boy, how do you feel?" he said. There was a note dangerously like compassion in his voice. My head swam as nausea overwhelmed me again. I did not answer.

"We're pulling out soon. The Japs are licking their wounds after that pasting we gave them!" Arthur went on cheerfully. "We are going to try to cross the motor road before more reinforcements appear from Mong Mit."

"We are going now?" I asked. I was conscious of a feeling almost of guilt as I said the word "we." I felt like a small boy who knows he has not been invited to go birds' nesting with the bigger boys because he is too frail to climb tall trees, yet he insists on including himself in their discussion of their plans.

"We shall be pushing off in half an hour or so," replied Arthur, watching me closely.

I was aware that both Arthur and Kulbahadur were looking at me thoughtfully. Their thoughts were in their

7

eyes—and I goose-pimpled with apprehension at what I knew those thoughts to be.

Kulbahadur moved up close to me. "Try to get up, Sahib," he said softly. Again the air of compassion was apparent. With surprise I realized that my wounded leg felt quite comfortable. I could feel the bandages tight around my waist and my thigh, and a thick pile of wadding was covering my hip.

"If only I could rest a bit longer, Arthur," I said. "Just a spot of rest to regain my strength and I'm sure I would be all right."

"I know, old boy, I know. But I'm afraid it's much too dangerous around here just at this moment and we've got to push on," he said. "By tomorrow there will be a chance for you to lie up a bit. We must just get away from this place and throw them off our trail and then we can lie up in the jungle for a good rest." Then, deliberately, because I realized I should have to face up to it sooner or later, I spoke of my wound. "How bad is it, Arthur?" I asked abruptly. I ran my hand gingerly again over the bandage which swathed my injured hip and leg.

"Oh, it's nothing much, old boy. The splinter is still in there. Doc Stocks says it's impossible to tell just where it is at present. Doc Lusk wanted to take it out right away, and they both agreed that that would have been best while you were still unconscious. But Colonel Alexander said we have got to push on." Arthur did not meet my eye as he finished his answer.

Then I knew that this was it; my death sentence. Although Arthur had not said so in as many words, he had said enough for me to know the horrible truth— "Colonel Alexander said we have got to push on."

"In other words," I said bitterly, suddenly conscious of the hoarseness of my voice and the parched dryness of my lips, "I am to be another Premsingh."

I felt Kulbahadur's grip tighten on my arm. Although I was speaking in English to Arthur my Gurkha orderly, who hardly knew a word of the language, instantly understood the implication of what I had said.

My use of Premsingh's name had told him. The tightening of Kulbahadur's grip was like a spasm of fear running through both of us, and drawing us closer to one another.

Arthur looked puzzled. The cut and thrust of jungle fighting against our savage Japanese hunters since the column was first attacked, had left no time for me to tell Arthur the story of the tragedy of Naik Premsingh Gurung. Tersely, sparing no detail, I told him how I had ordered Premsingh to be left—and he had shot himself. The telling of it to Arthur was like ridding my mind of a corrosive memory that would poison my very soul if it remained untold. The story of how I had left a brave fighting man and faithful friend to a fate that could be only death. With a sense of inner shame, I realized that I had another reason for telling of the death of Naik Premsingh. Because of it, I was hoping that Arthur would somehow persuade the Colonel that I should not be left.

Arthur Best's brow had clouded as I told him this story. But he attempted a reassuring smile as he said now: "Anyway, what rot! Because it happened to him it doesn't mean it has to happen to you." Even as Arthur said this two figures detached themselves from the surrounding darkness and loomed into the area of my night vision. They were Colonel Alexander, and Major George Dunlop, of the Royal Scots, whose No. 1 Column my little group of survivors from No. 2 had joined shortly before the battle of Mong Mit.

The Colonel spoke first. "Feeling better now?" he asked with apparent casualness.

"Oh yes, thank you, sir. I'm still a bit weak though," I said, trying to keep my feeling of desperate anxiety from my voice. Trying to sound strong and brave and ready to go on with the rest.

Colonel Alexander was a small, slimly built, regular soldier with black hair and a straggling moustache. He now had a ragged black beard which he had grown during our eight weeks in the jungle. He was C.O. of the 3/2nd Gurkha Rifles and had been Wingate's choice of Commander of No. 1 Group of this his first Chindit expedition. No. 1 Group comprised Nos. 1, 2, 3 and 4 Columns which, once into Japanese Burma, had split up to go for separate objectives.

"I'm not surprised. The Doc said you lost quite a lot of blood. How does it feel, anyway?" the Colonel was saying, with a degree of heartiness in his voice which I could not help feeling was somewhat false. Then suddenly I was hot and cold with fear. In the abject depression which engulfed me at that instant the pain of my wounds swept through me in a new spasm of agony. A vision of Premsingh leaped to my mind again; the tenderness that had come into his inscrutable almond eyes; the warmth and strength of his brave handshake as he said goodbye. The little smile that was both a smile of resolution and an acceptance of fate; all of these details flooded through my mind. Overwhelmed with an urgent desire to live, I could not make the Colonel's task any easier by unflinchingly accepting my fate as Premsingh had done. I just could not go out like that.

"Your wound is not fatal, your wound is not fatal!" a voice inside me shouted to my very being. "It is not even serious. All you need is a few days rest for the torn muscles to knit together again; just a few days."

But common sense, logical and cold-blooded, told me that "just those few days" were precisely what the Column must have for fast, unhindered marching, if they were to slip through the gathering Japanese cordon. They would have to be days of hard marching, of doubling back, of redoubling and then finally crossing the swirling mountain torrent which was the River Shweli. With all those hazards it had to face, the column could not afford to jeopardize itself. It needed every man to march and fight. None could be encumbered with a wounded subaltern who could not walk.

As I looked up again at Colonel Alexander I realized that he knew the answer even better than my conscience did. Firmly he rested his hand on my shoulder. Just as I had rested my hand on Premsingh's arm. I knew that what he was about to do was no easier for him than it had been for me with Premsingh. But I just could not help him in his unpleasant task.

"I know what you are thinking, my boy," said Colonel Alexander, his voice soft with compassion. "Do you think you can possibly keep up?"

Arthur's fingers were biting hard into my arm. I breathed in deeply. Then with a surge of resolution that bordered on defiance I looked up and full into the Colonel's eyes. I *would* tell him I could keep up. There was no harm in my saying so. Then possibly, somehow or other, the others would help to keep me going. They would not let me down. They would not let him leave me to die.

In the Colonel's eyes I saw nothing but pity and a deep understanding. Also behind the pity there was exhaustion, the unutterable tiredness and frayed-nerves look which told of the great burden of responsibility weighing down upon him and which had been on him for so many weeks now in the midst of the jungle.

I dropped my eyes. It was no good. I could not try to bluff it out.

"No, sir," I faltered. Premsingh's quiet smile was in my mind's eye once more. After all, it seemed to give me the hidden strength I so desperately needed and to encourage me to do what was the right and accepted thing. The thing we all had agreed we would do.

"We'll carry you down to the motor road, my boy," said the Colonel, softly. "You'll have a good chance if you give yourself up unarmed."

He let his hand drop from my shoulder to close gently over my wrist. He squeezed it, in the manner of a father at the sick bed of his son, seeking to give reassurance.

"Goodbye, and good luck!" he said quietly.

"Good luck, old boy," said Major Dunlop, his abruptness a painfully obvious disguise.

"And the best of luck to you, sir," I answered. I hoped the smile I gave was a brave one. I hoped they had missed the sob in my throat. Colonel Alexander and

Major Dunlop turned and walked off to be lost in the darkness of the jungle. They did not look at me again, nor spoke another word.

So the sentence of death had been passed. I was being left behind.

Now that it had happened and that I knew my fate, strangely the fear which had been clutching at my stomach seemed to dissipate. Instead, a feeling of lethargy bordering on complacency crept over me to lull my nerves and dull my brain. Somehow the tautness and strain had gone. My future had been ordained by the Colonel. I did not have to plot or plan, strive or fight, any more. Whatever lay ahead was no longer in my hands, nor in his hands, nor in the hands of anyone; whatever lay ahead for me now could only be in the hands of God.

As the lethargy increased, my will to fight against it waned. I knew my fate and preferred no longer to attempt to struggle against it. Tomorrow, in the daylight, when the first Japanese patrol came my way, I would shout out to attract their attention. I would surrender meekly. Perhaps, after all, those stories of how they murdered prisoners were exaggerated? Perhaps, after all, my fate would be no worse than that of any other prisoner in any other theatre of war? Boredom, frustration, maybe some indignities; but not death, never death.

But was there any hope of being decently treated— or even spared—if captured by these brutal little men of Nippon? Memory could not suppress what we had learned of the fate of the Marines and Commandos at Padaung, farther south along the Irrawaddy river, during the retreat up through Burma the previous year.

The British force, only a small one, had been sent to hold the west bank of the river to give the main force more time to withdraw. When the Commandos and Marines were welcomed with smiles and gifts of food, how were they to know the villagers were treacherous? While they were resting in apparent security a screaming horde of Japs who had been hidden in the village suddenly fell upon them. Most were killed, though some fought their way out. But the dozen or so wounded captured by the Japs were tied to trees, and methodically but slowly bayoneted to death by the little yellow fiends before admiring audiences of villagers.

Arthur stepped close and disturbed my gruesome thoughts. He bent down so that his face was almost against mine. I saw the gleam of his teeth as they were caught by the first slanting light of the rising moon. I was conscious at that moment of the ceaseless sibilance of the cicadas, and a distant cough of some wild beast deep in the further blackness of the jungle.

"You are not going to stay behind, don't you worry," Arthur whispered in my ear. "I happen to be at the rear of the column for the next few days. We will make a stretcher on the quiet and carry you!" As if to prove that his words were not just a false promise, Arthur raised his voice and called: "Kulbahadur! Get two men and make a bamboo stretcher! Chito! Chito!" (quickly.)

"Don't be a fool, Arthur!" I said, hoarsely, with a protestation I had no intention of sounding brave. "You know bloody well that you couldn't carry me even for one night through these mountains. Neither you nor your men could do it. In any case, nobody's going to kill me, I shall only be taken prisoner." I was conscious of the weakness in my voice, but I did not care. I wanted Arthur to hear it. I didn't want him to leave me.

"Yes?" said Arthur, and the dry note of sarcasm in his voice was inescapable. "Look what they did to those boys from Five Column. Don't you worry, my boy, we're going to take you along!"

Lieut. Duncan Menzies, a close friend of Bernard Fergusson, and L/Cpl. Gilmartin, of No. 5 Column, had both failed to return from a patrol to the village of Zibyugin. Later, when a force of Burma Rifles attacked the village, they found both men tied to trees. They had been shaved, maltreated, dressed in Japanese clothes—and then shot. Menzies was still alive, but only just. He was given morphia, and died soon afterwards.

Arthur Best knew, just as well as I did, that such a

thing was completely and utterly impossible. He would be jeopardizing not only himself and Kulbahadur, but the others who would have to take it in turns to carry me through the jungle.

Yet I still felt bitterness as well as the crawling hand of fear clutching my entrails as Arthur and Kulbahadur without another word took my dead weight upon their shoulders. I bit my lips to stop myself sobbing openly as, in the now brilliant moonlight, they struggled with my dead weight down the long undulating spur thrust out from the jungle-covered hillside down to the motor road to Mong Mit.

As we reached the roadway the rest of the column overtook us, threading their way down from the hilltop where we had fought the Japs. They started to cross the wide and dusty road. As if I were already dead they passed me unseeingly like a column of dark grey ghosts in the whiteness of the moonlight. One by one they passed across my immediate field of vision. One by one they disappeared, I felt sure forever, into the jungle the other side. Fascinated, I had to watch them until they had all gone—men I had marched with, men I had fought with, men I had laughed and talked with about the present, the past and the future. Now there was to be no more future.

"It just wants them to remove their bloody hats as they pass me!" I thought.

Slowly and painfully we crossed to the far side of the road, Arthur and Kulbahadur bearing up my dead weight. They carried me up the steep slope which was the beginning of the jungle and sat me down in a small basin overlooking the road, my back propped against a tree. Here I thought, here with my back against this tree in this unknown spot, here surrounded by these bamboos and the clustering undergrowth of jungle, will my life end. I felt sick.

I was aware that Arthur and Kulbahadur were standing silently beside me. The three of us were watching the rear party of the vanishing column carefully obliterating their tracks by brushing the low bushes and the surface of the road with huge banana tree leaves. Then they too were gone in the wake of the column, marching fast up a winding track which climbed with the ridge of an undulating jungle-clad spur directly opposite the one down which we had struggled from our mountain-top battlefield.

Then just the three of us were there—alone.

Arthur picked up my water bottle which was lying at my side and shook it. It was almost full.

"Good thing I used my bottle for the tea this morning," he said, in the dry almost rasping voice of a man trying to control emotion and talk about mundane things.

I reached out and grasped his hand. I had to make the final gesture that was needed. If they waited much longer I should break down completely, like a scared child.

"See you after the war," I said, with an attempt at cheerfulness.

"Good luck, Ian," Arthur gripped my hand hard, turned quickly and was gone. I caught a sudden flash of moonlight on steel which whirled me into the present. I realized that Kulbahadur had still not left me, and was wielding his kukri enlarging the clearing around me.

"Thank you Kulbahadur," I said. "That's quite enough cleared now. I shall be comfortable."

"No, Sahib!", he replied quietly. "It may be big enough for one. But it is not yet big enough for two."

I was astounded, for the moment, into absolute silence.

Kulbahadur paused and straightened his back from the cutting of undergrowth. Conscious of my silence he elaborated simply: "Sahib, I am your orderly. I stay with you."

The magnificence of his loyalty—a loyalty which was enriched by friendship—touched me deeply. The rush of gratefulness and relief which surged up within me nearly made me agree. To have just one companion in that desperate solitude in which I was to wait for the unknown would make all the difference.

But, "No, Kulbahadur!" I exclaimed passionately.

"You must not stay. What good would it do? I cannot walk and we would certainly be captured. Then we'd be separated, you to one camp and I to another. Go now and return for me next year or the year after. I will be waiting for you in prison in Rangoon."

The young oriental face, at first defiant, lost some of its resolve.

"Go now," I added. "It is my wish and," and I faltered as I said it, "it is my order!"

He hesitated, biting his underlip and frowning. Then discipline had its effect. Quietly Kulbahadur sheathed his kukri. Slowly he extended his right hand and we both gripped hard as we shook.

"Good-bye Sahib," he said. "We will meet again. I know that we will." Then Kulbahadur turned on his heel and, with a rustle of leaves, he, too, was gone.

It was only then, when I was all alone, that the utter hopelessness and desperation of my predicament really overwhelmed me. My stomach curdled with the gall of my bitterness against the circumstances that had brought me there. Wrong though it was—for I understood full well from both sides the "drill" regarding leaving wounded—I felt bitter anger against Colonel Alexander for having given the order to leave me. In my self-pity I felt he might have risked it and given instructions for me to be carried at the rear of the column.

At the moment when I gave up straining my ears for any last faint sound of my vanished comrades, my utter aloneness engulfed me. It was as though the tide of fear had been precariously held back by the dwindling, cautious noises, but now it rushed in upon me with all the sinister threatening of the vast blackness of the jungle night. It was then that the delayed shock of my wound struck me. Every tortured fibre of my being was strained to the utmost fighting against the fever and ague of this aftermath. The agony of it seemed as though it would never let up until exhausted and drenched with clammy sweat, I regained control of my muscles. I slumped back, played out in body and mind.

A violent shiver shook me, and reminded me that this place that was my hide-out must be many thousands of feet above sea-level. We had been climbing for days before the Mong Mit battle burst upon us. I wrapped my blanket more closely around my body. The blood was pounding through the torn muscles of my leg, but my brain was now languid, desperately tired by the stress of emotion. Save for the cicadas incessant susurration, there came only occasionally a distant definable noise, which could have been the grunt or cough of a hunting beast of prey. Occasionally there was an explicable rustle deep in the jungle, but otherwise all was strangely silent. I just had to sit and wait.

That was all, just sit and wait until the enemy arrived from the garrison at Mong Mit. For without a shadow of a doubt patrols would be out searching the highway for traces of the column with which the Japs had already twice clashed bloodily by day and by night in the past few days.

How would they come? With an air of fatalism my pain-dulled mind considered the problem, the solution of which held for me the difference between life and death.

Would they come by the truck load? Would I see the squat Jap transports come grinding over the brow of the hill on the motor road which lay immediately below me? Would I watch the trucks grind to a halt in billows of dust, hear the shrill, staccato orders of Japanese officers, and then have to lie helpless and sweating in fear as the men climbed out and probed the jungle with their long bayonets for any British stragglers who might be in hiding?

Or would they be marched down the road and halted near me, to be fallen out on the orders of their officers, just like a leave party being fallen out to scatter to barracks to prepare themselves for a boisterous evening in the nearest town? Whichever way they came what should I do about it? Should I call to them and wave in friendly fashion? Should I smile pleasantly at them when they closed in on me, to show that really

I meant no harm to them? (In my present predicament they would have little doubt about this!) Or should I just wait for them to discover me, hoping that they never would?

Perhaps it would be better to crawl to the side of the road and wave to them as they approached to make it quite clear that I meant to give myself up with the minimum of trouble; that I meant to co-operate with the "Invincible Japanese Army" and recognize them my masters. Or should I fire a signal shot with my revolver from where I lay up in the bamboo-hidden basin? On second thoughts, perhaps not. The sound of a shot was a hostile sound and however bland my smiles when the Japs came up to me they would surely suspect that the shot had been one that I had fired with evil intent. My end then could only be a skewering on the end of a bayonet!

Suddenly I was overwhelmed with revulsion as I saw all too clearly exactly how it would be!—First the Japs would stand still and look at me. Their eyes, their faces, their very attitudes would be coldly expressionless. Then they would look at each other and a meaning would creep into their looks. One would call out orders I could not comprehend, but whose meaning I would know only too well. Then, with a measured ruthlessness, they would tread towards me in their rubber-soled jungle boots, rifles dipped, bayonets pointing at me. Suddenly their expressionless masks would drop, slant eyes would gleam with lust for slaughter, and that would be It!

I needed no reminding that Jap soldiers preferred a living red-blooded body to a straw-stuffed sack for bayonet practice! The shudder that ran through me could have been a shudder of death already. Yet I was still alive. And any decision I might make at this moment could decide whether the future for me was to be life, or death. Faced with the necessity for a decision my tired brain gave up the struggle. Suddenly, unpredictably, I was asleep.

3

COMING OF THE JAPS

I awoke abruptly, my every nerve taut with fear. Something, some noise my brain had not yet assessed, had warned me of awful danger close at hand. It was the hour before dawn. No bird, nor beast nor insect stirred. The world was poised in absolute and ominous silence. Then it came again! A sound quite distinct from any jungle noise, the grumble of a distant motor!

Forgetting that any movement meant physical agony to me, I rolled over. Feeling my pain only as a thing apart I pulled myself up to the lip of my basin. From there I could look down on the motor road which ran direct from right to left below me. Although the moon had now gone down and dawn was near, my eyes were sufficiently accustomed to the fading darkness to discern that the road was still clear for all the two hundred yards that I could see of it. Instinctively I shook my tommy-gun free from the blanket and pack and clipped in a filled magazine. The magazine chattered against the cold steel of the gun as I did so. I looked down in exasperation to see that the hand that was loading was shaking.

This was it!

The noise of engines grew louder, approaching from the right, the direction of Mong Mit. I could tell now that there was more than one. I heard the drivers change gear to negotiate the steep slope on the other side of the pass which was beyond my vision behind the murmurous mass of the jungle. From sheer force of habit I pushed my tommy-gun forward, just peeping over the ridge in front of me. My left hand pulled back the cocking handle with a clack.

The first truck came over the ridge slowly. Then, as soon as it was on the downward slope, it increased its speed. It had been forced to come slowly up the incline beyond the hidden brow of the hill for the very good reason that it was loaded with Jap soldiers! The driver crashed into second and then into third gear as he muffed his clutch work. Now he accelerated. I could tell by the way he had gone through his gears that he had no intention of stopping just yet. My spirits rose slightly.

The first truck, with its load of Jap soldiers, swept past below me, and disappeared from view where the road was screened by jungle again. Then a second truck, similarly loaded, came into view. The driver changed gear in an equally inexpert manner, and accelerated to pass me by. Then a third truck came into view in just the same way and that, too, rolled by. My luck was in! They were not going to search this particular part of the jungle. Then a fourth truck came. This time the driver did not go swiftly through his gears in his eagerness to accelerate along the straight. Instead the truck maintained the crawl at which it had come over the brow of the hill. Then it pulled up with a squealing of brakes and little billows of dust on the roadway directly below my hiding place! I would not even have to move my tommy-gun! The windscreen was gleaming greyly right in front of my sights just where it had stopped. Almost abstractedly I observed the thick triangular foresight swing a little to the right as my hand pressed on the pistol grip. There was a group of ten Jap soldiers sitting upright in the truck so that now, in my sights, they were as if balanced on the very top of the triangle of the foresight. The encircling metal ring of the backsight completed the picture of potential slaughter with a neat frame of black metal. I had only to squeeze the trigger!

To this day the picture of those ten Japs, sitting stiff and upright in their truck balanced on the sharp point of my foresight and completely framed within the ring

of the backsight, remains indelibly imprinted on my mind. It is as sharp and clear as it was at that moment recorded by my right eye as I lay quivering with both fear and expectation in my jungle hide-out.

The Japs were just like toy soldiers. They were sitting so straight and stiff that one could hardly believe they were flesh and blood. I remember clearly how suddenly the hunter within me overcame the hunted so that, with a cold and fearless precision, I judged the range. I remember with absolute clarity the imperceptible movement I made so that my tommy-gun dropped its ugly snout as I aimed at their guts rather than at their heads.

This was no bravado on my part. This was no melodramatic testing of my sights to see what a truck load of Japs looked like when framed within them. This was the moment for which I had been so fully and rigorously trained. This was the reason why I had marched into

Burma behind Wingate. Now was the time to kill Japs, and go on killing them, until each one of those hideous little men in that truck was wiped out by my rapid bursts of fire. This was my hour!

These were the yellow creatures I had marched into this jungle hell to kill, and to kill whom I had already been through so much. I do not think I was unusual in my feelings that these Japanese soldiers were not human beings at all, but were a macabre, inhuman vermin which could be wiped out with equal inhumanity. These Japanese were not to be considered like German soldiers, or Italian soldiers, or any other foe that Britain had ever fought. They were sub-human, without conscience, without soul. They were evil things that had to be destroyed if the world were to be fit to live in. I do not think I was any different from any other British front line soldier in my feelings about the Jap fighting man. It never crossed our minds that Japanese soldiers had wives or children at home to love them, had mothers or fathers who were proud of them, had anyone in the world for whom they themselves could feel a human emotion or who could feel human emotions on their account.

No. As General Slim had already warned us, the Japanese were "the most dangerous insects in the world."—And there was I with ten of them, quite oblivious of my presence, beautifully ringed within the sights of my tommy-gun!

My brain sent the signal to my trigger finger to squeeze. Now was the moment. My lips tightened into a thin line as I drew in my breath on the instant of pressing the trigger. In another split second a stream of hot nickel-coated lead would go tearing into those Jap soldiers. Already the picture of their death throes was vivid in my mind. With the first burst two or three would be smashed over the side of their truck, their arms grotesquely flailing the air as their life-blood gushed out. My next burst would kill another two or three, jerking them about in sudden spasms of crazy agony as death swept among them from they knew not where.

But what if I did not kill all with my first magazine?
—Then I would have to change magazines!

As swiftly as it had come to my mind the picture of
the Jap soldiers, shattered and bloody in death in the
gory shambles of their truck, had been displaced in my
mind's eye by another one. This time it was a picture of
the survivors from my first triumphant hail of fire slipping into the jungle where I could not see them to shoot
them down. Even as I clipped on a fresh magazine the
roles of hunter and hunted would change. Now they
would be able to sneak up on me and stalk me
through the cover of the bamboo thickets and the
labyrinth of undergrowth until eventually they would
run me to earth. And what mercy should I expect from
them then?—The only possible mercy would be quick
despatch by a burst of light automatic fire.

Far more likely that they would drag me, heedless
of the jolting agony of my wounds, down to the road-
side. There they would strip me naked and tie me to a
tree. And ringed around me in maniacal glee, they
would bare their teeth in their flat yellow faces and
bayonet me to death in the most prolonged manner
possible to give the maximum sadistic enjoyment to
themselves!

This was the moment then. This was the moment
when I had either to squeeze the trigger or did not
squeeze the trigger. Whatever my decision in this quivering moment could make either picture come true. I
chose not to risk what imagination had shown me in
the second picture, however fierce my blood-lust to
bring about the first.

To press the trigger now would sound my own
death knell . . . !

My head sunk to the wooden butt of my gun. I could
not do it. My duty was to kill Japs but I had failed.
Failed because I was afraid to die. Here had been my
chance to show the Japs that they were not the only
supermen who scorned death in fanatical sacrifice of
self in line of duty to the fatherland. Here had been
my chance to show them that a young British soldier
was just as proud to sell his life dearly for the honour

of his glorious country, as was any fanatical Jap. Here had been my chance to fulfil the most important purpose of Wingate's daring raid with his 3,000 men penetrating hundreds of miles behind the enemy lines —to show that the Jap was *not* the incomparable and unbeatable jungle fighter that our ignominious defeat in Burma in 1942 seemed to have proved he was.

All I had been required to do was to squeeze the trigger. Then I should have proved the point and fulfilled my purpose. But I did not want to die. With a shudder I withdrew my right hand from any proximity to the trigger of my tommy-gun. I lay there dejected and ashamed. With increasing sense of shame I watched the Jap soldiers dismount from their truck, unmolested.

I heard the Jap officer, in a high and urgent monotone, gabble out instructions to his men. I watched them break up into two parties, one crossing the far side of the road, and the other taking up their positions my side. Fanning out from the verges into the jungle on each side of the road the two parties pressed forward slowly, each man searching the ground for any sign of the escaping column. Meanwhile they chattered away in the unintelligible talk, curiously menacing with a dangerous insect quality.

The Jap soldiers on my side of the road were so close that I could see every detail of their uniform, the puttees, the breeches and shirts done up at the neck. Some were wearing soft caps with large soft peaks and others the more conventional domed steel helmet. Their long rifles were slung over their shoulders. One man carried a weapon distinguished by its peculiar bent butt as a Japanese light automatic.

What had my plans been in the event of being confronted with a situation such as this? My mind despaired in a slough of indecision. Should I call to them for help? Should I surrender to the enemy and throw myself at their mercy? I could not stand up to wave to them, but I could certainly call and make myself heard. What should I call, anyway? Should I call: "Surrender. Peace. Here I am. I give myself up"? Is that what I should shout to them?

I licked lips which were cracked and dried despite the fact that sweat stood out in great sluggish globules on my brow. I knew that no voice would come.

What if they did not find me in their searching after all, and I did not give myself up to them? What would happen to me then? What fate could I expect other than to lie here, in this little basin, and here to die of starvation?

Better to lie here and starve to death than risk being bayoneted or tortured—or be starved to death in the filth and degradation of a Japanese prison camp. Thus said a voice inside me. And to that voice I listened. It would take several days to die of starvation and during those days a miracle might happen. Better to risk starving to death and trust myself to miracles than to give myself up to be the bayonet practice side-show at a Japanese jungle holiday!

An excited yell from one of the searching soldiers on my side of the road sent a shudder of fear down my spine. He had discovered something! Was that "something" the beginning of the trail that would lead up to me for the Japs to lay open my hiding place and reveal me to them in all my pitiful helplessness?

Chattering excitedly, all the Japs crowded around the one who had shouted. They were a few yards up the slope from the road and in my direction. From the urgent motions he was making with his hand, I guessed that the soldier had found a badly erased footprint or maybe a piece of broken bamboo.

The tall, slim Jap officer, the first light of dawn by now glinting on his helmet, took over the search from there. The men stepped aside to let him in. Methodically he examined the mark. Then he straightened up, and with a purposefulness that seemed to indicate he not only knew where I was hidden but was also fully acquainted with my name, rank and number, he began to push forward up the slope through the jungle.

I could see he was very excited. And he was coming straight towards me following the route Arthur Best and Kulbahadur had taken when they carried me to my hiding place! Up and on he came, ploughing through undergrowth, brushing aside branches and creepers. Up and on. Always towards me. Then, in the pregnant silence of the brink of day, the Jap officer loomed before me through the dapple of criss-crossed bamboo stems and saplings. It was as though all life held its breath. The very utterness of the silence shouted terror to my taut nerves. In that breathless moment the figure of the Jap officer filled the whole of my visible horizon.

This was it! This was that moment I had pictured (and guilty conscience had tried to disbelieve) would come to Premsingh, when we left him wounded and helpless, to face whatever fate might overtake him in the brooding jungle. Now it was happening to me!

Drenched in the cold sweat of overwhelming fear, I hoped with the hope of despration that the searching Jap officer would not penetrate my hiding place. Even the pain of my wounded leg constricted to nothingness in the palpitating concentration of mind and spirit.

The Jap was so close I could hear his laboured breathing. He was a keen officer, was this one. So eager to hunt down his human prey that he was himself taking a more than usually energetic part in the search. He was not content to stand around observing his men obey his commands.

So close was he to my hiding place, that I felt only a miracle could prevent those flat expressionless eyes searching me out. He was bigger than the average flat-faced square-looking Jap fighting man, who had charged screaming at us in their drab green uniform and rubber-soled jungle boots. He was taller and slimmer than the average. His cropped skull was domed by a steel helmet which, even as my gaze fixed on it in fatal fascination, caught the first gleam of another tropic day emerging greyly from the Burma night. Detail by detail I took in his officer's uniform buttoned at the neck, his knee breeches which even then I noticed were badly cut, and his black riding boots.

From the left side of his polished Sam Browne belt hung a sword scabbard. On the right side a pistol

Nambu Type 14 (1925)

holster. The Luger-type pistol was out and in his right hand, thrust forward accusatively as he had pressed through the jungle. I had heard the click as he cocked it just after he had leaped down from the truck to lead his men in the hunt for scattered British soldiers.

Had that been but three minutes back in time—or had it been three life times?

The Jap officer changed his pistol from right hand to left. In utter agony of mind I watched his right hand partly draw the sword from its scabbard—then push it back again with a sharp "clack." Apparently he was just making certain he could draw swiftly when he found his victim!

I was suddenly aware of the acrid reek of my body sweat and that my slashed and torn shirt and trousers, in places hard with dried blood, were clinging clammily to me. I shuddered. A cold trickle of sweat ran down my spine. A quarterway down. Stop. Halfways. Stop. Then suddenly all the way. I dared not shiver.

The Jap officer turned and called urgently to two of his men farther down the slope. Then he lunged away abruptly through the undergrowth—away from my hiding place!

By some miracle he had missed me, and was now following the trail leading away from me, following tracks Arthur and Kulbahadur had made when they left me. Stumbling in his eagerness, two of his flat-faced evil-looking soldiers now close on his heels, the Jap officer crashed his way back to the road and yammered out some rapid orders. Men crowded around him chattering shrilly, while he pointed animatedly at his open map.

Two of the Japs doubled back, rifles at the trail, and jumped into the truck. With a crash of gears it leaped forward, violently reversed, and roared off in a cloud of dust in the direction of Mong Mit. They were obviously losing no time in reporting to the Jap garrison there that a British party had crossed the motor road heading towards the Shweli river.

Instinctively, in the cold aftermath of its awful shock, my mind was assessing what the next move would be with these Japs. The officer and his men would almost certainly follow the column's trail until they linked up with the larger force that would go from Mong Mit. The combined party would then attack from the rear, hoping thus completely to trap the British on the south bank of the Shweli river towards which they were obviously heading. Undoubtedly there would already be strong forces of Japs hidden in the dense jungle on the north bank of the Shweli to ambush any British troops trying to cross.

The hurried crashing of men in the jungle beyond and above me told that I had anticipated the Jap plans correctly. The officer was leading his patrol away from my hiding place, and up the track on the jungle-clad spur where the British column had gone.

Soon the crashing of men hunting human prey through the jungle had died away, and I was alone once more in the vast solitude of the jungle. Night had now suddenly and completely melted away before the splendid march of the rising sun. Exhausted, as much by my inner shame at not having fought to the death and sold my life dearly, as by the apprehension which had strained my nerves to breaking point, I slumped back in my hollow. I fumbled for my pipe. As I lit it and took the first puff a feeling of comfort crept over me despite the desperateness of my plight.

In this new-found comfort I considered how the reason for my present comparative safety was because the Jap patrol had been diverted from my trail to follow the trail of the rest of the column. In the self-pity that welled up in me with almost childish petulance I felt that, after all, it only served them right. I could feel little else but anger at Colonel Alexander for giving the order that I should be abandoned to my fate. My mood towards the rest of the column was of petulant grievance because they had been party to that decision. I felt they should have refused to obey the Colonel's order to leave me. Surely, if they had really prevailed upon him, he would have changed his mind and agreed that I should be carried at the rear of the column until my wound had healed sufficiently for me to walk? Therefore it was their own look out if the Japs were at this very moment hot on their heels. When it came to leaving behind your wounded, and the "wounded" turned out to be oneself, it was terribly difficult *not* to feel that the rule should not always apply!

That the Japs had gone well away from me was very certain. Not even the faintest sound of them could be heard in the over-all murmur of the jungle. God, I felt, must have decreed that they would pass me by. It must be a sign that I would live. With this assurance growing in my mind, again the will to live, the insistent hope against hope, welled up inside me. Premsingh's leg had been broken. Mine was not. True the muscle was torn and useless and the leg so painful that to put it to the ground sent agonies of hot fire shooting through my body. True, if I put any weight on it the agony caused me to collapse completely. But somehow I would find a way to walk. I *must* walk! I *would* walk!

If I could manage only one mile each day I had a chance of getting through to China. One mile each day for three months, perhaps, and I could get through to China. I could get up into the mountains of Yunnan where the Japs never went and live there secure, my leg mending all the time.

I had not the faintest idea how I would live or where I would live. But surely, something inside me insisted, loyal tribesmen in the Shan mountains, here in North-east Burma, would come to my aid? All I needed was their goodwill, their friendliness, and food and drink. Then maybe some information as to the disposition of the Jap forces and I could, healed and rested, walk out north-eastwards through the enemy lines and thence into China, and get back to my own people from there.

Which way to go? I knew that if I went on through the jungle to the north-east ultimately I must fall in with the Chinese forces. Or maybe an American contingent, who we had been told were holding the Japs up against the borders of China? My spirits brightened at the thought of meeting up with friendly troops in Yunnan. Yes, I could do it! All I had to do was to manage to walk that one mile a day. My only danger lay in a chance meeting with the Japs on a mountain path, I felt sure. But that was a calculated risk. I would have a shot at it. I would walk out of Burma even if it meant hopping on one leg! There and then I determined to set about it, and strangely was overwhelmed with a feeling of elation. I was going to walk to China! And with that in my mind I set about my preparations with the light-heartedness of a youngster about to start on a holiday hike in the Chilterns or Trossachs.

First I had to lighten my load. I emptied my pack and rapidly and methodically sorted out in my shadowy refuge the things I should need for my journey. When we had set out from Imphal some two months ago, my pack, like the others, had contained a 50 lb. load. This included six days paratroop rations, fifty rounds of ammunition, an aluminum mess tin, and a sterilizing outfit capable of purifying even the foul sludge-water from dried-up buffalo wallows (which more than once was as nectar to us!). The theoretical day's ration allowed for each Chindit was twelve wholewheat biscuits, two ounces of nuts and raisins, two ounces of cheese, four ounces of dates, a small bar of chocolate, powdered milk, tea, sugar, salt and vitamin "C" tablets. Also there were twenty cigarettes and two packets of matches. But at the best we rarely had more than two-thirds of this ration.

What would a man need on a walk from the depths of the North Burma jungle to the Chinese border? —The top half of my mess tin, a pair of new socks, a large square of parachute silk, morphia phials and ten atebrin pills I pushed quickly into my small pack. The under half of the mess tin, two pairs of socks, a shirt and toggle rope, I bundled into the large pack, along with a balaclava helmet which had arrived in the last airdrop we had taken before the battle at Mong Mit. All of these I wrapped in my discarded blanket before pushing them into the large pack.

Of my equipment I decided that all I needed was my water bottle, hunting knife, compass, pistol and ammunition. My kukri, grenades, tommy-gun and other equipment I would cram into the big pack as well. I had two packets of biscuits left and I pushed these into the basic ammunition pouch clipped to my belt. Then I set about making a crutch.

I had only to reach up a hand to find a thick bamboo pole suitable for this. I cut it down with my sharp kukri, and, lying comfortably in my hide-out, trimmed and fashioned it into a make-shift crutch. The top I padded with the balaclava helmet, which I retrieved from the large pack. I folded the thick khaki wool around and over the top of the pole and secured it with a piece of parachute cord. My armpit would not now be rubbed raw as I hobbled my way out of Burma. Despite my plight, I could not refrain from chuckling

as I contemplated the balaclava helmet. My dear mother had sent it with a note explaining that "it can be
very cold in the Indian hill stations," where she presumed I was going on leave, and she felt sure that I
would find a balaclava indispensable! And I had found
it indispensable! But how worried poor mother would
be if she could see me now. The balaclava she had
meant to keep my ears warm in the thin cold air of the
foothills of northern India was now being fashioned
into the padding on a crutch on which her wounded
son planned to hobble out of the oven-heat of tropical
Burma!

How I blessed now the sentimental attachment which
had prompted me to keep that useless balaclava because it had been a present from my mother! I had
refused to throw it away just because it had come from
her with such tender thoughts.

I was ready to go. All I had to do was walk!

I rolled on to my right side, lifting my body up
so that I took all the weight on my arms, and twisting so
that at the same time I could draw up my right leg
underneath me. I pressed upwards with the right leg
and started to turn my body more fully. I could not
restrain a cry of agony, despite my gritted teeth, as a
vicious stab of pain shot through the gashed and torn
muscle I was twisting. The wounded hip joint, also beginning to take some of the strain, was suddenly hot
with a searing agony.

I slumped back to the ground, soaked with sweat
and sick with pain. My agony of soul was even greater.
It could not be done after all. Without someone to
help me I could never stand up! Just for that very
reason, just because I could not raise myself from the
horizontal to the perpendicular to lever myself on to
the crutch, my body could not set out on the journey my
ambitious mind had planned for it.

Tears of pain, and of rage and desperation, sprang
to my eyes. I ground the heel of my good foot into the
dry soil in a fury that was also an agony of despair.
I slumped back, my body clammy with cold sweat and
hot blood pounding at my temples. Now I had toppled

down the yawning chasm of despair and was stretched at the bottom, fingers clawing the earth around me.

I lay there for a long while, until the pains which had tortured my body subsided, and the pain in my mind gave way to a dull emptiness. Then I felt for my pipe once more and lit it, and lay back puffing at it steadily. Slowly my hopelessness drained out of me.

My pipe went out and I felt in my jacket pocket for my matches to light it again. As I did so my fingers came in contact with a folded piece of paper which I could not remember putting there. Perhaps it was a map that Arthur Best or one of the others had thrust into my pocket while I was unconscious? I drew it out. I opened it to find, not a map, but a printed text that my mother had sent to me in the last letter I had received from her. Against the day when I "might need some extra help," she explained, she had sent me that quotation from M. Louise Haskins which was made famous by King George VI in his memorable broadcast to the Nation during Britain's first war-time Christmas of the Second World War.

"I said to the man who stood at the gate of the year: 'Give me a light that I may tread safely into the unknown'. And he replied: 'Go out into the darkness and put your hand into the hand of God. That shall be to you better than a light and safer than a known way!'"

I read it. I read it again. Then, as I carefully folded it and returned it to my pocket, something of its message seemed to infuse itself into me. I felt I new courage and determination well up inside me. What if there was no known way for a wounded soldier, abandoned by his comrades as incapable of walking, to escape through hornets' nests of Japanese aroused by the Chindits in the hell of this Burmese jungle? Never in all my life had I been so alone and so friendless. Yet suddenly I was fully prepared to do just what the text said. I would put my hand into the hand of God —of whom I knew no more than an average schoolboy would—and set out into the darkness of the jungle believing that my faith in His love and protecting guidance would be better than any known way. It made up my mind for me. I would try again to walk.

Gingerly I buckled on my belt. Next I slipped the strap of my haversack, containing those articles I had selected as necessities, over my head and wriggled until it was comfortable upon me. Then I rammed my tommy-gun into the large pack and seized hold of my crutch. Holding the bamboo pole upright and firmly digging it into the ground I started to pull myself up hopefully. A sudden pain of sheer agony shot through me, radiating from my hip. I collapsed into my hollow retching, overwhelmed with nausea. Panting and bathed in sweat, I lay there until I could summon up the will-power to try again. But a second time the blinding pain that shot through me crashed me to the ground as if I had been flung there by a giant hand. It was no good. I had to find some other way if I were really to "go out into the darkness."

When the ague of sickness and pain had left me, I looked around me and gave the matter more thought. The lip at the rear of my hollow I now saw in the daylight to overlook a small clearing. To this there was a drop of about five feet. It could have been made for me! Slowly I crawled towards the lip, dragging my wounded leg painfully. Then carefully I lowered the crutch down into the clearing until it was leaning upright against the bank which dropped almost vertical from the lip of my hollow downwards to the clearing.

With my crutch in position I then wriggled slowly backwards into the hollow and turned myself right round to face once more towards the forward part of my hiding place, looking down to the motor road. Then I proceeded to wriggle my way, only this time backwards, up towards the rim. When I reached it I gently eased myself over the edge, feet first and backwards, and with my fingers providing firm anchorage in the roots and vegetation around me as I slowly lowered myself. At last my sound foot touched the bottom. I hung on to a clump of bamboo with my left hand while I gingerly manoeuvred the crutch in position under my armpit with my right. I was now actually standing, as comfortable as could be expected, and ready to go. I slowly shuffled round on the sound leg supporting myself with my crutch until I was facing a gentle slope which I could now see led up from the clearing to the track.

Aloud I said: "China, here I come!"

I was all too conscious, as I staggered up the slope, that I was going out into the darkness. It was the darkness of an ominous, dangerous jungle. I was alone as few men can have been alone. My enemies were many and cruel and they were everywhere—the Japs, possibly treacherous and murderous tribesmen, hungry carnivorous beasts, and venomous snakes. Even the very jungle itself was against me. And I was not only alone, but I was distressingly crippled.

The track ahead was a twilight trail into a gloomy and sinister cavern. My mode of progress was quaint and laughable, had it not been so painful and pathetic. I could not march face forwards, striding out boldly into the unknown up the steep slope of the track. Instead, like a skier walking up a snowy ski-run, I had to take shuffling side-steps all the time.

By the time I reached the first crest in the ascending track I was already at a point of acute exhaustion. Yet I dare not slump down to rest for fear that I might not again be able to get to my feet. Once down I would not be able to get up again unless I was fortunate enough to find myself at the top of a bank as convenient as the one behind the little basin in which I had so successfully hidden from the Japs. The jungle track of dirt and rock up which I was climbing was some six feet wide, and was quite even under foot. For stretches it rose very steeply and as I shuffled painfully onwards and upwards it became increasingly apparent that it was spiralling up the side of a mountain, clad so thickly in jungle that all sense of height was lost in the dimness.

After an hour of sweating agony, one side of the track had developed into a wall of sheer rock, covered with moss and lichen. On my other side it dropped away precipitously down into a vally which lay several thousand feet below in a weird dark green half-light. As I continued my shuffling crab-like progress still farther upwards I came to a point where suddenly bright light shafted down and I was looking below me on to the tops of giant trees. I could easily have lobbed stones to land right dead-centre on top of them so directly was I above them. In places landslides had cut great swathes down into the deep far distance through the trees, toppling them like children's playthings. The overwhelming undergrowth of jungle had covered up where the trees had stood in a riot of turbulent foliage and swathing vines and creepers.

After this break-through of light let in by the falling of giant trees, the track entered once more into a green and gloomy sepulchre of jungle. No man-made mechanical contrivance had manufactured this track. Its flat surface and polished stones had undoubtedly been worn by countless generations of naked feet. The dark feet of tribesmen who for centuries had lived their secret lives in the jungle's depths. On and on I hobbled, negotiating difficult slopes painfully, learning by sharp experience the best methods of progress.

I secured my injured leg tightly to my improvised crutch with a strip of parachute cloth, for as I hobbled it had jarred painfully on stones or against the crutch. Sometimes the crutch jammed between stones in the track. When that happened my leg was given a cruel wrench which sent pain shooting through my body. At times I nearly fainted with the pain, and half-stood, half-crouched vomiting bile, my whole body clammy with sweat. I knew that once I fell to the ground I should be as helpless as an overturned turtle. There I would have to remain until I was either discovered and murdered by the Japs, or killed by hostile tribesmen.

By nightfall I reckoned I had covered something like three miles—three miles of such physical agony that I could not even bear to think back on them. At this point I came upon a junction with another track. Here I found clear evidence of the spoor of the column which had left me behind—and unmistakably over-printed on it were the imprints of Japanese jungle boots! The pursuing Japs must have been hot on their trail!

These tracks of pursued and pursuers disappeared into the green depths of jungle where the left-forking path rounded a thickly forested spur. Not unnaturally, I chose the right fork! I followed it until the steep slope dropping away on its right suddenly became grad-ual enough for me to slither down. And with an ease and lack of painful jolting which was an agreeable surprise, I slid down on my back to emerge almost gracefully through some undergrowth into the seclu-sion of a miniature, well-hidden little valley. To my amazed delight there was even water. A crystal-clear mountain stream bubbled and chuckled over a stony bed, running through it before cascading over the side of the mountain to the floor of the greater valley I knew to be hundreds of feet below.

With a feeling of real contentment I wormed my way into a comfortable position at the bottom of my slide and lay there quietly to take stock. I liked every-thing about it.

Lulled into a sense of seclusion and safety I un-buckled my belt and placed it at my side with my small pack. Still determined to remain a good soldier I slipped my revolver out of its holster and cleaned it carefully. When I had done this to my satisfaction I reloaded it and placed it under my hat just a few inches from my right hand.

My immediate security taken care of, I ate a packet of biscuits, took an atebrin tablet, and quite calmly composed myself for sleep. Now that the die was cast, and I had decided to make my attempt to walk out of Burma, I had a peculiarly reassuring feeling that I could leave the rest to God. So now I slipped easily and willingly into a deep sleep. Weakened as I was by loss of blood and the continuous throbbing pain of my wound, I was in a decidedly light-headed state. My feverish mind had cast aside all fears of Japs or of four-footed beasts of the jungle as it welcomed the oblivion of sleep.

*   *   *

I awakened violently! Fully awake on the instant, my straining ears immediately caught and identified the sound of a stealthy footfall, and the sinister sound of leather scraping on stone.

My right hand reached for and found the comforting butt of my pistol. With intense concentration my eyes searched the darkness. I could see nothing. After a tense pause that seemed a lifetime, I could hear nothing either. Gradually my racing pulse slowed to normal. Then I heard it again, the stealthy placing of one foot on the ground and the easing of the body's weight on to it. As my eyes searched in an agony of suspense among the inky blackness of the moon-shadows around me, visions of the enemy stalking me tortured my imagination.

I pictured him distinctly. In my mind's eye he was a squat, expressionless Jap soldier whose face, hands, and uniform were all of the same yellow-green hue in the darkness. His lips were bared in a half-grin, half-snarl, and his slant eyes gleamed with a glitter that was both inscrutable and cruelly menacing. I saw him moving with the utmost stealth along the bed of the stream towards me. Deliberately he was choosing the damp earth just above the water line so that nothing dry should be snapped beneath his feet to give away his whereabouts to me. I pictured him with his rifle at the alert, thrust forward across his body, its long slender bayonet ready for the killing thrust. I could even see his finger crooked around the trigger, requiring only the very slightest extra pressure to set off that sudden staccato detonation and burst of red flame that would be all one explosive eruption plunging a .280 calibre bullet into my heart.

Perhaps he had not yet fully located me? Perhaps he had only heard my breathing in the blackness of the jungle shadows and was stalking me stealthily, his ears

cocked acutely to catch the sound of every breath
I took?

I pictured him again, his evil yellow-green face
turned slightly sideways so that his right ear was inclined towards me the better to hear any small sound
I might make. Undoubtedly the next thing I should
hear would be the muffled sound he would make as he
went down on all fours, so that he could creep up on
me and despatch me with bullet or bayonet as I slept.

Then I heard him again! But this time it *was* the
sound of a foot grating on stone. That could only mean
that he had now left the soft earth of the outer bed
of the stream and was treading on the stones at the
very fringe of the water as he came closer and closer
towards me. I panicked. That last sound could have
been the stealthy Jap moving into a firing position.
The sweat started from my pores and my teeth
chattered in the sudden cold clamminess of my body.
My mind pictured the invisible rifle slowly swinging
towards me for the black hole of the muzzle to point
at my heart. I jerked my revolver up, cocking it all in
one frantic movement. The double click of its hammer
shattered the silence of the jungle night and seemed
to reverberate to eternity.

Now I really had written my own death warrant!
Too late I realized my panic-action had betrayed me.
In utter terror I knew that the noise of my revolver
being cocked had now completely given my whereabouts away to my hunter. Even if he had not already
been aware of my hiding-place and was perfecting his
preparation for the act of killing, he must now know
without any doubt. As if my unseen enemy had suddenly switched on a searchlight to expose me completely
in my ineffectual hiding-place, a spear of light from
the rising moon slanted down through the upper darkness to bathe the jungle and stream-bed in white light.
In its light a terrified doe stood poised at the stream's
edge, ready for instant flight, and the next moment,
like a released spring, she abruptly vanished from
my sight!

I slumped back, shuddering and exhausted, too overwhelmed by my experience even to feel a sense of relief. I was conscious that my head was throbbing as in a fever. I lay drained of strength, both mental and physical, and felt death must still be near. Eventually I sank into a deep sleep.

Well before dawn I awoke shivering with cold and bitterly rueing the moment when I had decided to discard my blanket to facilitate my walk to China. I realized that I would have to walk now, or face the very real risk of dying from pneumonia. I had learned another lesson of survival in the jungle. I must walk by night and sleep through the heat of the day so long as I was so high above sea-level.

Laboriously I struggled back up the way I had come when I slid down through the undergrowth into my night's hide-out. Pushing my bamboo pole ahead of me, I wormed my way up on my stomach. By the time I was in reach of the track my whole body was bathed in sweat again and my wounded leg was throbbing with a fire that pulsated but did not pain. I was shivering as though seized by an ague. When six feet below the track I pulled my crutch into postion under my left armpit and tied my leg to it again. Then, clutching at trailing creepers with my left hand, and taking all my weight on my right foot, I forced myself up and forward on to the track with an immense effort both of will-power and body.

Despite my physical weakness and the agonies of mind I had undergone, I became intensely aware of the haunting beauties of the night which still enveloped the ever-rising track. The sky, now visible through the towering trees, was of the deepest of blues, almost midnight blue. Great stars stood out in it like resplendent jewels which seemed to hang temptingly down towards the world. Not realizing quite what I was doing. I stretched my free hand up as if to touch them. They were so bright and so clear and beautiful that they seemed to be almost within touching distance. Every dragging, painful, sidestep I took on-wards and upwards seemed to open to my wondering eyes a more and more beautiful vista. Beneath the dark velvet of the jewel-bespangled night sky I could clearly see the black range of peaks in the distance which I knew was the lofty range of the Yunnan Mountains on the China border. This picture of distant, dark mountains beneath the wondrous Burmese night was framed in a fairyland fretwork of silhouetted giant trees and bamboo saplings, which formed a sort of tunnel through which I looked up along the track and out into that enchanted world of night sky and mountains.

I knew that I must be getting very close to the tree-line now, where jungle ceased and bare mountainside started. My increasing awareness of the bitter chill in the air—which cut through my scanty attire of tattered khaki shirt and khaki drill trousers—made me realize that I could not go far beyond the end of the tree-line as I was. Not much farther up the bare mountainside I would be over the snow-line where I could freeze to death if I were not careful.

I calculated that I must have climbed a good thousand feet in my first attempt at walking sideways. At the rate I was now shuffling upwards I reckoned that by the time dawn broke I should be almost ten thousand feet above sea-level, and at that height nearly clear of jungle and trees. Then, almost as though a revolving stage had transformed the scene from night to day while I blinked my amazed eyes, the sun rose up into the sky, in splendid majesty. Before its sudden golden glory, the dark bowl studded with green and orange jewels that had been night, dissolved instantly. I gasped aloud at the sheer wonder of it. Then, in my fevered and weakening state, I staggered on, still upright and dragging my crutch-supported leg. The glory of the awakened day was one of the last things that registered on my full consciousness, and from then on my progress up and onwards was in a state alternating between waves of delirium and near oblivion.

Ultimately my increasing weakness became too much for me. Though my mind fought to rule my flagging body and to compel it to continue its tortured progress,

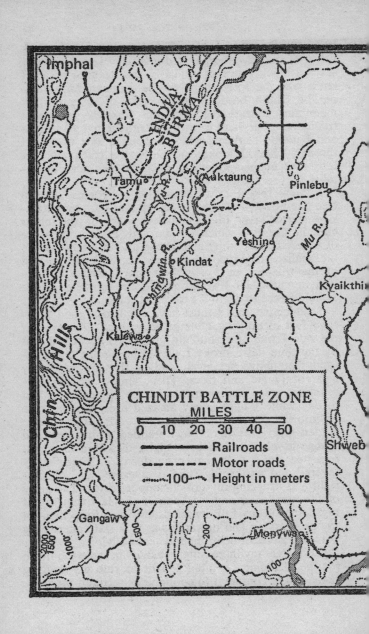

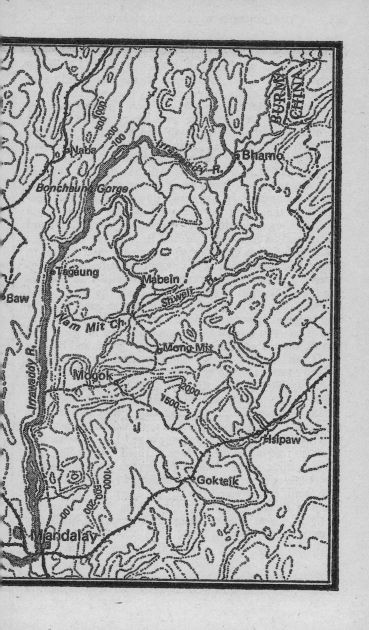

the end was very near. My bearded chin rasped my bare chest as my head sagged with a weakness that was both physical and mental. I had to lie down again. Either that, or I would collapse on the track and never be able to rise again. Feverishly my eyes searched from side to side for a slope down which I might ease my aching body, feet first, for somewhere where I could lie hidden in the undergrowth and abandon myself to complete prostration of body and mind until sufficient strength returned for me to shuffle on once more.

But I could find nowhere. All that met my fevered gaze was the steep, rocky bank at one side of the track, and a precipitous falling away down through the tree-tops and the deep, dark cavern of the lower jungle on the other. I would have to press on round the bend just ahead to see what fate had in store for me on the other side. I would have to get round that bend. In agony and frustration now amounting to frenzy, I staggered on, clutching desperately at the cliff-side bordering the track, until I reached my goal, the bend. As I rounded the bend the cliff beside me seemed to sway and bulge as spasms of nausea and faintness swept over me. The way ahead now appeared as a grey and brown mass, shot through with jungle green and blazing flashes of sunlight, all of which swirled and undulated as if to overwhelm me and engulf me completely.

Abruptly—through this swirl of pain-racked mist, there stood out starkly the figures of two men advancing on me! To my fainting senses they loomed like giant men. They were fraught with the most horrible menace! Even as my senses weakened I was aware that each carried a weapon: Japs, armed with rifles, advancing upon me! In one despairing movement I jerked my revolver from its holster, slumped back against the rock wall, and pressed the trigger again and again and again with the gun at my hip. Then, in a crescendo of noise, I was swallowed up in a great red-black fog of unconsciousness . . .

4

A JUNGLE SHANGRI-LA

The very next thing that I was conscious of was the coarseness of the texture of the blanket which covered my naked body. It prickled my skin as I turned on my side and vomited. From the wretchedness and exhaustion of vomiting I slumped back, and was overwhelmed once more by a wave of unconsciousness.

The next time I opened my eyes my head felt clear. My whole being was delightfully comfortable, lulled by a feeling of immeasurable content. I was conscious that my body felt warm and cosy. I was conscious that I felt clean, from head to foot, that my wound no longer throbbed, that all weakness and despair and wretchedness seemed to have been drawn from me.

Was I dead? Was this some other world where one wandered in green pastures and suffered no pain, nor fear of death? Were there clear and crystal streams tinkling and burbling through this new world which had washed me clean like the little sweep boy in "The Water Babies"? Had those same streams slaked my raging thirst, even as I slept? It could be so, for I could hear a distant, fairy-like tinkling. I stretched. And as I did so there came the sound of a creaking bed. So I was on a bed!

I turned my head cautiously. I became aware of a shaft of golden sunlight slanting down to my right. I turned my head and saw that the sunlight came through a small grille high up in a stone wall. It was the sort of grille that one saw high up in the walls of storybook prisons.

Good God! Was I in prison?

Then I was aware of the gleam of a polished brass jug just beside my bed where my hand could easily reach it. I eased myself up in bed and raised it to my lips. I drank deeply. As I placed the brass jug back on the floor, which I could now see was uneven and hewn out of rock, the gleaming, bulbous metal rang like a bell.

"Shshsh."

I nearly jumped from the bed in fright at this new sound. I turned my head wildly to my left to see a yellow-clad figure rising from the floor on the other side of my bed. Forgetting all about my wounds, I sat up in bed and shielded my eyes from the brightness of the sunbeam.

He was a tall and very thin man. From head to foot he was completely robed in yellow. I knew from his robe, which was made up of many strips of yellow cloth, that he was a Bhuddist priest of one of the Upper Shan tribes. He had grey hair and was clean shaven. His brown eyes were curiously penetrating and alive. I was aware that they glistened brightly as he fixed them on me. He looked me straight in the eye and raising a long thin finger to his lips, repeated: "Shshsh!"

The air of contentment which had lulled me so pleasurably a moment earlier drained from me. Horrified, I looked frantically around me for a way of escape. I saw now that I was in an underground cellar. The whole room was hewn out of solid rock, just like a medieval dungeon. A dungeon! That was it! The events of the immediate past—how long ago it had all happened I could not imagine, for I had no idea how long I had been unconscious—flooded back to my mind. The last thing I could remember was firing from the hip as the Jap soldiers, looming huge and fantastic through the mists of unconsciousness overwhelming me, had advanced upon me.

Who was this man, this yellow-clad priest who now stood over me? Why was he keeping guard over me in a dungeon? My luck must have deserted me from the start. Instead of falling in with friendly tribesmen, I had been captured by Japs and was now being held prisoner in a Shan village which was co-operating with the Japanese. I looked at my gaoler again. He was still watching me closely, his curiously luminous eyes first gazing straight into mine, and then assessing me detail by detail, my eyes, my nose, my mouth, and then my shoulders and arms. Was he thinking up some form of fiendish torture to please his masters, the Japs? Was he gloating by selecting the part of my body that would give me most pain and him the most delight?

I looked around me to see what were my chances of escape. The cell was about 12 feet long and 6 feet wide and was nearly 30 feet high. It was so high in fact that the ceiling was almost lost in darkness. The entrance was closed by a massive teak door hanging on three stout, highly polished, brass hinges. It was iron-studded and there were bolts to show that on the other side were brackets for an extra securing bar which would make it completely impossible to open from the inside.

My eyes examined the rock-hewn walls for the only other possible means of escape; the grilled window through which the sunlight was streaming. This was not wide enough for me to worm my way through. And I could see at a glance that the grille was too stout and firmly embedded for there to be any chance of me removing it and slipping through.

A shudder of horror went through me as I was suddenly aware of the boots and puttees of a sentry standing outside the grilled window. Only Japanese soldiers wore boots and puttees like that! So the worst had happened. I was a prisoner of the Japanese. Prisoner, presumed dead!

I took in more details of the cell. The bed I was lying on was a typical native charpoy and my exploring hands revealed that it was wooden framed and made of interwoven fabric strips. It was placed in the far left hand corner of the cell opposite the massive teak door. I was lying facing that door, the grilled aperture being high up immediately above my head. Overwhelmed by misery at my predicament, I slumped in the bed and closed my eyes. My hand went to my waist where my belt and revolver should have been, but my worst fears were confirmed. My hand touched only bare flesh. I had been stripped of all clothes and equipment.

Abruptly there came sharp commands in staccato Japanese from immediately outside the grille above me. There followed the stamp of feet and the clink of weapons, and the putteed legs that had been partly visible now moved so that they almost completely obliterated the light from the outside world. The golden, slanting sunbeams had been blotted out as though a light had been switched off. There came a further command in Japanese. The boots stamped and the rifle butt disappeared upwards and a fine dust came filtering down on to my bed. It came dancing down in the sunbeam which was once more slanting into the cell. The Japanese soldier had been marched away.

Where was he going from there? Did it mean that the firing squad was coming down to collect me? Or were they going to take me away and torture me to try and make me reveal the full purpose and the exact composition of Wingate's force? The lean priest who was my gaoler stood up, his yellow robe rustling. He put one long thin finger to his lips, again hissed: "Shshsh!" Then he opened the heavy studded teak door and stepped out silently, as noiselessly closing it behind him.

In the throbbing suspense that followed I ran my hands down my wounded leg. I could feel that it had been re-bandaged. I plucked back the coarse blankets and twisted over gingerly to look at it. The whole area of the wound had been neatly bandaged with clean white cloth and, my heart leaped as I realized it, the action of turning over had been accompanied by no twinges of pain.

I swung my feet to the ground. The next second I was standing gingerly on my sound leg. I steadied myself at the bedside as the cell see-sawed alarmingly in the waves of faintness that came over me. Then they passed off, and I was clear-headed again. Carefully I allowed my weight to be taken by both legs. A

slight spasm of pain shot through my hip, but it was
only a slight one. This time it was not the searing
agony which had been almost like a physical blow
from a giant hand, vicious enough to knock me down,
clawing desperately at the ground.

I steadied myself against the wall and took a step
forward. Cramping stiffness impeded the full swing
forward. I tried again. Another spasm of pain stabbed
the mending muscle, but it was not pain that I could
not bear. I thrust the leg forward in a full step and
this time let it take the weight of my body, just for a
fraction of a second as I brought my right leg into line.
Then I took two steps back to bed, confident that I
could at least walk again with two legs, however stiffly.
That was, so long as I had enough future before me to
be interested in walking!

As I lay down on the bed again I felt inexplicably
elated, despite the fact that I was a prisoner. Surely
I could escape now, somehow or other? Then the massive door creaked slowly open again. I turned at bay.
When the door had swung halfway back there entered
a three-man procession. I prickled with apprehension
as my yellow-garbed gaoler stood to one side to allow
a small, slim, white-clad man to come in. I looked
behind him swiftly for the inevitable Jap with rifle and
fixed bayonet, and to face those cold, inscrutible slant
eyes that boded no good for any British soldier. Instead
of a Jap soldier the third man, who was almost as tall
as my gaoler, proved to be another brown-skinned native. He walked in carrying a wicker-basket against
his chest.

The small man crossed over to the foot of my bed
and gabbled some words at me in a language that
was completely unintelligible. I shook my head defi-
antly, to make it quite clear to him that whatever he
was trying to get me to say I was not going to say it.
Then: "I thought perhaps you would understand Kachin as well as Gurkhali," he said, in perfect
Nepalese. "I am the Thugyi."

My heart bounded at the sound of the language of
the Gurkhas. This village headman (as he had

introduced himself by saying he was the Thugyi) must have recognized my battered Gurkha hat, and from recognizing it had deduced that I spoke Gurkhali. Surely this knowledge of Gurkha troops and of their British officers could only promise well for me?

I examined him closely. He was small and slender of build and was dressed in a white lungyi (an ankle-length, skirt-like garment worn by Burmese men) and a spotless white shirt. His hair was straight and white and was cut in European style. He had a high forehead and oval shaped face and his skin was the colour of dark tan. His eyes, as dark as ebony, were bright with friendship as they looked into mine. They were set in deep sockets accentuated by his high and widely spaced Mongolian cheekbones. The nose was thin and highly-bridged ending in sharp, sensitive nostrils. The prominent jaw bones which gave his chin a chiselled firmness spoke of strong character.

"I am honoured by your presence Sahib," he said. "I am delighted to see that you have recovered from your fever. You must be very hungry now."

I was completely overwhelmed with delight and relief. It was all I could do to resist throwing my arms round him and trying to dance him around in sheer joy of being among friends. From the depths of depression my spirits soared so that now the fact that I was in a rock-hewn cell underground, and that there were Japanese troops marching up and down outside, seemed of little consequence. Already, I felt, I had been led from the darkness into which I had gone out so hopefully.

The Thugyi beckoned to the man with the basket, who had been standing a little back. He placed the basket beside me, and then my three visitors stood back in respectful silence between my bed and the doorway.

"Thank you Thugyi. Please to be seated," I said to him. I felt that his old-world courtesy fully merited a courteous response.

The Thugyi sat down on the end of my charpoy and motioned me to eat. I opened the basket and discovered in it a heavy metal platter piled high with curried chicken and rice. At that moment there was nothing in all the world I wanted more than curried chicken and rice! Kneading the sticky rice into balls with my fingers, and dipping it into the highly spiced sauce, I began to eat ravenously. And while I was eating my first full meal for what seemed like an eternity the Thugyi told me more of how I came to be there.

Graphically, in his rapid Gurkhali, he filled in for me the missing hours from my life since that moment when I had collapsed unconscious after firing at the two Jap soldiers advancing on me so menacingly down the mountainside track. The two figures who had loomed so ominously before my fevered eyes, the Thugyi explained, had not been Japs at all! They had been two Shan charcoal burners walking through the forest, axes over their shoulders, going about their normal, everyday business. Fortunately I had been already toppling to the ground when I fired my pistol, and so the three bullets meant for them went wide. But apparently only just!

Scared out of their wits, for our sudden meeting had been as unexpected and alarming for them as it was for me, the two charcoal burners dived headlong into the jungle at the side of the track. It was only when nothing further happened that they ventured to look out from beneath the bushes, and saw me lying sprawled across the track.

Those charcoal burners were no cowards for they were descendants of wild hillmen who barely two generations back had been addicted to hunting strangers with poisoned darts fired from blow-pipes. But fortunately, like the inhabitants of the village in which I now was, these two sturdy hillmen were extremely pro-British and hated the Japanese. Because I had fired on them they had presumed I was a Jap soldier and when they saw me lying unconscious they came rushing down the track at me wielding their villainous axes. It was their intention swiftly to put paid to me and rid the British Raj of at least one of its yellow enemies!

Then fortunately they recognized, before it was too

late, that I was in fact a British officer. They refrained from hacking me to pieces and in the best traditions of the Good Samaritan picked me up and carried me back to the village in which I now found myself. Their kindness was the more remarkable because they were not even from this particular village but had travelled from quite a distance away in the jungle-clad hills. Obviously they could in no way benefit from going out of their way to succour me, and it would have been much easier and safer for them either to have handed me over to the Japs and claimed a reward or to have rolled me off the track down the steep slope. But it was not in their simple and loyal natures to do so.

As soon as they had delivered me to the Thugyi of the village I had been carried down into a cell deep below the village pagoda. There I had been stripped, washed, and put to bed. That very evening a Japanese patrol had arrived from the south seeking stragglers from the ambushed British column. The Japs had requisitioned some of the houses and spent the night in the village. The next morning the officer had decided to give his men some foot drill up and down the dirt road outside the pagoda, and it had been the feet of one of the drilling soldiers I had seen through the grille when I recovered consciousness. Even as the Thugyi had come down the steps to my underground hiding place the Japs had finally marched off from the village, still heading north in pursuit of British stragglers.

What with this news and the new strength that now coursed through my body from the excellent meal I had eaten, life was suddenly very good indeed! The Thugyi smiled with an almost smug satisfaction as he eyed me, approving my obvious enjoyment of the food and my relief at having discovered I was among friends.

"And now bring the Sahib his clothes!" he called, in the voice of a man about to produce the *pièce de résistance*. The native who had brought in the basket of food stepped forward again, this time with my khaki drill slacks and shirt. They had been cleaned and pressed as neatly as though they had just returned from the cleaners in a more civilized land, and the rents and gashes had been repaired. It was hard to realize that these now immaculate looking clothes had been stained and filthy with blood and sweat, sliced by jagged mortar splinters, and ripped by jungle thorns. As I pulled them on and buckled my revolver at my right hip once more, the Thugyi and his two companions stood grinning at me as though enjoying a huge joke. So far as they were concerned it was a huge joke against the hated Japanese! It was a joke I was very inclined to share!

"Now come out and look at our village," invited the Thugyi. "The Japs have gone and will not come back without us first having good warning."

Without assistance I climbed stiffly up the steps from my cell and followed the Thugyi through the deep, cool shadows inside the pagoda. The tap of my crutch echoed through the long cool passage we followed as we made our way up from the subterranean cell. We emerged suddenly into the full, dazzling brightness of the morning. Once my eyes were acclimatized to the brilliance of the day I appraised the village and was overwhelmed by the beauty of it. It nestled at the top of a long, sloping valley, and straight up behind it rose two towering thickly forested mountains sloping steeply down to each other to intersect immediately behind the village.

Along the full length of the valley on each side of it an almost vertical strip had been cleared of forest and carved out beautifully into terraces. On these terraces were grown the vital rice which was the staple diet of the people. As my eyes travelled onwards from the beauty of this valley they took in next the grandeur of the vast, glorious stretch of the Shan states. The glistening emerald undulations of tens of thousands of acres of forests and jungle dropped gently away to merge into the blue, shimmering heat-haze that lay along the lower foothills of the next range of blue-green mountains. Beyond them rose fantastically the snow-covered peaks of the Yunnan range, the sparkling spectrum of dancing sunbeams softened by haze in the distance to a rainbow glow in which the white peaks seemed to float in ghostly majesty.

Not a leaf stirred anywhere. It was all the most perfect peace. The smoke from many village fires rose in faintly brushed wisps straight up against the azure sky. Individual sounds, both from close-by village and more distant jungle, seemed blended naturally into one happy murmuration.

In the village itself the long, deep brown houses of teak stood on short piles. All were within the high shelter of the huge pallisade which completely encompassed the habitations. The main gateway at the lower end of the pallisade was adorned by great carved wooden Chinthes, mythical beasts associated with China which serve the dual purpose of keeping out evil spirits and discouraging warring tribesmen from attempting to enter the stronghold. The same Chinthes that Orde Wingate had chosen as insignia of his Chindits.

Mentally intoxicated by the sheer beauty of the vista before me I turned to see what lay behind. There right before me was the pagoda standing on a small hillock in the very centre of the village. Its bulbous base was cleft by the shadowy cave of the main entrance and its tall, slim, gold-painted spire gleamed and glistened like a thing apart from the rich green of its jungle background. Two enormous elaborately carved and coloured stone Chinthes protected the doorway at the top of a flight of wide, stone steps. Their bared teeth and bulging eyes gave them the full ferocity of both the Griffon and the Lion, their traditional parents. In the silent and breath-taking beauty of this scene the distant chatter and yapping of monkeys was the only touch of reality, and a coucal crooned interminably somewhere unseen. Otherwise it might have been a painted fairyland against a painted ocean of jungle green.

Indeed, a man could be at peace here. The very atmosphere had the quality of eternity.

"Yes, we are proud of our village," said the Head-

Chinthe

man softly, obviously pleased at my enraptured appreciation of the beauty of his homeland. "My people came here a century ago and now we rank as one of the most important communities in the Shan States."

"Where did you come from then?" I asked. I had always imagined these people had lived in Northeastern Burma since that land first became known.

"We came from Nepal," he replied. "There are many Nepalese villages in northern Burma, especially in this area which is very much like our homeland. Legend says that when the men from Hindustan invaded Nepal their cruelty drove thousands of my countrymen eastwards into Burma. Here the people are very like ourselves, hardy, hill folk, so our ancestors settled here. We have, of course, intermarried extensively, but we retain our language and customs. Our young men even join the Assamese and Gurkha regiments. I myself was a naik in the Fourth Gurkhas twenty years ago." His voice rang with a great pride as he said this. His white, thatched head was held high and he looked up into my eyes, every inch of him bearing the martial air of a soldier who is proud of his regiment.

We walked together through the village until we came to the Thugyi's home. The yellow-clad priest who I had at first feared was my gaoler joined us and helped me to mount the wooden steps to the veranda. The Thugyi disappeared into the dark interior while the priest and I sat down at an enormous brass tray. After a few minutes he came out carrying a beautifully carved box about the size of a small attaché case. With deep reverence he opened it. Then: "Look, Sahib," he said breathlessly. In the open box lay some medals and a kukri. Embossed on the kukri's leather scabbard were miniature crossed kukris surmounted by the Prince of Wales' feathers. It was the badge of the Fourth Gurkha Rifles.

"I was in the Burma and Assam Military Police," he began to explain. "I volunteered to join the first battalion of the Fourth Gurkha Rifles at Gallipoli in 1915. We were too late for the fighting there and returned to India—to the North-west Frontier. There I was wounded while attacking an Afghan fort and I was discharged from the Army in 1921." I told him then that my father too had been at the Dardanelles and had been seriously wounded there. This forged a further bond between us. So I became the honoured guest of the headman of this Shangri-la lost far out in the mountains of North-east Burma, with the foothills of the mountains of Yunnan on the immediate horizon and the ghostly floating white peaks of the great mountains behind them my ultimate goal. The beastliness of war, the ferocity, the slaughter and the hate of man for man, seemed far, far away in this idyllic oasis in time into which fate had brought me. So soon after my taking the way out into the darkness it seemed to be proving better than a known way.

Much of the time that I now spent in the Shan hill village I slept stretched out luxuriously on the wide veranda of the Thugyi's house. I lay on a thick durrie rug which had been woven by women of the village. It was of deep pile wool into which had been woven a sumptuous scene depicting an Eastern hunt. It was beautiful and strangely virile carried out in many gorgeous colours. The faces of the hunters were all pale-complexioned and were depicted full face, in spite of the most awkward contortions this demanded of their bodies.

Food arrived regularly. It consisted of a huge main meal of curry at sundown, and various delicious fruits and melons at intervals during the day. Breakfast was in the Chinese fashion—a cup of hot water. Cups of tea appeared in never-ending succession throughout the day. The cups themselves were sheer delight. So exquisite, in fact, that I often lay back contentedly examining them after draining the contents. They were made of very fine, almost shell-like china, and were hand-painted with the most intricate and colourful designs. The saucers matched the cups in their gay and fragile beauty. These cups had no handles and were wide and shallow, the tea served in them being always steaming hot and a delicate shade of translucent green. "Ghoor", a coarse texture brown sugar, was added to suit my taste, which proved to be decidedly lavish as I was determined to satisfy the craving for sugar which possessed me after being without it for so long.

From where I lay on the Thugyi's cooly-shaded

veranda I could gaze down on nearly the whole of the village. His house was built at the foot of the pagoda hill and, as befitted the headman of the community, it commanded the most magnificent view in the village. All through the heat of the day I could, from the cool shadows of my little place of peace and security, hear the tinkling of the tiny temple bells.

Below me in the streets the villagers passed to and fro, going about their work in cheerful contentment. Beyond on the rice terraces men were at work, bending their backs effortlessly beneath the hot sun and working with smooth, unhurried efficiency. The women, in the way of village women the world over, mostly busied themselves in the houses or gathered at the well, ostensibly to collect water in heavy brass vases, but in reality to chatter animatedly among themselves.

The men were dressed in brightly coloured lungyis, favouring mostly vivid purples and glowing reds. Some wore shirts which were not tucked in European fashion but hung outside, while others wore a type of cloth waistcoat. The majority, however, went about bare chested, covered only from the waist down by their lungyis. The women also wore a version of the lungyi secured above the breast and flowing in graceful folds to their calves. Some of them wore a belt of twisted leather or woven beads. The women's hair, which was long and black and in deep, curly waves, flowed to their shoulders and was held in place by ribbons. Most of them wore a beautiful orchid above one ear or on top of the head like a small hat, which accentuated in many cases the bright-eyed dusky beauty of the woman herself.

The sounds of the village drifted up to me as in a lovely dream scattered with the tinkling of the pagoda bells and drenched with a benevolent sunshine. All day long there came, muted and delightful in its friendliness, the chatter and laughter of the children punctuated by the merry yapping of their dogs. Every one of these villagers, from the oldest men to the youngest tots, seemed full of real joy and contentment.

As I lay there alternately sleeping and waking, I

was inescapably drawn into the exquisite peace of this little lost dream-world in the midst of jungle-clad mountains. A voice inside me began to whisper that if I stayed here I could attain that simplicity and peace of mind which seemed to be common to everyone. It was a joyous peacefulness I had never experienced before and have never discovered since. It was something that I am convinced the Western way of life will never capture, and will always remain the poorer for it.

During my waking hours I received many visitors, all of whom had been personally vetted by the Thugyi. Needless to say most of them were relatives of his and in the main they were divided into two types. Some of them came to chat trivialities with me in Gurkhali, and others just came to sit quietly at the far end of the veranda, gaze at me with smiling benignity, and say nothing. All of them were completely welcome so far as I was concerned, and each one, whether loquacious or mute, exuded friendship and goodwill.

Every one of these visiting villagers brought me gifts of some kind, which they set down around my bed. Soon I was practically surrounded by countless varieties of fruit and flowers, cooked meals in gleaming brass vessels, quantities of raw rice, little platters of river fish, all set close together or balanced one on top of the other. One of the Thugyi's innumerable nephews even brought me a freshly killed deer which he laid out beside my bed, while another gave me two long bamboo spears and a raw hide shield. Although no word was spoken, these were obviously an invitation to join the tribe—an invitation that I found it very hard to resist. I gave all of these gifts to the Thugyi, and the majority of them I expect he sent to the temple.

By night only the main tower, which stood up foursquare and strong over the main gate, was manned. But all the time both by day and by night, it was perfectly safe for me to remain at my ease on the veranda of the headman's house without fear of surprise by the Japs. Very ample warning could be given by the men in the watch towers, quite apart from the information grapevine operating for miles beyond. However, as an extra precaution. by night the Thugyi insisted that I return to my cell beneath the pagoda to sleep the deep sleep of complete security.

5

"GENTLEMEN, YOU ARE THE DECOY"

It was during these idyllic days in the hillmen's village that I told the Thugyi the full story of how I had come to be wounded, alone and desperate in the depths of Jap-occupied Burma. He listened with avid eagerness, an eagerness accentuated by his own martial background. I took the Thugyi right back to the very beginning of the story of Wingate's fantastic expedition deep into the heart of Japanese-held territory, made at a time when the Japanese fighting men had been built up by countless stories into a sort of savage little superman whom nobody could defeat in jungle warfare. It had become painfully obvious that the morale of troops facing the Japs in this theatre was not too high. The Jap soldiers were becoming bogeymen and someone had to debunk them! So, General Wavell had decided that a limited offensive against the Japanese in Burma would, if successful, have not only a good effect on world opinion and on the opinions of our allies, but would also show the British troops that the stories of the Jap invincibility in the jungle were no more than a myth.

Thus the year 1943—less than six months after the disastrous British defeat in Burma—opened with this limited offensive planned down the coast of Northwest Burma to Akyab, and also in the far northeast. There the Chinese armies under the American General "Vinegar Joe" Stillwell, assisted by a small American force, were to start an offensive on that front. And this was where Brigadier Orde Wingate's Chindits came in. The Chindits had been intended to co-operate with the advancing Chinese, and surprise the Japs by suddenly appearing right across their lines of communication in the very depths of the Burmese jungle far behind the Japanese lines. This surely was a bold British answer to the Japs' dream of invincibility and world domination! It had all the boldness of Wingate at his most unorthodox!

But something had gone wrong with the plans for the Chinese army to move down to the attack from those distant blue-hazed mountains of Yunnan. While on the British side of the campaign preparation was nearing completion, and the word to go was confidantly awaited, it had become perfectly clear to the British headquarters back in India that the Chinese move against the Japs would not take place. Despite the massing of several Chinese divisions away up behind the mountains of Yunnan, there was no apparent eagerness to come down and get to grips with the Japs. It was then that General Wavell decided to send in Wingate's force alone. This was not so much because of any lasting military damage it might do, but to prove that the British soldier was as brave as, or braver than, the Jap, and could be more skilful, enduring and cunning as a jungle fighter than these so-called supermen of the jungle.

There was another reason, too, for Wingate and his Chindits to go marching out into the unknown. This was that the Japanese High Command was thought to be planning an offensive to sweep the war deep into India, and Wingate's modern "Charge of the Light Brigade" would confuse and distract the Japs sufficiently to disrupt their plan. At the very least, the British hoped, this disruption would give them a chance to forge new armies to fling against the Japs in full-scale warfare and defeat them before they could execute their plan to invade India.

We of the Chindits had been told in the beginning that part of our task was to fight for time. The plan for our campaign was entirely of Brigadier Orde

Wingate's conception and was, typically, a masterpiece of simplicity and daring. The name "Chindits" was his own conception too. He decided to call his raiding force this after the Chinthey because the object of these statues outside Burmese pagodas was very similar to ours, to drive away evil spirits and loathsome things which might haunt a jungle night! The symbolism behind Wingate's choice of the Chinthey, however, was the fact that his deep-penetration force was to be supplied all the time by airdrops, making it possible to march and fight entirely without lines of communication. One only had to keep one's radio set working to ensure the swift arrival of friendly planes dropping food, drink, ammunition, weapons and medical supplies, like manna from the heavens. That was all! (As our column radio operator so succinctly pointed out on the occasion when our set was blasted to smithereens by a hail of Jap machine-gun fire!)

The Chindits comprised three battalions of infantry, numbering 3,000 men, made up of the 13th Battalion the King's (Liverpool) Regiment, the 3rd Battalion of the 2nd King Edward VII's Own Gurkha Rifles and the 2nd Battalion the Burma Rifles. These were split up into seven columns, each a major's command consisting of eight officers, 250 other ranks, and some 50 mules and horses. The columns were numbered from 1 to 8, but there was no No. 6.

With these seven columns Brigadier Wingate had set out to sneak through the Japanese forward areas. These extended right up to the line of the River Chindwin, the east banks of which were closely patrolled by the Japs, while on the western banks were the most advanced British outposts. The ways in chosen by Wingate were tracks believed to be secret. Supplied regularly by airdrops, he aimed to take his columns deep into Burma where they could strike at the Japanese lines of communication hundreds of miles behind the front. The expedition's only link with the British forces back in India would be a long-range radio set. Everything was to be carried on man or mule and every man was to be counted a fighting man. "We're even going to sharpen the ruddy mules' teeth, sir!" a grinning Chindit told me when I first joined them.

In the crossing of the Chindwin five of the columns (Wingate called them his "killing" force) were to march with complete secrecy straight to their objectives, and descend upon them before the Japanese realized what was happening. The other two columns were to cross the Chindwin farther south with a studied lack of secrecy, and were deliberately to attract the Japanese towards them acting as a decoy. Thus, it was hoped, the "killing force" would be able to carry out their devastations in comparative peace.

My particular job in this set-up was that of commander of the support section in No. 2 Column. With No. 1 Column we were the lucky fellows chosen as the decoys! Looking back I fail to see how we in those two columns so confidently—even light-heartedly— took on the task of literally inviting the vicious and cock-a-hoop Japanese "supermen" to attack us and test their mettle against ours. Put it down, if you like, to the magic of Wingate and the complete trust he inspired in men. It was difficult, indeed, to realize that most of the British soldiers taking part in this seemingly crazy and highly dangerous long-range raid, were townsmen born and bred who only a few months back had been considered second-line troops on garrison duty in England. Yet now each one was imbued with the Wingate creed, drummed into them during their tough and exacting training in torrid jungle in the depth of India's Central Provinces.

"Jungle fighting is a matter of swift, close-quarters encounters. A man's life will depend entirely on his own cunning, speed and skill. Man will suddenly find himself fighting man, with no one to come quickly to his aid. Then the better man will win. You will be the better men."

And, despite all the odds against us, despite the long trail of defeat suffered by the British through Malaya, Singapore and Burma only a few months earlier, we felt we were the better men.

The story had started for me at Jhansi, a cantonment in Indian jungle country where the Chindits had done most of their training. In the sweltering heat of the afternoon I arrived I sensed at once the atmosphere was electric. Newly commissioned, I was joining them on the very eve of entraining for Dimapur, on the Assam-Burma border, from where the great march eastwards was to start.

Captain Bertwhistle, 3/2nd Gurkha Rifles, Adjutant of No. 1 Group, was sitting at a blanket-covered trestle table in the 180-pounder tent which served as the orderly room of the 3rd Battalion, 2nd (K.E. VII's Own) Gurkha Rifles. I stamped in smartly to announce my arrival and the interior of the tent engulfed me in heat, like an oven. Sweat was coursing down the Adjutant's face as he looked up sharply. It ran in rivulets down his chest, and dripped steadily from his armpit hairs. Sweating as liberally, I stood at ease before him, and watched him pick up his fountain pen and dry his fingers on the blanket table cover before attempting to write my name in capital letters on the *pro-forma* before him. As he wrote the date "January 7, 1943," sweat from his brow dropped on the paper and smudged the ink, so that he had to dab it with a corner of the blanket and write anew beside the smudging.

"Rank—2nd Lieutenant," he mumbled, seemingly to himself, as he began to fill in the details. "Regiment— 8th Gurkhas." He looked up: "Date of present commission?"—

"The fourth of October, sir, 1942," I replied.

"Age?"

"Nineteen."

"Next of kin?"

"Father, sir."

And so, in between pauses to mop sweat from his brow and chest with a sodden handkerchief, and to blot it from the paper in a hopeless attempt to keep the *pro-forma* neat, he filled in all my particulars.

"Right. Now you are to join No. 2 Column," he said tersely. "Major Emmett is in command. You had better report straight away, there is not a lot of time."

I took one pace to the rear and saluted. The great adventure had started.

Major Arthur Emmett, who had been a tea planter in North Bengal before the war, I found to be a kindly man with a quiet smile that instantly put one at ease. He told me I was in charge of his support group, a command concerning which I knew next to nothing, having rather skipped the subject at the Officers Training School I had been at in India. However, I speedily discovered my Gurkha troops to be as helpful and friendly as they were obviously brave and tough. My platoon havildar, Lalbahadur Thapa, made it quite clear he would take a real delight in teaching the new young "Officer Sahib." In the days that followed I rapidly made up the deficiencies in my education.

Captain Bertwhistle had been right, however. There was not a lot of time! Within three days of my joining the unit Major Emmett gathered together all his officers at Column Headquarters. "We move tonight at 0200 hours," he announced quietly. "It will take us at least four days by train to Dimapur if all goes well, and from there we have a 150 mile trek to Imphal, where we will have a rest." In fact, the Major had exaggerated slightly. It was only 143 miles from Dimapur to Imphal, and we marched in there on January 28, 1943.

We marched every one of those 143 miles in dead of night. For security reasons by day we were hidden in the jungle leaving the Manipur Road to the line of communication troops ferrying forward supplies to the fighting troops up in the no-man's-land that flanked the Chindwin river. We marched onwards and upwards, until we were tramping stolidly forward at heights of over 5,000 feet. The piercing cold of those nights on the march were sometimes momentarily compensated for by visions of distant beauty which burst upon us in the sudden splendour of the burnished dawn.

Once we had reached Imphal, the sprawling capital of Manipur State, on a lofty plateau in Assam, we started to put into practice some of the jungle training we had received hundreds of miles away back in India. On the night of January 28 I made myself a bamboo shack, just as I had been taught, and sat in it as the rain teemed down over the low hills in which we were encamped. By its sheer weight the rain forced itself through the flattened pile of leafy bamboos which formed the roof and dripped monotonously upon me. Around me were many more huts similarly built by British townsmen. Merged skilfully into the surrounding undergrowth as the huts were, it was apparent that already the British soldiers were adapting themselves to the conditions that they would find in the jungle. For the Gurkhas, of course, such adaptation required far less change in mode of living.

Despite the rain, high spirits seemed to pervade the whole of the Brigade area around me. With a start I came back from a dream of home to realize that there was quite definitely "something in the air." And so, of course, there was! We had just been told that tomorrow was "D" day. The week of rest that had followed our arrival at Imphal was over. On the morrow we were to be unleashed to strike, swiftly and stealthily, into the very depths of Japanese occupied Burma.

Wingate had told us: "Gentlemen, you of No. 1 and No. 2 columns are to be the decoy!" And we had then been told how we were to march south-east on Kyaikthin once we had crossed the Chindwin—for the express purpose of drawing the Japs off from the other columns who would be marching north-east. It had been a bit of a shock. But then, because Brigadier Wingate had said it, because we knew he had planned it, we were prepared to accept it uncomplainingly and with quiet confidence.

The whole thing was so new to us that, with the exception of the few who had been in the 1942 retreat, no one had any real idea what jungle warfare would be like. Generally, we were prepared to regard it as something of a daring adventure. We knew the principle of air supply and had a firm faith that we would receive from the skies the food, mail, and ammunition required to keep us in fighting trim physically and mentally. And I am sure that almost to the last man we all had implicit faith in Brigadier Orde Wingate. The fact that he told us we *would* go through the jungle in such a manner and that we *would* come out in such and such a manner, was good enough for us. When he told us we would both outfight and outwit the Japs in so doing, the troops were prepared to take this "as gospel."

It was, of course, significant, although I did not realize it at the time, that the British soldiers were mostly men of quite an ordinary line battalion, and were by no means young super-fit commandos. They were, in fact, of an average age somewhere in the region of thirty, many of them being married men with families. Few were volunteers, although they had all been given a chance to withdraw at some point early in the preparations. This was all in accordance with Wingate's plan to show that, with the right training, weapons, and leadership, the average British soldier could safely be pitted against crack Japanese troops in the most unusual surroundings of so-called impenetrable jungle. .

There were high spirits among the Gurkha and Burmese troops that rain-swept night. Above the laughter and chatter around I caught a snatch of animated conversation from a group of Gurkhas in a bamboo shack nearby. They were priming a box of grenades in readiness for battle. As they did so, they were laughing and joking, and telling stories of what they were going to do to the Japanese when they got to grips with them!

Already I was greatly attached to these stocky little warriors of Mongolian origin, with their wide-set, almond-shaped eyes, flat noses, and faces on which they could grow hair only with the utmost difficulty. By disposition phlegmatic, bordering on lazy in anything that was not directly concerned with fighting, they were always good tempered and cheerful. They hardly knew the meaning of the word fear. They loved soldiering and adventure, and the ambition of every virile young Gurkha was to join the British Army. Many quite genuinely joined "to win a V.C."! Like all other British soldiers who came in contact with the gallant little Gurkhas, I was instantly attracted to them. Truly they lived up to their native proverb that, "It is better to die than to live a coward". Kulbahadur Thapa, who was appointed my orderly, was typical of all that was brave and most loyal in the Gurkha race.

I suppose it was at that moment, when I heard the Gurkhas joking about the slaughter they would wreak among the Japs, as they primed grenades in their rain-lashed bamboo hut and lovingly fingered their razor-edged kukris, that I really realized I was about to learn the full meaning of war.

It was, I suppose, the first time that I had let myself consider the full implications of our training and the magnitude of our task. One brigade of 3,000 men, sneaking through the heavily garrisoned and patrolled Japanese forward areas, has been set quite a job of work! There was to be blowing up of railway lines, bridges and gorges, ambushing of motor traffic and patrols, and attacking barracks and troop concentrations. We knew we would be outnumbered by at least ten to one, but such had been the thoroughness of our training that I am sure that each one of us felt he had enough of self-cunning and ruthlessness to meet the Jap at more than level terms.

The thousand-mile-long front line along which the Japs and British were at that time only clashing sporadically in localized patrol actions, wound its tortuous way through country generally accepted as largely impenetrable. But Wingate would accept no barriers. And in the end he sufficiently convinced higher authority (not without considerable opposition) that the so-called impassable could be penetrated by bold and resolute men. With proper training, in fact, he insisted they could turn to good account that very unfriendliness of the jungle.

Wingate had emphasized again and again to us that with no supply lines to retard us and advertise our presence, and no vulnerable rear echelons to swallow up men in their defence, we should be a far more

potent force than the Japs could possibly anticipate.
Supplies would fall like manna from the heavens in
answer to our prayers rising up on wireless waves
through the ether. Provided we could keep going and
retain our fighting spirit, the enemy would never be
able to pin us down. Our job was to strike unexpectedly
from the depths of the jungle, to kill and disrupt, and
then to vanish as suddenly as we had come. We were
not to allow the enemy to draw us into a pitched battle
in any one particular place. Our strength was to lie in
speed and surprise at all times.

That Wingate's raiders were something of an unusual force became evident quite early on at Jhansi.
Deliberately anything that appertained to the barrack
square and square-bashing was avoided, and a certain
amount of latitude was permitted in the matter of
uniforms. "Dress for comfort" was the order of the day.
Shirts and slacks, secured at the ankle with puttees, a
wide-brimmed soft felt bush hat, and a belt hung with
grenades, water bottle and a revolver, was a general
rule. There were of course exceptions. One officer
favoured a Seaforth kilt, with socks, boots and puttees
completing his below-the-waist ensemble. As a con-
cession to his local surroundings he crowned this
somewhat spectacular outfit with a huge flat wickerwork
Burmese hat of the sort the coolies wore. Another officer swaggered around with a pair of pearl-handled
.45 automatics which dangled on each side in the best
two-gun Wild-West manner!

Not the least flamboyant was the Brigadier himself.
Orde Wingate's battered East African sun-helmet, of
course, had already become immortalized. No-one
thinks of Wingate today without picturing him as a
slightly stooping, predatory figure crowned by his old
topee. His trousers were a faded pair of well-worn
whipcord, and he liked to carry an enormous bamboo
pole which gave him the air of an ancient prophet
striding out into the wilderness. Wingate's bush shirt
had one red tab, his Brigadier's badge of rank, missing
from the collar, to complete the unorthodox picture.

But his unorthodoxy did not detract one iota from the

respect and the awe in which everyone of his men held him. On those occasions when he strode among us holding a large metalically ticking alarm-clock no one laughed. No one ever suggested he was "round the bend." We all knew the clock was to remind us that time was ticking away with every moment that passed, and that no one must waste time if the war were to be pursued to its ultimate victorious conclusion. When he arrived in India to form his Chindit brigade, he was already a legend. His pre-war cloak-and-dagger work in Palestine, and later leading the Abyssinian guerillas against the Italian Army to such fantastic effect, was all part of the Wingate story known to every man serving under him.

The moment when Orde Wingate told No. 2 Column exactly what our mission would be in this desperate adventure is perhaps my most vivid memory of him. His thin lips pursed, his unruly brown hair falling forward over his right eye, he crouched even farther forward over his prophet's pole so that his acquiline nose was almost touching it.

"You will make for Kyaikthin," he said, tersely. "There you will destroy the railway south of the village. In going there and in so doing you must draw as many Japs as possible after you. The success of the northern group which is the main striking force, and therefore of the whole operation, is in your hands. Gentlemen, you are the decoy. Good luck!"

His blunt instructions delivered, Orde Wingate ran his cold blue eyes calculatedly over each one of us. They seemed to be penetrating deep into our inner thoughts, to be deliberately assessing each one of us before we set out to do his bidding. Then our hour struck, and we were off. Each man weighted down by his bulky Everest-type pack, and fairly bristling with weapons and ammunition,* we swung into the march from our bivouac area—due east!

Just before we left General Wavell himself arrived to wish us God speed. In words which filled us with

---

*Fully laden, a Chindit carried 72 lb. of kit and weapons.

intense pride he told us that the eyes of the Allied world would be upon us as we marched out into the great unknown of the Burmese jungle to do battle with the Japs behind their own lines. I remember how the tears of pride sprang to my eyes as we marched past the General, and he paid a wonderful tribute to the spirit of Wingate's daring campaign by himself saluting us before the Column Commanders could give the "eyes right" for us to salute him.

Little did most of us realize why General Wavell had really come up to Imphal to visit Wingate's Chindits. It had been to cancel the North-Burma offensive of which our deep penetration raid was only a part. Higher command had just learned that the other part, the advance by the large Chinese force down from the Yunnan mountains to attack the Japanese in the Lashio-Bhama area, had fallen through. Although there were several Chinese divisions deployed there, and apparently only one Jap division to fight them, Generalissimo Chiang Kai-shek just wasn't interested unless the British would mount a large-scale amphibious assault down the west coast of Burma at the same time. So the three thousand Chindits—meant only to cut the Japs communications and disrupt their rear while they came to grips with the Chinese divisions—went in nevertheless. It was a calculated risk which Wavell agreed with Wingate his force could take.

For a full nine days out from Imphal we marched hard before we reached the Chindwin river. The latter stages were very much like marching through no-man's-land. The broad and fast-flowing Chindwin, east of the British concentrations at Imphal and Kohima, was the recognized boundary between Jap-held and British-held territory in northern Burma. Except for the broad plateau in which Imphal lay, on our side of the Chindwin were hundreds of square miles of thick jungle flowing unendingly over hill and valley all the way from Imphal right down to the banks of the Chindwin itself. Across the river in the Japanese-held North Burma a great dusty escarpment, a hell of razor-sharp towering grasses, flies and scorpions, extended as far south as Kalewa. But apart from that, on the Jap side of the Chindwin the jungle was quite as wicked as anything on the British side. And, of course it was full of vicious, jungle-wise Japs.

During the last two or three days of our march towards the Chindwin we became acutely aware that it was a no-man's-land. Except for a section of Burma Rifles returning from a patrol, and a small detachment of Sikhs, we saw no-one. The British forward troops within one or two days' march of the Chindwin river were, in fact, no more than a scattering of small patrols. They were mobile "listening posts," keeping keen eyes and ears open for any sign of an attempted Jap invasion. Any indication of increased Jap patrol activity coming across the Chindwin into our side of the no-man's-land might well precede an all-out attack. It was in this no-man's-land between Imphal and the Chindwin that we, the "decoys" of No. 1 and No. 2 Columns, parted company with the other columns of the main force and Wingate's brigade headquarters. Under the overall command of Lieut.-Colonel Alexander we marched some forty miles south of the main body to make a crossing at Auktaung. Wingate led the others to a far more secret crossing point at Tonhe.

The split up of forces took place just south of Tamu whence we, the decoys, marched on boldly by day while the main body lay low during the light hours and marched only by night. An even more ostentatious approach towards Jap-held territory was made by a still smaller party which split off from Colonel Alexander's force immediately we had crossed the Chindwin. This, led by Major John Jeffries—grandly dressed up as a Brigadier—headed deliberately for a village of which the headman was known to be a very willing tool of the Japanese.

John Jeffries was quite a character, by anyone's standards! An Irishman, it was perhaps quite typical of him that he should have started his professional service career in the Royal Navy, and was in line for promotion to Lieut.-Commander when he decided to resign his commission to go into business. When the Second World War broke out he was doing very well with a chain of super petrol stations around Southampton and Portsmouth, but he straight away volunteered for the Navy. When told it would be several months before he could be assigned to a warship for active war service John Jeffries could not wait! He joined up as a private in the Royal Ulster Rifles, with whom he served in the ranks for six months before being commissioned. It was only natural that he should have volunteered for the Commandos, and should have been in the Lofoten Islands raid. It was also only natural that he should have volunteered for an unspecified "special duty" in the Far East just at the time the enemy there were right in the ascendancy. Thus he turned up in the Wingate circus!

Major John Jeffries was not content with being "just a Brigadier" when he marched into the pro-Jap village across the Chindwin. In a deep, dark spot in the jungle before he arrived there, he halted and decked himself out with the full insignia of a General—red tabs, hatband and all! Once in the village with his "staff officers" he lost no time in billeting himself on the traitorous headman's house. He lost even less time in pulling out important-looking campaign maps and discussing the best tracks to use for the movement of a big force of British far south down the Chindwin. The headman was extremely helpful, and then undoubtedly sent runners hot-foot to warn the Japs of this strong thrust to be aimed at them far to the south.

Having had lots of fun (which included the bringing in by his "staff officers" of a number of important-looking messages, one to announce that he had won the Irish Sweep!), John Jeffries and his deceptionists marched off importantly into the jungle whence they had come. Within forty-eight hours they had completely changed direction to strike out eastwards to overtake Nos. 1 and 2 Columns, which by then were marching strongly through dense jungle towards their date with the railway line at Kyaikthin.

Just to make sure the Japs knew which way we

were heading, the whole of Colonel Alexander's group had taken a big supply drop two days' march before we reached the Chindwin. The air had fairly throbbed with Dakota transports, and a blizzard of parachutes had descended on us from the skies so that even a blind and stone-deaf fifth columnist could not fail to know all about it. It was fascinating, somehow—in a creepy sort of way—to be proclaiming so blatantly to the little yellow "supermen of the jungle" that we were on our way to meet them.

Thanks to that drop we had full stomachs, enjoying a vast meal of bully beef stew, with lashings of potatoes and onions, followed by tinned fruit, bread-and-butter and jam, and mugs of hot tea. This was destined to be the expedition's last meal of field service rations until well over two months later. From then on they averaged half-rations if they were lucky.

Each man had five days' paratroop rations in his pack as we marched on eastwards after the supply drop. This consisted of biscuits, cheese, raisins, and dates, with tea, sugar and milk. A few lucky hoarders carried also such luxuries as a tin of bully beef, or a half loaf of white bread. Armament and equipment carried on the back, or clipped to belts, included a groundsheet, spare trousers and shirt, four pairs of socks, a canvas life-jacket, mess tins, both metal issue water bottle and a canvas one, mending materials, a toggle rope, rubber shoes, a jackknife and kukri, three grenades, and a bayonet, while all carried rifles or tommy-guns. The mules with each column carried the Bren-guns, extra ammunition, and blankets to the extent of one per man.

We had been nearing the end of the last stage of our march to the Chindwin, when Wingate made a sudden and unexpected final appearance to bid us God speed. He had left his part of the force, now nearing the Chindwin forty miles to our north, so that he could read to all his officers his order of the day. His surprise visit could not have been better timed, nor his message more inspiring. It was filled with the fire of a crusader's zeal, and aroused a flame of pride and determination in even the most unimaginative of his troops.

Brigadier Orde Wingate's "Order of the Day," dated 14 February, 1943, ran thus:

"Today we stand on the threshold of battle. The time of preparation is over and we are moving on the enemy to prove ourselves and our methods. At this moment we stand beside soldiers of the United Nations in the front line trenches throughout the world. It is always a minority that occupies the front line. It is a still smaller minority that accepts, with a good heart, tasks like this that we have chosen to carry out. We need not, therefore, as we go forward into conflict, suspect ourselves of selfish or interested motives.

"We have all had the opportunity of withdrawing, and we are here because we have chosen to be here: that is, we have chosen to bear the burden and heat of the day. Men who make this choice are above the average of courage. We need, therefore, have no fear for the staunchness and guts of our comrades. The motives which have led each and all of us to devote ourselves to what lies ahead, cannot conceivably have been bad. Comfort and security are not sacrificed voluntarily, for the sake of others, by ill-disposed people. Our motive, therefore, may be taken to be the desire to serve our day and generation in the way that seems nearest to our hand.

"The battle is not always to the strong, nor the race to the swift. Victory in war cannot be counted on, but what can be counted on is that we shall go forward determined to do what we can to bring this war to an end, which we believe best for our friends and comrades in arms; without boastfulness or forgetting our duty, resolved to do the right so far as we can see the right. Our aim is to make possible a government of this world in which all men can live at peace and with equal opportunities of service.

"Finally, knowing the vanity of man's effort and the confusion of his purpose, let us pray God may accept our services and direct our endeavours so that when we shall have done all, we may see the fruit of our labours and be satisfied."

It was signed: "O. C. Wingate, Commander, 77th Indian Infantry Brigade."

6

THE HELL OF BURMA'S JUNGLE

After the Brigadier's departure, Nos. 1 and 2 Columns tightened up their equipment and accoutrements and set off in "column snake" (as we called single file) to cover the last few miles to the Chindwin. The Brigadier was off to lead the secret crossing by night up at Tonhe, we to make the daylight crossing at Auktaung that would draw the enemy after us. If our diversion worked according to plan Wingate would be able to slip his "killing force" through the Japs forward position completely unobserved along secret forest tracks leading out to the Mu Valley beyond.

I have never forgotten my first vision of the Chindwin river, that final definite division between the ominous jungle that was no-man's-land on the British side and the dark forest on the other side we knew to be strongly patrolled by the Japs. We were breasting a rise in the track when, because of the increased light ahead and the wave of excited anticipation that ran through the troops in front, I realized that there must be a big break in the green twilight monotony of the jungle. A break which could be only the River Chindwin.

Although we were soon to find it was a turged, swirling expanse of water more than a quarter of a mile wide, from this point it was a silver snake lazily coiling between an eternity of undulating green forest. It gave one a shiver of apprehension to realize that vast areas of this jungle were officially "impenetrable," and that through an unthinkable number of ages only solitary adventurers had risked its perils. Some of the areas before us indeed had never known the presence of man.

A look behind, before we dropped down over the brow of the hill and on to the steady decline which ended at the Chindwin, gave a view of the fantastic territory over which we had already marched. The steep risings and fallings of the Chin Hills appeared to go on forever, and we had already marched over them, for as far back as the eye could see, and even beyond. Every one of those hills was clad in thickest jungle, and the unending vista of dark green and shimmering lighter greens was all around us, seemingly for ever and for ever. Sometimes it was obscured by a drift of mist hanging above an unseen watercourse, sometimes broken by an abruptly rising barren peak, but otherwise on and on for ever, jungle, jungle, everywhere.

The column snaked man behind man, man behind animal, silently but in determined spirits, down to the river itself. The last quarter of a mile was over flat paddy, deserted and neglected since war had enveloped the country. But by the time the main body of the two columns had reached the Chindwin's west bank, opposite the large village of Auktaung, we found that our advance party of Burma Rifles had already fully organized the transport across. The villagers had proved to be genuinely glad to see the British back, and readily hired their boats out and provided boatmen to manipulate them back and forth across the river. Thus we crossed without incident or alarm.

We fed well at Auktaung, on heaps of curried chicken, fish and rice bought from the villagers with some of the silver rupees the columns carried. Then, after a good night's sleep, we set off marching strongly due south at first light, and marched due south all the daylight hours to continue our plan of deception. Next night, after a few hours sleep, we of No. 2 Column were up and off again. Only this time we were heading due east for Kyaikthin and had split off from No. 1 Column. Now we were in earnest, marching through enemy territory on our own straight towards our target, the distant Myitkyina-Rangoon railway!

There followed for us then a week of absolute hell, clawing our way through the heart-breaking humid green inferno of the Chindwin's eastern watershed. The dense impenetrable bamboo jungle through which we had to fight our way now consisted of closely packed clumps of spiky bamboo rising twenty or thirty feet to merge into a tangled mass of creepers and foliage overhead. We hacked and crashed and slashed our way through this frustrating, infuriating, maddening jungle with its sharp-spiked stems and razor-edged leaves and giant grass blades. For days on end foliage completely obliterated the sun and compressed the hot and motionless air down upon us so that we hacked and fought forward laboriously, always in the torrid heat of an oven that bathed us in sweat and sapped our strength. Yet nowhere, at no time, in the midst of that geen hell, did we encounter sight or sound of our enemies. After the steaming heat of the gloomy forest there came next the fury of the sun-blistered escarpment. This, a barren stretch of higher ground, thrust in a long arid wedge of desert upland north to south straight through the endless jungle.

Conditions here were possibly even worse. Parched bushes and elephant grass offered such bitter opposition that we had to march for days along a river bed, up to our knees in water. Hands were torn and blistered, and feet cracked and split because the constant immersion in water softened and crinkled them to the consistency of white bloodless pulp. Every day and all the time we sweated, so that our clothing and equipment was black and stinking and becoming rotten with it, and half the time our eyes were blinded with sweat. Every day our muscles ached and our bones almost groaned aloud in the agony of our exertions. Every day our filthy and sodden clothing became more and more torn, ripped and ragged until most of us looked like walking scarecrows. It was true that each night brought a pause from this agonizing slavery, but not before each bivouac area had been prepared and manned against possible attack, and weapons had been cleaned to ensure complete fighting efficiency. And the stinking obstinate mules always had to be "maintained." Mostly the meals that were all we had to sustain us during this terrible march were made up of a hotch-potch of crushed biscuit, with sometimes some dried fruit thrown in. Always there was a cup of hot tea to wash it down.

Even as early as this in the campaign, there were lice in our clothes to torment us in those moments when we could slump down in sheer exhaustion to rest from our back-breaking labours. Nagging ticks attached themselves to us, too, and in the river leeches fastened on to legs and arms and sucked blood greedily further to sap our strength.

Then, thank God, we at last reached an end to that hell east of the Chindwin. There came the days and nights beyond the escarpment when we marched through terrain where majestic teak forests flourished, and the ground was mostly flat and sandy. Those mighty trees, rising a hundred feet and more into the air, were well spaced out and the ground between them clear of bush and creeper. Magnificently they stood there, the cultivated wealth of Burma. Still more important to us, it was pleasant country through which to march, with cool, leafy shade and no humidity! And still there was no sign of the Japs we knew must be all around us. But at no time did our watchfulness relax. Always we carried out the strict security measures in which we had been so rigorously trained.

We cooked meals in pairs. One man would boil the water while the other ground into powder with his bayonet hilt two Shakapura biscuits. The lukewarm water was poured on the powder until it became a gooey paste in the bottom of the mess-tin. Then this would be gently stirred over a slow fire until it began to bubble. Next more water would be added, together with chopped bamboo leaves and any jungle fruit, pieces of meat or nuts which a soldier mighty be lucky enough to have unearthed—either from the living jungle around him or from the bottom of his ammunition pouch.

Making tea in the jungle bore little resemblance to the making of tea in any civilized home or, indeed, to making tea in any more static military establishment.

Water was boiled in a mess-tin and as soon as it started to bubble a bag of tea leaves would be speedily immersed in it, and as quickly withdrawn by a deft flick of the wrist. Almost simultaneously two strong fingers would squeeze the water out of the bag into another mess-tin; and that would be tea made while with great care the bag with the leaves in it would be wrapped in a teak leaf and safely deposited in an ammunition pouch from which it would not be withdrawn again until the evening (perhaps to make its eleventh pint of tea!).

Once breakfast was ready it would take approximately two minutes to eat. Then we would loll back on the dusty ground and drag our equipment towards us with a minimum of movement. Ammunition pouches would be methodically opened and bullets and grenades cautiously extracted. The reason for this carefulness had nothing to do with fear of sudden destruction by an unexpected explosion. It was because it was the usual practice to hoard any reserves of tobacco leaf at the bottom of an ammunition pouch. With the air of misers secretly counting gold we would carefully tap the dust remaining in our pouches on to a scrap of a tattered letter, a piece of toilet paper, or a dry teak leaf which would then be rolled into the semblance of a cigarette. It would be kept roughly in shape by winding around its middle a piece of cotton torn from the seam of your shirt. The exposed end would then be folded over and the cigarette placed between the teeth. A burning ember from the fire would supply a light—and in spite of the acrid fumes which poured forth and the belly-straining coughs brought on by the smoke, we would lie back and really enjoy our after breakfast cigarette.

Next, before thoughts had time to crystallize into dreams of home, would come the crisp order: "Load up!" Boots would be fastened tight once more about aching feet, and rifles would be propped against trees. Then the mule loads would be laid out in neat avenues along the forest track. Soon the muleteers would appear leading their surly charges up from the mule lines to bring them up the avenue in proper order of march to be halted at their respective loads. In a trice four men would have each animal saddled with its load equally balanced on either side, and a circingle would be deftly bound around each animal to secure the whole load. Then the men would shrug themselves into their equipment and gird on their heavy packs, weapons and ammunition, and so the column would be ready to move off on another day's hard marching.

We had not long fought our way clear of the arid agony of the escarpment when we took our first supply drop east of the Chindwin. Now, far into Japanese territory, we quite deliberately advertised our presence by halting at the large village of Yeshin and waiting there for the Dakotas to fly over in answer to our radio signals, and cascade down to us a snowstorm of parachuted supplies. A full ten days supply drop we gathered there in full view of the villagers, who stood agape as we methodically and unhurriedly received from the skies fresh food, clothing, ammunition and other stores.

Whether or not we were to expect treachery from the people of Yeshin we did not know. It was part of the Wingate plan that we should deliberately lay ourselves open to the risk of reports being passed on to the Japs. We had heard numbers of stories of treachery by the Burmese. When the defeated and scattered remnants of the British forces withdrew from Burma in 1942 they brought with them stories of atrocities committed by Burmese villagers as well as by the Japs. A typical one was the story of a R.A.F. sergeant pilot who had been shot down over Central Burma by a Jap Zero, but who had succeeded in bailing out and landing quite unhurt on a nice, soft strip of paddy near a village. Feeling quite pleased with himself at his escape he had cleared himself of his parachute harness and set off walking briskly to the nearest village. There he hoped, indeed, quite expected, some assistance from the natives in continuing his escape. But his hopes were as short-lived as he proved to be. A party of between fifteen and twenty Burmese, armed with dahs (native swords) rushed out on him and literally cut him to pieces.

There was no doubt at all that hundreds of Indian residents in Burma, fleeing dazedly before the Jap onrush, had been murdered by Burmese villagers who lay in wait for them beside the jungle tracks. But then there never had been much love lost between the native Burmese and the Indian immigrants, usually either town dwellers who had become successful and wealthy, or else the village moneylenders. There were, of course, also inducements offered by the Japs who sought to encourage the Burmese to attack British stragglers, or to report the whereabouts of British troops, and offered rewards for every British soldier brought in dead or alive.

Also, as further persuasion for the natives of Burma to co-operate with the newly arrived Japanese, and to throw off any sentimental attachment they might have for the recently ejected British, the Japs meted out the most savage punishment to any village known to have harboured British refugees. The Japs would burn whole villages to the ground, slaughter all the men and youths, and often take away the women and girls to provide more "recruits" for the "comforts battalions" which were attached to the Japanese fighting units.

Japanese "comforts battalions" were squads of young women sent in as "second wave" after the front line troops. They would be put into hastily constructed camps in the jungle behind the Jap front line. Their mission in life was to provide the full amenities of a mobile brothel, and the supply had to satisfy the demand whenever a battle-weary Jap superman came their way. To start with, patriotic Japanese girls (of rather doubtful morals) were persuaded they were gloriously serving their country, as well as their countrymen, by enrolling in the comforts battalions. But the jungle conditions proved less inviting than the life they had expected to lead in the rather more luxurious quarters of captured Hong Kong, Singapore, Rangoon and Mandalay. So the unfortunate Burmese women were called on to provide a quota of compulsory volunteers. For many of these poor wretches the end was death as well as degredation.

The Japs did have some less violent, even if equally lethal punishments which they would mete out to villages suspected of sympathy towards the British. They would stop their rice supplies. The whole of the rice grown in the area would be confiscated by the Japs and taken away, which would mean that most likely the whole village would starve to death. Their only chance was to disappear *en masse* into the jungle to try to start a new, if rather less civilized life.

In view of these savage punishments it was all the more remarkable that the bulk of the people of Burma remained loyal to the defeated British who, after all, might have seemed to the natives to have no more right there as their masters than the Japanese. The loyalty of the Kachins and the Shans in the hill country of northern Burma was particularly inspiring. They faced the most terrible dangers and privations purely out of loyalty to the British. They provided a spy network and guerrilla forces who worked and fought with intrepid valour. Britain should never, never forget them and their loyalty.

In view of the barefaced manner in which we took our big supply drop at Yeshin, and the way we courted treachery, it was not surprising that we soon had our first clash with Japanese troops. Two nights later there was a slight skirmish between a section of the Burma Rifles platoon and a Japanese patrol. It ended in the Japs being driven off and the Burrifs bringing back a wounded prisoner. To me, still very much a boy as yet untried in battle, it was strangely fascinating to go over to the bivouac area to look at my first Jap!

The fight had been at night, and the wounded Jap prisoner brought in had been dumped down under a tree. He had been hit in the chest by a tommy-gun bullet, but the wound did not seem likely to be fatal. The blood did not pulse from his breast or drool from his mouth as it would have done had he been hit in the lungs.

The Jap was dressed in a khaki shirt, now blood-stained, and was wearing khaki breeches and puttees and rubber-soled jungle boots. He looked to be well fed and in good healthy condition. He had been very carefully searched for grenades because already the British had learned to their cost that Jap wounded had a very bad habit of unexpectedly whipping out grenades from their clothing, snatching out the pin, and blowing themselves and everyone handy to Kingdomcome. They usually chose the moment for this inconsiderate practice carefully so that they had the largest possible number of British soldiers around them at the time!

My impression of this, my first Jap superman, was not so much that he was a little yellow man, but that he had a large wide mouth, full of very uneven square teeth. His hair was close cropped and he wore no hat. I stared at that Jap good and long, wondering how many more like him I was going to see, and hoping that most of them would be dead ones. This one was soon dead himself. Though his wound did not appear to be serious it seemed to be his intention to escape at any cost the indignity of being a prisoner of the British. Lying there under the tree he just made a point of being stiff and dead when the sun rose to shine on him next morning.

After this brush with the Jap patrol outside Yeshin there was an air of increased alertness and anticipation throughout the column. Fingers itched to be on triggers, eyes peered more intently into the jungle depths for the slightest trace of enemy soldiers, the ground was watched even more closely for the imprint of the Jap jungle boot, and ears were constantly cocked for the slightest sound that might precede a hail of enemy bullets from the dark jungle around us.

As we approached the River Mu, the next water obstacle that lay across our route, we carried out a subterfuge aimed further to confuse the Japs, and maybe hold them off a bit longer from attacking us. In our heart of hearts, of course, we knew they could be holding off only because they would be building up a still bigger killing force to launch upon us!

As we advanced in twisting single column on a small village near the river the order came quietly down the line that we were to march round it for the next two hours. As soon as the head of the column had passed out of sight of the village around a bend in the track it turned off left into the jungle and cut across to rejoin the track we had already traversed before the village. Thus, soon after the tail of our column had vanished from sight and the gaping villagers had started to go about their normal business again, what should turn up but the head of another column! And after this column had wound its way past, what should happen but yet another one arrived!

In just the same way that every Chinese, every Jap, every Burmese or every Indian looks to the average Englishman to be the same as the next Chinese, Jap, Burmese or Indian, so did every soldier in that marching column appear to the wondering Burmese villagers to be "just another English soldier." They never tumbled to the fact that it was the same 250 men marching past them again and again during the two hours British soldiers were passing near their village. The result, we learned later, was that spies reported village gossip back to the Japanese exaggerating our numbers so greatly that No. 2 Column was entered down as a complete brigade on the Japanese Order of Battle maps!

We waded the shallow Mu river still untroubled by Japanese attack and on March 2 were on the very threshold of our objective. Less than a day's march from us lay the railway line from Mandalay to Myitkina on which we were to descend from our jungle cover at Kyaikthin and so to tear it asunder with the demolition charges that it would disrupt for many a day to come, Japanese rail communications feeding their forward troops.

Soon after the crossing Major Emmett ordered No. 2 Column to lie up in the jungle. We were on the very verge of attacking our objective. I felt strangely satisfied and buoyant of spirit as I lay, drowsy and content, vaguely conscious of the endeavours of a radio operator near me to contact rear H.Q. at Imphal. Here, in our jungle hide-out 150 miles behind the Jap lines, he was our vital life line, our one link with the only people who could succour us if calamity befell us.

"Hallo X-Ray. Hallo X-Ray. Report my signals. X-Ray, over." On and on he droned in the heat of the noonday sun which blazed with savage intensity high and invisible above the roof of the jungle. His presser switch reminded me of the repetitive clicking home of a rifle bolt. But it only reminded me in a lazy sort of a way. I felt peace and content, and there was no alarm in my mind. To add to the drowsy sense of peace a gorgeous pink and white butterfly drifted down from the shadowy world of creepers and foliage above us and settled on the radio operator's bush hat, spreading out its wings to flaunt itself before me, a thing of a mysterious beauty almost out of this world. The radio operator, quite unaware, made a sudden move with his hand to dash sweat from his brow, the butterfly, startled, flapped upwards from his felt hat and then lazily spiralled away high up to be lost again in the roof of dense jungle above.

I rolled over, dimly conscious that the operator was still unsuccessfully trying to contact Imphal. I gazed out through the trees, as though through a dark green tunnel, upon the railway line, a section of which was now framed by the end of the tunnel where it lay burning like gold in the afternoon sun. Along that single metre-gauge track the Japs were carrying all the arms and ammunition required by their troops in all parts of Upper and Western Burma, bringing them right up from Rangoon in the south to Myitkina in the north.

Individual flints on the four foot high embankment, hot in the sun, themselves blazed back its glare so that the burnished track seemed set in a dazzling diamond setting. Each side of the railway line was a 20-yards wide strip cleared bare of vegetation so that as far as one could see the track upon its embankment ran like twin lines of fire from end to end of a wide avenue between towering walls of darkest jungle.

No. 2 Column, now at long last poised to make our

kill as planned by Wingate, were lying up on a small teak-covered hill overlooking the railway. We had been concealed there for some hours resting through the heat of the day before the arduous task that lay ahead of us for that night. Our zero hour was at long last nearly upon us, the hour of the destruction of the railway line at Kyaikthin! I was dreamily conscious that the radio operator had abandoned his attempt to contact base and was drowsing now like the rest of us. His back against a tree, his feet up on his radio set, felt hat tilted over his eyes, he, too, appeared completely at peace with the world. Somewhere through the high, hot oven of the jungle, a brain-fever bird spilled its rambling, sibilant monotony.

The butt of a rifle pushed into my ribs awoke me. Arthur Best was standing grinning at me. "Tea is ready. Come and get it!" he said. Arthur turned away from me and resumed his crouch over a tommy-cooker. A look of exasperation clouded his normally cheerful face.

"What's wrong with you, Arthur?" I asked chidingly. "You look like a frustrated vulture!"

"Any more cheek from you, youngster, and you'll brew your own bloody char!" he growled. "These tommy-cookers are no earthly use at all, it's taken me half an hour to get the water warm." Tommy-cookers certainly did not do the job as efficiently as a fire, as I came to realize when Arthur handed a mess-tin of warm water with tea leaves floating on top!

In the hot stillness of our jungle hiding-place I could at that moment afford to look with affection upon Arthur, and to contemplate my happy association with him since I had joined the Chindits. He had been my instructor, confessor, and continuous companion since I had joined the column. Though he was a few years older than I, we had discovered many mutual interests. In fact, during many hours of jungle conversation our only serious difference of opinion had been over our respective views on the works of Mr. Ivor Novello and the value of the ballet as a medium for the expression of art! Differences hardly likely to cause a rift between us as we fought our way, often side by side, through the dense jungle to fulfil our task as decoys for Wingate's main striking force.

So new a soldier myself (except for O.T.C. training at school the total of my military experience was at the Officers' Training School, Bangalore, from April to October, 1942), I regarded Arthur with all the respect that a recruit should give to a veteran. A bank clerk in civil life, Arthur Best had been a rifleman in a crack Territorial Army battalion of the London Rifle Brigade. He had known the ferocity and carnage of war and the heat of battle in the very early days. He had been one of those battered, bewildered, exhausted, outnumbered but indomitable British soldiers who had fought the rearguard action against the Germans all the way down to the beaches of Dunkirk. Sometimes at night, before we rolled over to sleep deep in the whispering jungle, Arthur would paint for me lurid pictures of fighting against the Germans in France.

I was proud that I, even though only a schoolboy of sixteen, had played my very small part in helping with the evacuation from those famous beaches. My father had owned a 35-ft. launch which was moored in Weymouth Harbour, and I had accompanied him on the high adventure of ferrying rescued soldiers back to Weymouth and Poole, from Dover, Beachy Head, and other places where they had been put down by the little ships shuttling valiantly backwards and forwards between England and France. To be serving now with a man who had been through the real thing was quite something.

After his showing in France and at Dunkirk, Arthur Best was put forward as the right material for an officer, and was eventually commissioned into the 9th Gurkha Rifles, during 1941. He had found his work tedious at his Regimental Centre and had volunteered for "special duty" with the 77th Independent Infantry Brigade. It was only natural that, by virtue of the fact that he was a keen amateur mechanic, he should immediately have been appointed animal transport officer in charge of No. 2 Column's mules when he joined the Wingate force!

All through those days now behind us, of fighting our way through bitter jungle always beneath the unrelenting blaze of the Burmese sun, Arthur had been a strong and staunch companion. He had been a stout friend to whom I could look for help and advice whenever I needed it. And now, on what was likely to be the eve of my first battle, I was more glad than ever to have him beside me.

I had no illusions now, for all the peacefulness of the jungle around us, for all the immunity from Jap attacks which had been ours thus far. I felt sure we could not hope to live many more hours without being involved in the full fury of a pitched battle. I looked again on that burnished stretch of railway line which lay down there below me, darkly framed by the fronds and leaves of the jungle that was our cover. As far as the limited view permitted it stretched shimmering with heat-haze, impersonal, dazzling bright, disturbed by no man, nor by any beast. Yet I knew that somewhere, not far away down that line, lay the Japanese installations at Kyaikthin. In and around them were the tough, savage, fanatical Japanese soldiers whom we had been told to engage and destroy. Although I knew well the reputation of the Jap fighting man, I was also confident in the courage and skill of my companions, in the uncanny brilliance of Wingate's leadership, and in my own weapons and ability to use them.

I drank the tea Arthur had made, grinned at him, and settled down to sleep again.

7

AMBUSH ARMAGEDDON

That night, while the world was ghostly still and silent around us, we slipped stealthily from our cover and formed up on the railway line. The jungle we had left behind looked black and inscrutable as we stood out there bathed in the silver light of the Burmese moon.

For two hours we marched along that railway line, with never a sound or sign that there was a Jap within a hundred miles. We were 250 men and 20 mules, all strung out in our habitual single file marching in the moonlight 150 miles behind the enemy lines. Then, from somewhere way up ahead of the Column, Major Emmett gave the order to halt. Faces glistened and teeth flashed in the moonlight as we stood there on the railway line. A stray moonbeam touched off a gleam along the purposeful-looking barrel of a Vickers machine-gun on a mule ahead of me. Farther up the column another moonbeam danced whitely on the naked blade of a kukri a Gurkha was fingering with a sort of idle longing.

I wriggled my shoulders to ease the weight of my pack. My immediate companion of the march, Nelly the mule, flicked her tail playfully at my bare forearms. From force of habit I withdrew just six inches, sufficient to keep me clear of the rasping hairs of her tail. I could claim to know Nelly and her habits intimately by now, for I had trudged so many miles behind her. Through forest and over fiery escarpment, through jungle thorns and turgid torrents, on and on in her approved place in the column Nelly had plodded, bearing on her back the column radio set. And with me, mostly just out of "swishing distance," directly behind.

As we stood out there on the railway, patiently awaiting the next move, the moon slid behind a cloud. Immediately the world of silver and soft grey was transformed into one of shadow and darker shadow. Suddenly Nelly started forward, pulled by her muleteer. This was the signal for me, the next man down the line, to move forward in my turn. The man behind me followed until the whole column was advancing again.

Although we were marching in silence we could not move without noise. The clank of steel-shod boots on the railway line, the crunch of hoof striking sparks from flint, were part of the unavoidable sound of our progress. I had felt uneasy from the moment we had emerged from the jungle and had begun our march along this naked railway line. We were sitting ducks out here, just right for ambushing from the flanking jungle. We had halted several times while guides went to search the black uprising walls of jungle on each side for a possible track to lead us back behind cover and through to our objective, Kyaikthin. So far there had been no luck.

Once the jungle track was located, and we were at long last in striking distance of our objective, we would be completely silent. Silent until, from the black cloak of our cover, we would debouch from the jungle to bring down a hail of fire and destruction upon the sleeping Japanese. All according to plan.

Again we shuffled to a halt as the guides probed for the elusive track. I yawned as the column stood there out in the moonlight, awaiting the outcome of whatever was going on up at the front. There were carried back to me the restless sounds of man and beast. I yawned again. There came the sound of just one bang up at the front somewhere beyond my vision. But only for a split second, then an inferno of noise engulfed the world around me!

There came the high-pitched staccato scream of a machine-gun. Instantly my battle training told me it was a Japanese light automatic. Then overwhelmingly many other machine-guns joined in an ear-splitting chorus. The crash—ping of rifles and banging of grenades, joined in to swell the noise of sudden battle to a fearful crescendo. Somewhere ahead there was an uncertain scuffling. A hoarse voice cried: "Take cover!" and another screamed "Christ Almighty!" and was silenced.

I swung my tommy-gun from the slung position to the ready in one instinctive movement. Cold sweat stood out on my brow in the hot night. I peered forward, completely befuddled. As if jerked upwards abruptly by wires Nelly the mule reared up highly before me to black out the moon. She spun round even as she reared up, then crashed over backwards and slid down the embankment to lie jerking convulsively at the bottom. And in that split second the sense of being overwhelmed by unaccountable disaster which had numbed my brain and frozen me to the spot, vanished before the urgent instinct for self preservation. I dived after Nelly.

All was turmoil along the column. The file of men and mules which but a moment ago had been a compact warlike force advancing with measured menace through the moonlight, had now completely changed its nature. Men and mules were lying, twisted and contorted, twitching and writhing, as far as the eye could see along the track. Others were still erect, stark in the moonlight, heaving and jerking in the midst of this chaos. Frightened mules reared and kicked and bucked and some men still fought to quieten them. In the midst of it, around it, below it, and above it and beyond it was the noise! The shrill scream of the Jap light machine-guns, the metallic chatter of bren-guns, the cracking of rifles and banging of grenades, the ricocheting bullets and the deeper whine of grenade fragments all sang their songs in the hellish symphony of sudden battle.

A bren-gun opened up right beside me, so close that its sound was shattering. Bullets were suddenly ricocheting off the metal rails at the embankment's top above my head. A mortally wounded soldier some-where in the blackness near me screamed with hor-rifying shrillness. Somewhere, everywhere, men and animals were uttering cries that belied description and which were new in my knowledge of human and animal sounds. Over all there was that sinister scuffling noise made by men of all kinds in close combat. The close combat of bayonet and kukri, of dagger and hunting knife, the fanatical, personal slaughter with blood-dripping cold steel which was at the core of the more impersonal killing by the high-velocity metal of machine-gun, rifle and revolver.

A fiery swarm of tracers swept over my head. Above and beyond me grenades exploded, and a shower of small stones descended on me from the embankment above. Then, as though washed clean by a draught of icy well-water, my brain cleared. I was suddenly, startlingly conscious of the smooth metallic grating of a round being levered into a breech beside my ear.

"Fix bayonets!" shouted a high-pitched, near-hysteri-cal voice. Wonderingly, I realized it was my own. As though my voice vibrations had touched off the button of some responsive mechanism, there came the answer-ing reassuring clicks of bayonets being fixed. Once more I was an integrated part of an effective fighting ma-chine.

A mule charged back down the line where men still appeared, disappeared, then loomed again. One side of its load was missing and the other was swinging dangerously from a solitary metal ring. As it bucked and snorted past me I saw that the load swinging thus dangerously was a box of 808 explosive! Then I saw that the Gurkha muleteer still hung on to the reins in an endeavour to halt the terrified beast. I hugged the embankment so close that I thought I must physi-cally merge into it. Then the mule and its box of latent death was gone.

I raised my head above the rails on the top of the embankment, just as the moon-splashed wall of grey-green jungle opposite appeared to disintegrate. Parts of it detached themselves, and were suddenly howling, screaming Jap soldiers, weapons glinting in the moon-light, charging across the thirty yards of ground which separated us! "Banzai! Banzai!" they screamed blood-curdlingly, the fanatical Jap war cry I had secretly dreaded to hear. Automatically my right hand flew to my belt. Closing over a grenade hanging there it pulled it free with that drill-book downward jerk that left the pin still fastened to the webbing. I lobbed it, and saw it arch over in the moonlight with leisurely ease to drop down and explode in red and black fire and singing metal just as the line of yelling Jap soldiers lurched over it.

As if it had been the first rocket signalling a fire-work display to commence, tommy-guns, rifles and brens opened up all along the embankment in frantic cacophony. The night palpitated hate and blood and fire and hot metal, behind and before, above and below and around.

With a murderous exhilaration I brought the sights of my tommy-gun into line on the chest of a Jap officer not fifteen yards from me. With the cold and calculated exultation of a professional killer I squeezed the trig-ger. But there was no comforting recoil at my shoulder. Suddenly I was ice cool no longer. Frantically now I pulled the trigger, and snatched it, and pulled it again and again. Still nothing happened. The clammy perspi-ration of fear burst out all over me and ran down my forehead into my eyes. What did I do now? Oh God, what did I do next? The Japanese officer, samurai sword weaving in the air suddenly somersaulted like a drunken acrobat and was a twitching heap between me and the rest of the charging Japs. The line of stocky, screaming, yellow fiends that had been charging towards us close on his heels seemed to wither and vanish.

I wiped the sweat from my eyes with the back of my hand and gasped my relief. There came a deep chuckle at my right side. I turned to find that Kul-bahadur was grinning broadly. Then he leaned towards me in a confiding manner and whispered in Gurkhali: "Sahib, the book of instruction does say that the

Thompson 1928 A1

Thompson machine-carbine must first have its action
cocked if it is to be fired. This is carried out by pulling
the cocking handle smartly to the rear." He chuckled
again, quite audible above the noise of battle. I
laughed—whether from embarrassment or hysteria I
could not say. I realized that even in the fury and desperation of the fighting Kulbahadur had seen the joke
in the fact that his officer had been trying to fire a
tommy-gun without first cocking it!

As suddenly as it had begun the battle died away
to a mere splatter of shots. Then, somewhere in the
near distance, it was a matter of just one stray rifle
shot. In the deep and sinister silence which followed,
I lay shuddering in the aftermath of my first battle.
The very silence steeped me in an uneasy feeling that
all was not well. I tried to assess what sort of force

of Japanese had ambushed us. For ambushed we most certainly had been!

Mentally I totted up the various types of weapons the Japs had brought to bear upon us as they opened fire from the jungle along both sides of the railway embankment. There had been heavy mortars and light mortars, light machine-guns and rifles, and at least two heavy machine-guns. I had never been under fire before but I estimated (and in later years learned that my estimate was quite reasonably accurate), that at least a Japanese battalion of some 800 men had engaged our column of 250. In all probability it was a whole Japanese brigade!

Now what?

From that ominously silent jungle across the railway track whence most of the firing had come, would there burst forth another charge? Or, even as we lay low waiting, were the Japs in the jungle behind us massing silently to complete the encirclement? An ammunition clip rang like a bell on the night air in the midst of the silence as someone to my left re-loaded his rifle. Someone to my left! Kulbahadur, I knew was by my right-hand, but who was at my left? My next duty as an officer was suddenly urgent. We must close up and keep contact. Whoever was on either side of me must be formed under my command into an integrated fighting force.

"Kulbahadur!" I whispered: "Eh! Kulbahadur!"

"Huzoor?" he answered softly.

"Is there anyone on your right, Kulbahadur?" I asked. There was a pause of some seconds and then, having peered into the darkness: "I can't see anyone, Sahib. Shall I go and look?"

"Yes. But very quietly" I said.

There came the clink of his empty cartridge cases, dislodged by his movements, striking the flints as they rolled down the embankment. Then silence again. A few minutes later, with a stealthy scuffling, he crawled up beside me to whisper in my ear. "I have found no-one, Sahib. Except four or five dead men."

So I turned to the Gurkha soldier lying immediately to my left to find out from him who I had with me on that side. "Pass the word down," I told him. "Make contact with the man on your left!"

As if lost in thought the Gurkha soldier continued to stare fixedly at the impenetrable shadows of the jungle ahead of him across the embankment. His honey-coloured hands held his rifle in readiness, the taut readiness of a trained soldier ready for the next Jap attack. His obvious vigilance gave me an added sense of security. What better fighting soldiers could a young British officer wish for on each side of him than Gurkhas? For all his eagerness to be ready should another Jap charge come, this Gurkha must do what he was told. Impatiently I repeated my order, and when he still took no notice I exclaimed: "Eh—timi!" and stretched out my hand and pushed his shoulder roughly. He rolled over languidly and, amid an avalanche of small stones, slithered to the bottom of the embankment. He lay there in a crumpled heap, his upturned young face glistened in the moonlight. I lay paralysed.

The hasty hot words of reprimand were never said! I could only stare in horror at the smiling Gurkha boy who was younger even than I. I knew men were killed in war but it had never occurred to me that those I knew and liked would be killed. And killed beside me at that! Rifleman Lal Bahadur Thapa would never answer to my orders again.

Lal Bahadur had been close to me from the day I joined the Chindits back at Jhansi. Somehow or other he had always seemed to be there. All through those days of marching since we had crossed the Chindwin I had been somehow aware of his smiling young face, his virile young presence, marching onwards close to me. He was I knew little more than sixteen years old, and it was almost impossible to reconcile the grinning, tireless, Lal Bahadur with that body, which I could now see had a ragged hole the size of half a saucer in the back of the head, lying grotesquely at the embankment's foot.

I was jolted back into reality by a new outburst of firing behind us. It was unmistakably a Japanese light machine-gun. I reacted at once. It was as though I were someone else in a dream. Shouting for my men to follow me (not even knowing who "my men" were), I jumped up and ran crouching down to crash through into the cover of the jungle. Jap .280 calibre bullets hissed close over my head as I did so. We ran on, crashing through thickets and clawing aside creepers, towards where the head of the column had been. My instincts directed me there as the likeliest place to find my commanding officer. When I assessed I was there I flung myself down in the midst of the undergrowth with the Gurkhas who had followed me thudding down around me. Then, having listened tensely to ascertain whether or not we were being pursued, I crept up to the embankment again. What I saw told me one thing above all others. Number 2 Column had done their decoy job to perfection! The weight of fire they must have drawn down upon themselves as they marched into the moonlight up the railway track had been quite devastating!

Bodies of men and beasts lay in all manner of positions over the railway track and were heaped down the embankment. Tumbled mule-loads were everywhere, wrenched from the animals' backs as they were flung about after being hit by Japanese bullets, grenades and mortar bombs. Squat men of the Nippon Army were mingled inextricably in this scene of death. The Japs looked grotesque and evil in death. But they *were* dead! That at least was cause for satisfaction.

Where was the column now?

A menacing crashing in the jungle back along the way we had come warned us that it was time to leave this horrid scene of slaughter and desolation. In a rasping voice that surprised me by its strangeness I ordered: "Follow me!" Then we burst back through the undergrowth to seek again the cover of the jungle's deep shadows. The crashing behind us was still coming in our direction so I swung blindly off at right angles. Suddenly we were on a track. Panting from our exertions, the straps of our heavy packs now seeming to bite through flesh and into the bone as we continued our precipitate flight, we staggered up to some higher ground. There we had to fling ourselves down to regain our breath. As quietly as we could we lay there and listened for sounds of pursuit, but they seemed to have disappeared. It was time for me to make some sort of plan.

With a sudden shock I realized that I was alone in the jungle with seven Gurkha soldiers and had not the faintest idea where the rest of our column were. Or, indeed, even if any of them had survived the ambush! We were 150 miles behind the enemy lines, that I did know, and it could be that just me and my seven Gurkhas were left. Just me and seven Gurkhas against the entire Nippon Army! My thoughts ran away with themselves all at once so that any semblance of a plan vanished from my mind.

Then, as if to reassure me that I had friends, an obviously British bren-gun opened fire. It was barely a hundred yards away. Immediately its challenge was answered by the popping and crackling of scattered Japanese rifle fire. We rolled over on to our stomachs into the firing position, weapons thrust forward at the ready towards the new sounds of combat. At that moment the moon came out from behind the great cloud bank which had obscured it to reveal in sharp relief a small hillock which was apparently the British position. A dry river bed at its far circumference concealed the Japanese. The deep shadows of the jungle from both sides were broken by the red and yellow flames of bursts of automatic and rifle fire. Both sides had located their foes' hiding places.

Kulbahadur crawled up to me. He motioned towards where the ferocity of gunfire flared like summer lightning among the massive teak trees, so that these forest giants loomed in towering spasms from the over-all blackness of thicket and scrub. "What do we do now, Sahib?" he asked quietly. Kulbahadur's question brought me to reality with a jerk. Suddenly I was the officer again, and once more in control of my own particular part of the situation. I had had my baptism of fire on the embankment. Here was some more, and now I knew both from training and experience what I was supposed to do.

"Get Naik Premsingh Gurung!" I ordered.

Kulbahadur wormed his way through the bushes to my left, and in a few moments I was suddenly aware the naik had silently joined me.

"Stack the heavy packs here, Premsingh," I told him. "We will drop down into the chaung and work our way round away from the firing to the back of the hill. We can then try to get into the British position after attracting their attention and letting them know that we are friends."

"I think the Japs firing over there are those who were following us," said Premsingh. "They think that it is us up on the hill. Could we not attack them in the rear? They will not be expecting two parties."

I was surprised now how my mind seemed to be coping with the situation, coolly and without effort. The next move was logical and easy to decide. "Yes, we could do that," I agreed. "But first of all we must contact the rest of the column up on the hill there to let them know what our plan is."

"I'll go, Sahib!"

"No!" I said: "We will all go together. There are not enough of us to split up our force."

I gave orders then that all heavy packs should be stacked beside the track. Sweating and breathing hard in the jungle's oppressive heat, we wriggled out of them and left them there together in the shadows. Then stealthily we wormed our way forward to the lip of the chaung, farther along which lay the enemy. The chaung was about six feet deep and its sandy bed was tufted with small bushes. As I started foward to lead my Gurkhas up to the chaung, towards where I assessed the rear of the British position would be, a concealed light machine-gun opened fire on us, but fortunately, as so often happens at night, the gunner was firing too high. The bullets whipped and sang over our heads to smack into the jungle behind and above us.

We flung ourselves flat, crawling frantically to the shelter of the steep bank of the chaung between us and the hidden machine-gun. Beside me Kulbahadur was cursing horribly in Gurkhali. The only words intelligible to me were: "It was a ——bren-gun! It was a——bren-gun!"

"The silly bastards!"—I joined Kulbahadur in cursing the efficiency and foresight of the British commander, whoever he might be, who had posted this hidden bren to cover his forces flank and rear. But he might at least have found out who we were before he fired! As another burst ripped past us I lay there frantically trying to think out a solution to this problem of being between two fires. Then dramatically it solved itself!

"Japun Ayo," rang out with crystal clarity the shout of one of my Gurkhas. "Japun Ayo!"

Even as he blazed away with his rifle up the chaung in the direction of the enemy I was suddenly and alarmingly conscious that shadowy panting figures were almost upon us. Smooth domed steel helmets reflected the moonlight balefully. They were Nips all right! The moon now picked out the new and more menacing glint of the cold steel of bayonets!

I shouted with the utmost power of my lungs. I do not know what I shouted. My only consciousness was of a series of shuddering vibrations along my arms. I was passing hot lead in spasms at the enemy. This time I had remembered to cock my tommy-gun! My immediate world dissolved into soul-satisfying vibrations and burgeoned bloodily with flailing arms and the bite and crunch of steel-shod wood on flesh and bone. In split seconds it was all over and we stood shouting and yelling in our triumph over the Japanese supermen!

We stood erect, the victors of an unmarked and unnamed chaung, literally with our heels on the faces of our crushed foes. Through flared nostrils we exulted amidst the intoxicating smoke and tang of victory! The gleam on the steel in the moon-stippled chaung was now a dark gloss on our cold steel, the gloss of

Japanese blood on bayonet and kukri! The dead who lay twisted at our feet were useless creatures who but seconds ago had thought themselves Japanese supermen!

A groan echoed eerily along the now silent chaung. Stepping forth from the carnage fresh and bold in my triumph I saw a form writhing in agony at the fringe of the crumpled heaps on the ground at our feet. Suddenly two Gurkhas were beside me and we stooped over the moaning man. Lying face downwards on the bloodstained sand was Naik Premsingh Gurung. The naik stifled his groaning by biting into his lower lip until the blood ran while we turned him over tenderly to look for his wound. It was not hard to find. His right thigh bone had been smashed by a bullet fired at such close range that the acrid smell of burned flesh still hung about him. As we gently turned Premsingh over on to his back we exposed what lay beneath him. It was a Jap soldier, almost decapitated by the Gurkha's kukri which was still cleft deep into the yellow neck. In the moonlight the dark stain of the blood pulsing from the severed jugular veins was spreading like a red-black shawl over the dead Jap's shoulders, and out on to the silver sand.

My gorge rose to vomit, but the upsurge of nausea was checked and forgotten as a sudden shout rang out above us. It was in Gurkhali. We returned the hail, and a few seconds later my platoon havildar, who had disappeared in the ambush, bounded down into the ravine with two men at his heels.

We carried Naik Premsingh Gurung carefully to the top of the tree-clad hillock. There the havildar gave him a shot of morphia while a field-dressing was applied to his wound. As from nowhere ready cut bamboo splints were produced and applied to the shattered leg. Premsingh's eyes, which told of the depths of pain his clenched lips refused to reveal, signified his thanks as we made him as comfortable as possible among the undergrowth of the little hillock.

I sent two of the Gurkhas off to collect our packs. The Japs who had been attacking this position had obviously been wiped out. Those who were not scattered across the blood-soaked sand down below us in the chaung were dead in the undergrowth on the other side, the victims of the hill-party's fire. I stood up to take stock of the position and the others who made up the small force with the havildar. There was just Havildar Lalbahadur Thapa and five Gurkhas from the column infantry company. Like us they had neither seen nor heard of the rest of the column since the ambush.

On our hilltop position we lay down to await the dawn. I must have dozed, for I awoke with a start to a touch on the shoulder. Kulbahadur was lying close beside me. He smiled and said nothing, and conscious of the lessening of the darkness I realized he had roused me because it was the hour of "stand-to." The hour before dawn. The hour when jungle fighters on both sides were awake, watching and waiting. Often the fatal hour.

I watched the first grey streaks of dawn steal through the towering black mass of the teak trees around us. As I watched their foliage merged almost imperceptibly from black to deep purple and then from purple through lessening darkness until finally they were green. Once more jungle night was becoming jungle day. But this was a day different from all the others. As far as I could see there was myself, my six Gurkhas and the badly wounded Premsingh, and the havildar and his five Gurkhas. Were we the sole survivors of the whole column?

We waited through that first hour with fingers on triggers. The thumping of my heart drowned for me the many noises of the awakening forest. The insistence of its pounding, and the burden of the question which oppressed my brain, dominated the grating of crickets, the chattering and whistlings of the arousing birds, and the distant jibberings of the monkeys. What to do now—that was the question? Was I the only officer left? And were these twelve Gurkhas, and one wounded Gurkha, my sole command?

"Tuck-too. Tuck-too." Almost by my elbow a vivid

green lizard with scarlet throat started up its maddening repetitive call. I would go on, from him and a thousand other lizards, all through the sweltering day. "Tuck-too. Tuck-too."

"The dawn comes up like thunder, on the road to Mandalay," I found myself singing under my breath. Why I shall never know. "Come you back you British soldier. Come you back to Mandalay."—When would that be, I wondered. Some time a long way off. Would I live that long?—The minutes ticked past . . .

"The others must have gone away," said Kulbahadur suddenly, breaking the silence. He was expressing the very thoughts running through my mind at that moment. Where could they have gone? I asked myself. Why hadn't they returned to look for us? Weren't we of any consequence? Worried, I searched for any possible answer that might make sense. There could be no doubt about it, the Japs had been lying in wait for our column and must have strong forces around this area bent upon hunting down and destroying all British stragglers. There was probably a whole brigade of Japs in that area searching for us at that very moment.

There could be no doubt about Wingate's deception plan having been successful! The enemy had obviously concentrated his forces at Kyaikthin and we had walked slap bang into them! The whole locality must by now be absolutely alive with Japs! That being so, why had we not seen or heard any more of them during the night? Why had not a stronger party come after us after that fight in the chaung?

The answer I ultimately arrived at was that the enemy must be pursuing larger groups of the scattered column. From what I had been taught of the Jap mentality one might presume that Japs would think that no one would possibly be stupid enough to hang about near the railway at Kyaikthin after the bloody ambushing the British force had suffered. Well, luck was apparently with us, I decided. We had got away with it. But the sooner we cleared out of the vicinity of Kyaikthin the better it would be for us!

According to the plan of operation in which we had all been fully instructed, the column was to have split up into pre-determined dispersal groups in the event of meeting heavy enemy opposition. These would meet at an already established rendezvous. I decided that I might quite reasonably presume this was what had happened, and that even now the survivors of the column were marching forward to the rendezvous in the hills which formed the western watershed of the Irrawaddy river. It might have helped, I told myself with some truculence, if the bugler who was to have blown the dispersal had blown it loud enough for us to hear down at the rear of the column!

My mind was made up now. The way ahead was clear. I would lead my little party to the rendezvous and join up with the rest of the survivors from the ambush. I stood up to call the others to their feet. It was good to be on our way again. But was not there something else, something unpleasant, before I gave the order? Yes. There was the problem of Naik Premsingh to solve! I realized it with a sinking of spirits. I knew all too well what I had to do about Premsingh, but with someone as close as he had become during our weeks behind the Jap lines it was going to be hard. Premsingh Gurung had come into my life as one of the Gurkhas in the same unspecified "special operation" that I volunteered for. He was from a Nepalese village on the northern slopes of the Himalayas, and his father before him had fought for the British Raj. He never had more than one ambition in life, and that was to be a soldier like his father.

As soon as he attained enlisting age (it is quite customary for the Gurkhas boys to add a year or so and join up at sixteen), he had left his village and gone to the Headquarters of the 2nd Gurkha Rifles. There he had proved himself a willing learner and was soon a tough and competent soldier. Then he had joined the 3rd Battalion 2nd Gurkha Rifles which formed part of the 77th Independent Infantry Brigade and was sent on a machine-gun course. He came back with an excellent report and the two stripes of a naik. Naik

Premsingh was a machine-gun No. 1 under my command when Brigadier Orde Wingate gave the orders for his force to set out and led them into the dangerous unknown of the Japanese-dominated jungle of Burma. And as a machine-gun No. 1 he had acquitted himself stoutly at the battle of Kyaikthin.

I ran my eyes over Premsingh's wounded leg and then, with a feeling bordering on guilt, let them come to rest on his face. I found that he was gazing at me steadfastly with those almond-shaped expressive Gurkha eyes. From his pain drawn face they searched mine with a frightening insistence for a hint of the decision he knew must be inevitable.

There was no likelihood of him being able to walk before undergoing an operation and a prolonged stay in hospital. Naik Premsingh knew as well as did I, and every other Chindit, that unless a man could walk unaided he had to be left. The compassion I felt for Premsingh flooded irresistibly to my eyes and as the tears welled from mine I was conscious of the resolution hardening in his. Revulsion at the order I knew I had to give rose like bile in my throat. Naik Premsingh Gurung, who needed only hospital treatment to restore him to full physical fighting fitness, had to be left to die at this nameless spot in this Burmese jungle. He must die because twelve lives must not be jeopardized for one.

I crossed over to Premsingh and knelt beside him. I placed my hand on his arm and squeezed it hard. Feelings just could not be expressed in words. The heart of his friend was full of a yearning to save him, through thick and through thin to strive to get him back to the British lines and certain salvation. But the heart of his Commanding Officer, which was one and the same, was too well aware of the dictates of duty. No words passed between us as I knelt there. But in that silence he knew that I, his senior by barely two years, was sentencing him to death.

His eyes still holding mine, his tightly compressed lips relaxed. The shadow of a smile played around the corners of his mouth. By now the rest were standing up and adjusting their packs ready to move. I sensed they were well aware of the agony of the moment, but rightly turned their backs on it.

I squeezed Premsingh's arm again. Then I stood up.

"Carry Naik Premsingh over to the railway," I ordered.

"Sahib, no! May I remain here?" He smiled up at me winningly.

I decided that maybe Premsingh was right. It was shadier beneath the mighty teak trees which towered majestically over the undergrowth where he lay. From here he had a commanding view and would be able to attract the attention of any passing Burmese who might turn out to be friendly. They might hide him in a village until the broken bone had knit and he was strong enough to escape back through the jungle to the British lines. Any slender chance of survival was preferable to capture by the Japs, inevitable if he were left beside the Japanese-patrolled railway.

"All right, Premsingh," I said. "Just as you like."

Premsingh reached out his hand towards his tommy-gun and held it up for Kulbahadur to take.

"Give me your rifle," he said softly. "You take this. It will be more useful to you."

Dispassionately the two Gurkhas exchanged weapons.

Then Premsingh looked up towards me again. Now there was an almost tender look in those usually inscrutable eyes. Again that little whimsical smile playing around the corners of his mouth.

"Goodbye, Sahib," he said softly.

Our hands met in a firm clasp. Then I turned abruptly and led my men down the scrubby hillside through the undergrowth into the dried up chaung at its foot. My eyes were hot with unshed tears. From behind us came the sound of a single shot.

Naik Premsingh Gurung had been the bravest of the brave.

8

THE SURVIVORS FIGHT ON

Stealthily, treading like cats in the sparkling freshness of the newly dawned day, we crept soft-footed out from the jungle and back to the scene of the ambush. The crumpled corpses of the Japanese soldiers we had killed, we passed on our way. On the fringe of the forest we halted and peered out through the bamboo thicket on the wreckage of the bigger battle of the ambushing on the railway embankment. The horrible evidence of the defeat of No. 2 Column was spread out starkly for us in the bright morning sunlight.

Every conceivable type of mule load lay scattered and abandoned on and around the railway embankment. Heavy packs lay everywhere, just as they had been shrugged from the shoulders of the British and Gurkha soldiers diving to cover from the sudden murderous hail of Jap bullets and grenades. Immediately in front of us three British soldiers lay sprawled on their faces diagonally across the railway line. Another lay stretched out and stiff on his back on the embankment with his head down and his feet up and slightly apart as though he were standing at ease on his head.

It was not until this moment, when I looked on the all too tangible signs of our ambushing, that I realized clearly that fire had been poured into us from both sides. The Japs had obviously been lying in wait for us both on the right and the left of the railway embankment as we marched up in the bright moonlight completely oblivious of their presence. By sheer

bad luck we had been caught in the open while our
scouts were searching out the jungle track which we
had been forewarned would lead us straight into the
village of Kyaikthin to surprise the Jap garrison we
knew to be there!

Brigadier Wingate had told us we would do this
and that, that we would march here and march there,
would kill Japs this way and that way, and so far as
I was concerned I had believed it would happen just
that way. In fact it had all happened almost exactly
as Wingate had said, until this incident of our ambushing at Kyaikthin. Now I had to admit to myself
I was no longer the cocksure victorious young soldier who had marched with such growing confidence
deep into the heart of Japanese-occupied Burma. I
had tasted defeat.

I snapped out of my gloomy forebodings as I felt
Kulbahadur suddenly stiffen at my side. A sudden
movement on the edge of the forest fifty yards away
caught my eye and sent my right hand sliding to the
tommy-gun's pistol grip. My heart pounded with
alarm. Three stooping figures were creeping from the
jungle cover ahead of us and advancing cautiously
towards the crumpled heap that last night had been a
cheery, stoutly marching, Gurkha soldier. Then one of
the indistinctly-seen men had his hand at the Gurkha's
throat. The sun flung out bright beams of light from
something in his other hand. It was a dagger! Had the
Japs returned to knife any wounded who might still
be lying out there on the embankment? My spine
crawled. I thrust my tommy-gun forward to cover the
men who had come from the jungle.

They moved forward, with equal stealth, to the next
body. This time it was that of a British soldier. Again
I caught the flash of the knife at the throat of the
immobile soldier. Then the man with the knife stood
up and as he did so turned so that his face was towards me, with the bright light full upon it. I could
not restrain a shout of delight. It was Arthur Best! I
burst through the green jungle waving my arms and
shouting greetings as I ran towards him, my little

band close on my heels. Thus in joy did we make our reunion. Arthur's joy matched mine. He told me he had come back there, accompanied by a couple of Gurkhas, to collect the identity discs from our dead. That was what he had been doing with a knife in his hand. We sat down then on the grass at the embankment's foot and swapped stories.

Arthur's experiences had been much the same as mine. After the ambush and fighting he had ducked for the cover of the jungle accompanied by a handful of Gurkhas. Through most of the night he had patrolled a wide area but had failed to locate the rest of the column. He had, however, been lucky enough to meet our column R.A.F. officer, Flt./Lt. Eddie Edmonds, who had been in charge of a special deception group attached to No. 2 Column, along with another officer, Lieut. John Griffiths. Between them they had collected together a few men and were now busily salvaging as much kit as possible. They had managed to recapture a few frightened mules which were roaming up and down the embankment in the vicinity of the battle.

With my few Gurkhas I quickly set to work to help Arthur's party. Within a very short time we had collected and loaded one medium machine-gun and boxes of ammunition. We also secured a mule-load of demolition charges and detonators, and another one with boxes of various types of ammunition. Arthur and I superintended the loading up of two mules with abandoned packs picked up from the scene of the ambush. It was our intention to share out the food they contained among our party when we were all together. We refilled the magazines of all our weapons from ammunition scattered beside the rail track. We shot one badly wounded mule which was dragging itself around aimlessly in the midst of the scene of death and desolation and was in a pitiable state.

Back in the shadowy jungle I was glad to shrug off the foul scene behind me and to march behind Arthur Best back to where he had left Eddie Edmonds, John Griffiths and the rest of their party. Our rescued mules slunk behind us in the file of Gurkha soldiers, bearing their loads of vital food and ammunition. While there was still nothing before us but the jungle, Arthur surprisingly turned to me and said: "Here we are." Then he turned right off the track and we pushed through a bamboo thicket to come across the rest of the party sitting silently, some with their backs against trees, others leaning on their packs, around Eddie Edmonds.

Eddie was quite a man to have with you in the jungle! By profession he was a big-game hunter but by inclination, he would explain, he was now a rodent exterminator. He had one object in life—and that was to kill as many Japs as possible in the shortest time possible. He was a massive man who on the outbreak of war had joined up in the Royal New Guinea Air Force. That was his homeland and it was in New Guinea that the Japs had murdered his mother and father when they overran the country. Eddie Edmonds was officially in Burma as a fighter pilot with the avowed intention of shooting down as many Japs as possible and an insatiable desire to swoop down and machine-gun any Japs he spotted. He was afoot in the Wingate show because he had heard that air-crew officers were required for a secret mission, "not necessarily in the air." Working on the assumption that any secret mission in Burma must necessarily lead to the slaughtering of still more Japs, he had volunteered.

When they told Eddie that it would mean fighting on the ground and walking all the way, he declared: "I couldn't care less about that. One way of killing Japs is as good as another and it looks as though this is going to give me plenty of chances." With more jungle experience that anyone in the whole of Wingate's force, Flt./Lt. Eddie Edmonds had got himself properly "organized" during the march in. He had always been accompanied by a sure-footed little Naga hill pony which followed him patiently and unfalteringly wherever he went with all his kit loaded on its back. "You lazy dog, Eddie!" we used to chide him. "You're big enough to be carrying that pony instead of making it carry all your junk!" Unfortunately, Eddie's pony had been one of the casualties in the Kyaikthin ambush. Now, although he was officially a flying man, his jungle knowledge and strength of character made him automatically our leader.

"Well, if it isn't the boy!" he grinned, on seeing me arrive through the trees. "Come and join our hiking party, youngster. We've got quite an interesting trip before us."

Eddie thereupon called a council of war to decide which way we should march out of Burma. He was all in favour of heading south-east to cross the border into Indo-China. His tactical reason for this was simply that he "knew a chap there who would be delighted to help us."

Without more ado we therefore set off, heading south-east. The fearless Eddie was at the head of the column and myself, Arthur Best and ginger-bearded John Griffiths, a Lieutenant in the 9th Gurkha Rifles, attached to the 3/2, a good man to have with you on such a job as this. Tall, gaunt, and lean he was nevertheless very strong and quite imperturbable.

Feeling definitely "re-organized," with the extra food and ammunition we had taken from the packs giving us added confidence, we found marching along the track through the teak forest quite pleasant going. We pressed on at a good steady pace and did not halt until we once more reached the jungle's fringe at that ill-fated railway line, the vital link from Rangoon to Myitkyina.

A well-worn footpath crossed the open, grass-covered strip which flanked the railway and led to a culvert in the embankment. A track like that could mean Japs or hostile Burmese. At a motion from Eddie Edmonds we silently fanned out to drop down on the jungle's edge to watch and wait from its shelter. Nothing stirred. As far as we could see, both north and south, the line ran like twin-snakes of metal dazzling in the sun. The flints on its embankment glittered beneath the sun's rays, a heat-haze shimmered upwards all along its length. Nowhere was there sight or sound of any human being, neither enemy nor friend.

We decided it was safe to cross. Eddie in the lead and Arthur and I bringing up the rear, we ran across the open patch of ground, ducking as low as we could in case we were observed. As we reached the embankment, Arthur and I glanced at one another meaningly. We were struck by a mutual inspiration.

"Yes. I think this will go very nicely," grinned Arthur. "In fact it must have been built for the job!"

I halted the mule just in front of us long enough to unfasten a box of high explosive and detonators. Then I let the Gurkha muleteer drag the animal on to make the final dash for cover, from the embankment across the far cleared strip to the opposite jungle.

It took me rather less than a minute to push the box of explosive into position in a hollow between the rails where they ran over the culvert. I packed it in with a layer of flints. Meanwhile, Arthur was clipping the detonator with its length of instantaneous fuse to the inside of the rail. The fuse was connected to a slab of gun cotton which we placed in the box of explosives. Here was a nice little surprise packet for any Jap supply trains which might happen to come along! All we hoped was that a train would come before a Jap patrol discovered our handiwork and spoiled our little gunpowder plot! Then Arthur Best and I bent low and scurried across the open ground that lay between the railway embankment and the jungle. We pressed on, sweating but curiously satisfied, to overtake the others.

We did not receive an answer to our prayers until that night, when our small force had pushed on a further ten miles east through the jungle. Then an explosion, tremendous even to us, told us that an enemy supply train had done just what we required of it!

Despite the frenzy and the furore the success of our train trap must have caused among the Japanese who obviously seethed around that area after the

Kyaikthin battle, we passed a peaceful and undisturbed night. As the light touch of Arthur's hand on my shoulder brought me instantly alert for yet another stand-to in the hour before dawn, I felt fresh and rested and eager to press on. The presence of jungle-wise Eddie Edmonds gave us all a real sense of security. When he told us he calculated we should soon reach the rendezvous, pre-arranged in the event of No. 2 Column splitting up, we felt that it would turn out just as he said.

In fact it did. Quite suddenly, round a bend in a track which was narrow and gloomy between towering walls of greenery, we were at the entrance to an enchanting little valley through which burbled a boisterous brook. And there was Doc Lusk our Irish Medical officer.

"Aha! Flight-Lieutenant Edmonds, I presume?" he chuckled, in best Livingstone-Stanley manner. He seized Eddie's hand and pumped it up and down in delight.

Then we all burst into uproarious laughter, partly at this sally but mostly with the sudden relief of friend meeting friend when he needs him most. After which, crowding round the fire, we each recounted our experiences. Our stories bore a remarkable similarity. It was from Doc Lusk that I learned that the dispersal signal had most certainly been sounded by the column bugler. He had heard it, and being in no doubt about what to do next, he had broken away with his section and made direct for the chosen jungle rendezvous. He had already been there for a day and a half when we arrived and had seen nobody else.

When I awoke, as the first grey fingers of dawn began to probe down through the highest tracery of leaves and creepers of the jungle roof, I was chilled and stiff. Feeling a desire for the jovial doctor's company, I threw off my blanket and walked across to where I could see him sitting, still wrapped in his blanket, on a log. We sat side by side on his log contemplating the beauty of the sky.

For no apparent reason the eyes of both Doc Lusk

and I fixed contemplatively upon one of the medical orderlies whose recumbent figure was even now becoming steadily clearer as the night around him faded. Then, (Doc Lusk and I both saw it in the same instant), there was a swift and sinister movement behind and over him. Horrified we saw, menacingly, the ugly brown length of a Russell's viper*. rear up behind the stirring form. Its head was back, its mouth open, and we knew its poison-filled fangs, as deadly as any snake living, were on the point of striking down into the man's bare flesh. At that moment only split seconds stood between life and death for that man. My hand flashed to my revolver holster and I had it out, hammer pulled back and sighted on the serpent's head, faster than I had ever done before in my life. In the instant of time as I slid my foresight up the two inch wide brown body of the viper, so that it was in line with the back sight and covering the snake's open jaws, I knew that this had to be the best shot of my life! My finger tightened on the trigger. There was a flash and a bang and a cloud of burned cordite whirled around me. But no recoil kicked at my wrist. In that same moment the snake's poisoned head became a mass of bloody pulp. It slumped, a writhing, dead thing, into the dust.

Before my startled mind had sorted out exactly what had happened the whole camp had leaped into wakefulness at the sound of the shot. In the next second all eyes were turned to where Doc and I stood, revolvers in our hands. Stupefied, I looked at his gun and mine to realize that my hammer was still back whereas his muzzle, held at his side, was smoking.

"Good heavens, Doc!" I burst out. "Where on earth did you learn to shoot from the hip like that?"

Doc Lusk grinned broadly. "You know, Ian, it's strange, but I've never fired one o' yon things before in all my life!" he declared. The whole camp relaxed and grinned too as the doctor strode over to grind the writhing body of the Russell's viper into the black

---

*One of the few snakes that will attack unprovoked.

earth. The orderly whose life had been saved was profuse in his thanks.

We spent two days and two nights in that little valley with its babbling brook. They were days which were comparatively blissful after our weeks of marching and the recent shock and horror of being ambushed. All that time we received no interruption from Japs, nor were we disturbed by any alarm. Our sentries and patrols neither saw nor heard anything to cause suspicion, so we just stayed there and made the most of the rest and of the companionship.

At the end of two days No. 1 Column, commanded by Major George Dunlop, which had accompanied us as the other half of the decoy force of Wingate's expedition, marched into our bivouac area. They had been operating some ten miles north of No. 2 Column at the time of the ambush at Kyaikthin and had suffered no similar calamity. It seemed No. 2 column had been the decoy force *par excellence!*

Major Dunlop told us they had heard at least two long train-loads of Japs pass by *en route* for Kyaikthin shortly before the ambush. It seemed No. 1 Column had heard the subsequent sounds of battle but with ten miles of thick jungle between them and us had no hope of coming to our help. Arthur and I enjoyed a certain amount of smug self-satisfaction when George Dunlop spoke also of the big explosion they had heard the following night—*our* explosion under the Jap supply train!

My world became very real and very sure once again now that I was part of a smoothly organized and well armed force still operating according to plan. Best of all, we were once again in communication with the outside world for No. 1 Column still had its long-range radio. It was in daily contact with headquarters back at Imphal on the British side of the Chindwin, and still in touch with Wingate and operating within his over-all plan.

From the officers of No. 1 Column we were soon put into the picture regarding the fate of the rest of the survivors of our column. Very early in the action in which we had been ambushed the bugler had been ordered to sound the dispersal and with the exception of a few stragglers such as Arthur Best, Eddie Edmonds, John Griffiths, myself and the men with us, the survivors of No. 2 had been led away by Major Emmett. Even now, apparently, they were heading for the Chindwin and home as fast as they could go.

Major Dunlop told us that the survivors of No. 2 Column were already probably nearly halfway back to the Chindwin. They had been followed by a very large force of Japanese which they had been unable to shake off, so they had shed their heavy equipment and were marching light. The Japs were continuously harassing them with heavy mortars and had sent in attack after attack by infantry, but the survivors of the column remained a cohesive fighting unit. They were still holding off the pursuing Japs when George Dunlop had last heard of them over the radio a few hours earlier.

Our new-found friends of No. 1 Column did, in fact, have all the news, thanks to their continued radio contact with the rest of the Wingate force. They told us that the main force operating up north had apparently been having a wonderful time! For our part, we few survivors of No. 2 Column felt we had done our bit.

While we enjoyed our rest in the valley, Major Dunlop, by radio with Wingate, was scheming the next move of his column's campaign. We survivors from the Kyaikthin ambush had now become officially integrated as part of No. 1 Column. At present all we knew was that we were to press on due east, deeper and deeper into enemy territory and were to cross the mighty Irrawaddy. Once over Burma's greatest river, we would receive our next assignment from Orde Wingate.

"I wonder what it'll be?" said Arthur Best. "Nothing like a nice surprise to keep the interest from flagging, is there Ian, m'boy?"

Speculation ran high among the officers. Odds-on favourite for our next objective was the Mandalay-

Lashio railway. Second favourite was the Goteik Viaduct, which so far had proved invulnerable to any attack from the air. Kalbahadur had his own private theory as to what "the great British Raj" intended to do next in Burma. "We are going to raid the Mogok ruby mines, Sahib," he assured me earnestly. "After all, the war costs the British Raj millions of rupees daily. If we attack the mines and get away with plenty of rubies we will be able to help the British Raj pay for many more months of war-making."

We were all in good heart when we set out to march the few miles between our peaceful bivouac area and the Irrawaddy river. It was Major Dunlop's plan to cross at a point where the village of Tagaung lay close to the river bank on the opposite side. It was a large village by Burmese standards and it was thought to be friendly; but just to make sure, an advance party of Burmese soldiers, under Captain Charlie Bruce, had left camp the previous night and, under cover of darkness, had slipped across the Irrawaddy in a scrounged dug-out canoe.

Shortly before dawn they had stealthily crept into the village and from their careful reconnaissance had been able to report back over the radio that the immediate vicinity was certainly free of Japs. Meanwhile they had not wasted their time in the village which they had found very friendly. It was with pleasurable anticipation that we learned that they were buying up all available rice, chickens and vegetables that they could lay hands on in Tagaung. This was really great news for none of us had eaten a square meal for some time. We were all very hungry and my last meal, the previous mid-day, had been a handful of boiled rice and a small and sickly-sweet mule steak.

There was more than just the normal anticipation of setting out on an unknown adventure when we fell in and moved off in single file following Major Dunlop to the banks of the Irrawaddy. There was also the good healthy anticipation of a square meal! When the lazily flowing waters of the great Irrawaddy at last came into view we found ourselves marching down into a dry chaung. There we crouched, bunched together in the undergrowth a little way from the track, awaiting the word to embark for the river crossing. This had already been fully organized for us, we were told, by the Burma Rifles who had gone on ahead. The silver rupees were certainly coming in useful!

As we crouched there I gazed with contentment and a happy awareness of the beauty of the mighty Irrawaddy. So intense was the sun's heat that a shimmering haze arose over the river which almost obscured the village on the far side. But through the haze I could see the golden spire of a pagoda gleaming in the sunlight, and the gentle tinkling of many tiny bells around the spire came to us on a light and fragrant breeze.

To complete the picture of fairy-like beauty there arose in the far distance the jagged grey-blue peaks of the Shan Hills soaring ten thousand feet up into the cloudless sky. Somewhere in the midst of those mountains lay our next objective. Somewhere out there was the vital Mandalay-Lashio railway, crossing its vulnerable Goteik Viaduct. That railway, we knew, carried all the supplies for the Japanese divisions facing "Vinegar Joe" Stillwell's Chinese Army massed along the Chinese-Burma borders farther to the north-east.

In the drowsy noon-day peace which now enveloped me I was lulled by the beauty of the scene and the deep stillness to day-dream comfortably of the campaigning still before us. I glowed with a deep satisfaction at a vision of a great stretch of the railway erupting skywards in the dust, smoke, and flame of a mighty explosion. With equal clarity I imagined the exultation of the moment when the Goteik Viaduct would be wrecked beyond repair.

"Get down! Take cover!" My fairy castle of cards was scattered with the urgency of the order, jerking my thoughts back to reality. Idling men were galvanized into action, fading from sight instantly. I dived under a bush!

Its twin engines throbbing, a plane that was unmistakably a Jap had suddenly materialized in the midst of this scene of beauty. Men who had been out on the sandbank at the river's edge had thrown themselves flat on the sand. They pressed their faces into the gritty surface like human ostriches fatuously trying to disguise their presence by themselves not seeing the enemy.

As we ventured once more to turn our faces upwards we saw that the sky was dotted high up with falling white pieces. These materialized into thousands of pamphlets, each the size of a page of an ordinary book. We scrambled to gather them up, and this is what we read (printed in English, Urdu, Hindi and Burmese):

SUMMONS TO SURRENDER TO
THE PITIABLE ANGLO–INDIAN TROOPS

Do you not realize the predicament you are in—that you are being taken to your deathbed by the cruel and selfish British Officers?

Your allied forces were annihilated in the battle on the morning of March 8 and your retreating troops were almost completely captured by the Nippon forces. Not a single one of your force has been able to cross the Chindwin River.

Recollect the dismal fact that in the battle in this locality last May your brother soldiers were deserted by the British Officers and left in the jungles of Upper Burma to die of hunger and epidemics.

Death nears you! Come immediately to the Nippon Army and be saved.

Display this pamphlet to any Burman who will act as your guide. The Nippon Army is determined to crush all forces who oppose it but will save those who surrender.

Do not hesitate to surrender immediately!

A British soldier standing next to me read his through carefully, as though determined to assimilate every word. He spat reflectively in the sand, then an expression of delight spread across his face as though a wonderful truth had dawned upon him: "It's going to

be lovely using paper again!" he said making appropri-
ate signs to point his meaning.

"Yes. Most considerate of the little yellow bastards.
Always think of something to help us just when we
want it," observed another. "Up the bloody Nips, I
say!"

"And down the bloody pan!" summed up the first
speaker on the subject. Thus did the Japanese supermen strike terror from out of the sky into the "pitiable
Anglo-Indian troops".

Soon the loading operations for the crossing were
in full swing and we were detailed off into boatloads
to await our call. Meanwhile, those detailed as rear
guards were back behind us in the jungle, in position
on each side of the track to give warning of pursuing
Japs and to hold them off.

Captain Vivian Wetherall, a lean young officer who
spoke fluent Gurkhali, and was adored by his Gurkha
troops as greatly as he was admired by his brother
officers, was in charge of the loading operations. So re-
vered was he by the Gurkhas that I am certain if he
had told them to swim across instead of using the
boats, every man Jack of them would have set out to
do so, even the non-swimmers!

Vivian had spent his adolescence on his father's
tea-plantation in Assam and it was there that he had
perfected his Gurkhali and had himself come to love
the friendly people of the Gurkha race. As I watched
him with his easy authority going about his task of allocating the men to their boats, I could not help re-
calling an incident which had made a deep impression
upon me while we were at Jhansi awaiting our marching orders.

A three-tonner load of us had gone to the Jhansi
Club for dinner and a bit of a party developed. Towards midnight the spacious teak-panelled lounge had
filled up to capacity and the long polished bar had
become invisible behind the scores of officers in khaki-
drill. The drabness of the uniform was relieved here
and there by the shimmering evening dresses and
sparkling jewels of the ladies, mostly the wives of

regular officers who had been stationed in India at the outbreak of war.

Harold James, like me, straight from O.C.T.U. to the Chindits, and Arthur Best and I, had been invited along by Major Arthur Emmett to join his party. Vivian was there as well and it was with obvious pride and pleasure that he introduced his mother. A charming woman in her late forties, with a quiet but firm voice, I found myself almost under a spell when in her presence. Somehow I was not surprised when, after tongues had been loosened by alcohol, and barriers of shyness broken down, someone asked Mrs. Wetherall to read our palms. For some reason most of us seemed to be eager for this. Possibly despite the light-hearted buoyancy of the party, our subconscious minds were reaching ahead of the unknown future, and our unspoken innermost worries were urging us to seek some foreknowledge of the dark and unknown ways that lay ahead.

There were several who knew Mrs. Wetherall well among our party and who had been greatly impressed by her talent for foretelling the future in the happier days of peacetime. Now it was with some reluctance that she took Arthur Emmett's hand and fixed her deep intelligent eyes upon his palm. Suddenly her serious face broke into a smile as if she were overcome with relief.

"It will be difficult for you," she said. "But have no fear. It is going to be all right ultimately."

She said much the same of most of the other hands that were eagerly thrust before her by men who would soon be marching out into the unknown alongside Arthur Emmett on this great and daring adventure.

Then "Come on Vivian!" cried Major Emmett, "it's your turn now!"

Vivian had been returning from the bar with another round of drinks as Arthur Emmett light-heartedly called him into the circle to face his mother. Suddenly her face clouded. I noticed that her hand trembled a little as she took the drink Vivian handed to her.

"Read my son's hand?" she said, unable to hide

an almost imperceptible tension from her voice. "Most certainly not. I know too much about him already."

At that we all laughed and we began to tease Vivian about what he had done on his last leave. But the smile that had accompanied his mother's remark had been a forced smile. I came away from that party with a curious feeling of apprehension for Vivian.

9

BEYOND THE IRRAWADDY

The shout: "Support group forward!" snapped me out of my reverie. This was my section and I led them to the boats with no little eagerness. First we had to unload the packs and panniers from the mules and transfer them to the long, narrow, native dugouts which our advance party had hired from the Burmans. Then twelve to fifteen of us sat in each precarious craft, one behind the other on our packs. Equipment was unbuckled and our boots were around our necks—just in case we had to do an emergency swimming act!

The loading party shoved us off and with apparent ease the two Burmese boatmen in our dugouts pulled strongly on their paddles and thrust us out into the wide waters of the Irrawaddy. The mules were strung out swimming easily behind their selected leader, which was secured to the boat. Out there on the great wide river I could not help feeling uncomfortably helpless and obvious. My ears were straining for aero-engines and I could not stop myself imagining our plight should even one Jap fighter or bomber discover us making our way across. It took us the best part of three-quarters of an hour to cross the Irrawaddy, three-quarters of an hour of apprehensive nakedness under a burning sun. All the time our ears and eyes were straining for the sounds or sights that could mean we were trapped in the open as surely as rats in a trap. That the Japs knew we were crossing we hadn't a doubt, for the leaflet raid had been very deliberate.

The two Burmese boatmen paddled on like automatons. Their pace never varied. Their expressions never changed. After a while I realized that no longer was the heat haze so thick before us that it obscured the village, but on turning round I could see that it now shimmered in a wall of heat behind that almost obliterated the bank from which we had set sail. This meant that we were well over halfway across and would soon be where we could once more merge ourselves into the jungle which was both our day-by-day salvation and unending scourge.

After an eternity, our bows grated gently on to a sandbank some twenty-five yards offshore. We swung our legs over the side of the dug out, slipped down into the water of the Irrawaddy, and started to manhandle the stores ashore. Meanwhile the muleteers brought together their panting and rather dejected animals, while we, with as much gentleness as we could manage, burdened them with their loads once again. A few minutes later we were tramping through jungle, still barefooted and with our boots round our necks, heading for a hot meal and shelter of the village of Tagaung.

Tagaung was typical of many other waterside villages up and down the larger Burmese rivers. The thatched wooden houses without windows stood up, apparently precariously, on stilts to keep them clear of the annual monsoon flooding. Before each house was a little vegetable garden which formed an attractive border to the sandy main street of the village, and this, as we marched in from the jungle track, came alive with inquisitive natives in their gay multi-coloured lungyis. All of them were apparently overjoyed to see the British soldiers once again, despite the fact that at first it must have been difficult to reconcile this handful of bearded, ragged and filthy men with the British soldiers they had known before the Japanese swept through Burma.

We did not have to wait long for the good food we had been anticipating ever since that radio message had come like a promise from heaven the night before. The column quartermaster, Lieut. John Fowler, whose equipment always gave the impression it had wound itself around him rather than that it had ever been fitted on to him, had a mess tin heaped with cooked rice and a slice of melon for each one of us. They were doled out to us as we marched through the archway in the high pallisade which surrounded the village. John was aided in this most popular duty by Captain George Carne, and as an extra delicacy they produced one chicken for every eight men as well! I led my support group through the village to the sector allocated to us, and we rapidly mounted our machine-guns and mortars. Then, our duty as soldiers fulfilled, we set about the most important part of this operation, eating our wonderful meal!

There followed a few idyllic hours in Tagaung in which we were able to get down to such domestic pursuits as washing and mending our torn and tattered clothing. I washed my shirt, already ripped and rent by jungle thorns, and spread it out over a bush beside the lapping waters of the Irrawaddy. Selecting a Jacaranda tree exotically aflame with gorgeous blossoms, I settled myself down under its shade, clamped my home-made bamboo pipe firmly between my teeth and shielded my eyes against the sun's glare to relax into the contentment of mind and body that follows a well-filled stomach. Without meaning to, I fell into a deep sleep.

A shout right in my ear and a violent slap on my back awakened me rudely. "Hey, rise and shine, we're on our way! Come on, wake up! Wake up!" It was Arthur Best standing all girded and ready to move on. "The column's already loaded up and we'll be moving out soon!" he bellowed. Then: "It might be a good thing if you come along with us, Ian," he grinned. "We're not a bad lot of fellows, really. Only you'd better be quick."

Hastily I climbed to my feet, pulled on my shirt and clipped on my belt and equipment. Then I shouldered again the weight of my pack. I followed Arthur up to the track and took my place in the column. We marched off a minute later, all of us feeling decidedly more content and happy about the future, still heading eastwards and deeper into Japanese territory. We had crossed the Irrawaddy, our greatest obstacle.

If we kept on marching due east according to our maps we should pass just below a big loop in the Shweli river and would soon afterwards strike into the spectacular hill country which continued on to the Salween river and the Chinese border beyond. The Shweli river joined the Irrawaddy to the north of our crossing point at Tagaung so that roughly speaking the Irrawaddy formed the perpendicular side of a triangle of which the hypotenuse was the Shweli, leading down from it to another big loop north of Mong Mit and Mogok.

Colonel Alexander was intent on leading his force away from the Irrawaddy as quickly as possible. We had no illusions—particularly after the incident of the leaflet plane—that the Japanese did not know of our whereabouts. And the river crossings along the Irrawaddy were certain to be the first places to which they would rush their forces by lorry wherever there were suitable roads, or on foot through the jungle along existing tracks. As we continued to march eastwards we avoided any tracks the enemy might be likely to use. Which meant that, in a hot and humid jungle half-light, we had to hack and tear our way through unending bamboo thickets which arose in front of us wherever we were. We were marching no longer. From now on we were fighting our way forward yard by yard, foot by foot, sometimes inch by inch.

We had been struggling eastwards for something like 72 hours in this fashion (I calculated it was ten days since the Kyaikthin battle) when we suddenly met No. 3 Column headed by Major Mike Calvert. Colonel Alexander decided that our two forces (both being under his overall command) should for the time being combine and go into bivouac hidden in this bamboo jungle. There would be organized our next air drop of supplies.

The situation which was selected for our bivouac was deep in the jungle beside a dried up chaung. Everywhere about us was the dense bamboo jungle which was generally and so truthfully referred to as "impenetrable." Our torn clothing and slashed and bleeding hands, legs, and bodies, already showed the price that mere men had to pay for deciding that "impenetrable" was "penetrable."

The laagar area was designated and split up as it was to be occupied by our force and No. 3 Column. Mike Calvert's force had with them a few members of No. 5 Column who brought the exciting news that within the next few hours monocled Major Bernard Fergusson himself would be leading the main force of his column into our area to link up with us temporarily for a rest. The prospects of this were rather fun, even in our exhausted condition, because each one of us had friends in the other column. I lost no time in seeking out my very good friend Harold James, who was in Mike Calvert's force.

I learned from some of his brother officers that Harold had put up a really splendid show in a battle farther up the railway line in which Mike's column had distinguished itself. When the main body of No. 5 Column marched in in good spirits to join the rest of us, there were still more yarns of successful exploits against the Japs.

Having caught the rough end of the stick in playing our part in the Wingate expedition we were somewhat envious, though impressed, to learn how the columns led by Mike Calvert and Bernard Fergusson had fared since we parted company way back west of the Chindwin. Once over the Chindwin, Calvert's No. 3 Column, nearly a day's march ahead of Fergusson's No. 5, had learned from friendly Burmese that there was a force of about two hundred Japs in a village called Metkalet. This was some five miles south of the route that Wingate had proposed the main force of the

Brigade should take. Eager to draw the first real blood of the campaign Calvert had pressed forward. But the Jap force they had expected to surprise had apparently got wind of their coming and had vanished swiftly southwards taking with them four elephants for transport. Having been robbed of a chance to bring those particular Japs to battle, No. 3 Column had continued to press on eastwards, on radioed direct orders from Wingate.

The Brigadier told them to cross the Irrawaddy and then move down towards Mogok, where Wingate intended concentrating his whole brigade. From there Mike Calvert's men were to go still farther south to destroy the Mandalay-Lashio railway. Wingate's overall plan of battle called for both No. 3 Column and No. 5 to make swift and, it was hoped, entirely unexpected marches over steep and jungle-clad hills to descend upon the railway. Those Japs not already interested in the decoys, No. 1 and 2 Columns, were to be drawn off towards Pinlebu by a section with orders to march that way hell for leather.

On 6 March, three days after we had been so savagely mauled in the battle of Kyaikthin, a patrol headed by Tommy Roberts of Bernard Fergusson's force had collided head on with a Japanese force in a village near the Bonchaung Gorge. In the ensuing fighting some twenty Japanese had been killed and it was there that Bernard had himself been confronted for the first time with the problem: What do we do with the wounded? Eventually he had been forced to leave three of them, with their packs containing food and earthen jars of water beside them, in the shade of one of the houses in the village. Two others had to be left beside a jungle track because they were too badly wounded to move.

Captain Roberts' patrol had surprised a lorry-load of Japs just settling down in their truck ready to drive off and look for British soldiers. They found them without having to look! The hail of fire the British brought down on the lorry was thought to have killed every Jap except the driver, who unfortunately had been able to drive away. Undoubtedly he would lose no time in returning with reinforcements.

The advance guard of Bernard Fergusson's column now in the bivouac area with Mike Calvert's troops, were enthusiastic in their admiration of the execution wrought by one sturdy naik standing no more than 5 ft. 2 in. high. By name Jhuriman Rai, he had pressed his attack home with such ferocity that he had killed five Japs single-handed. Three had fallen to his rifle and two he had slashed down with his kukri. The fact that five bullet holes were later found in his clothing showed how fearlessly the grinning little Gurkha had gone into the fight!

While the men of No. 5 Column had been so furiously fighting the Japs, Major Mike Calvert had given himself a birthday treat (the day happened to be his thirtieth birthday) by blowing up large slices of the railway line. The sounds of Tommy Roberts' private battle had hardly died down before Bernard Fergusson's first mission had been resoundingly executed by the blowing up of the Bonchaung Gorge, through which the vital railway ran. For good measure he had destroyed an important bridge just nearby at the same time. One span of the blasted bridge had been toppled completely from its piers, while another section had been up-ended and left with one end down on the chaung bed. The piers, too, had been left in a sorry state.

Both Bernard Fergusson's and Mike Calvert's columns had become increasingly worried at the lack of news from No. 1 and No. 2 Columns, who they knew were acting as decoys for them. Then they received a high priority message from Brigade telling them: "No news has been received from No. 1 group for ten days. The crossing of the Irrawaddy is possibly hazardous. There is no news of No. 4 Column either. It is left to your own discretion whether you continue movements or make a safe bivouac in the Gangaw Hills to harass the reconstruction of the railway."

So far as Fergusson and Calvert knew at this time,

the only columns still remaining to carry out Wingate's plan of sabotage and slaughter behind the Jap lines were their own, with the headquarters force personally led by Wingate operating farther north. It was not until they had caught up with us in our present bivouac area that they learned differently.

There came another surprise for them. Brigade came up on the air with news that they had crossed the Irrawaddy in full force with No. 7 and No. 8 Columns. With this message came instructions that No. 5 Column was to attack the Goteik Viaduct on the Mandalay-Lashio railway line under the direct orders of Mike Calvert, who was appointed local Lieutenant-Colonel for the occasion. The same message had information for us as well. No. 1 group (now comprising No. 1 Column plus the few stragglers of No. 2 such as myself) under the orders of Lieut. Colonel Alexander, was to march on to Mogok.

"You see, Sahib, I was right," said Kulbahadur with a sly grin. "Do you think there will be rubies to spare for you and me?"

These latest instructions from Wingate came as something of a surprise. However, they greatly delighted Mike Calvert, who had always wanted to blow the Goteik Viaduct. This yearning dated back to that day in the retreat of 1942 when he had fully prepared it for demolition, but the order had never come for him to blow it. Mike had, in fact, waited for ten days beside the viaduct in the face of the swiftly advancing Japs begging and praying for the word from Higher Command which would give him leave to push down the plunger and send the vital viaduct skyhigh. But that word had never come and Mike Calvert just couldn't get the viaduct off his mind. Now he was obviously itching to march there straight away, despite the mountainous jungle which lay between him and his goal.

All this we heard with considerable satisfaction and not a little envy. For me it was particularly good news for it made me feel that once again I was an integral part of a strong and well organized fighting force about to be led with skill and daring to wreak still greater destruction among the Japanese rear lines of communication. And I was particularly keen to do some major work of destruction myself, for my column had certainly come off second best in its engagement with the ambushing Japs at Kyaikthin. I had quite a score to pay off!

For Mike Calvert and John Jeffries this reunion in the bivouac area in the midst of this inhospitable elephant grass jungle could not have happened at a better time. It was 16 March, the eve of St. Patrick's Day, and both were as Irish as Irishmen could be. They brewed a fiery punch of hot rum mixed with water which had had raisins boiled in it, and it was as well for the Japs they did not put in an attack on us that night!

We spent some four days in the bivouac area, resting and repairing our tattered clothing and equipment. We were able, through our radio contact with Brigade farther north and H.Q. at Imphal, to form a more complete picture of Wingate's campaign to date. All of the eight columns, with the exception of the battered No. 2 and No. 4, were now over on the east side of the Irrawaddy. Roughly they were operating in the quadrangle of jungle-covered territory with the Irrawaddy forming the west side, its tributary the Shweli river (of which the source is in China) running along the north side, and then bending down sharply to form the eastern end of the quadrangle, and the River Nam-mit forming the southern boundary. This represented at least 300 miles of marching, most of it up steeply rising mountainsides and through dense jungle, always in a heat that was blistering in the open, and stifling in the shade. Quite decidedly we had penetrated to a depth in enemy territory which could fairly be described as the point of no return. We were just as far from British-held India to our west as we were from China to the east and Tibet to the north. Whichever way we might seek to escape we had the same distance to go.

Brigadier Orde Wingate himself, with his Brigade

H.Q., was at that moment advancing in a south-easterly direction towards Baw. His headquarters force was in company with No. 8 Column, under Major W. P. Scott, of the King's Regiment, and No. 7 Column, led by Major K. D. Gilkes, of the same regiment. They were some thirty miles to the north of our bivouac area. The missing No. 4 Column, under Major R. B. G. Bromhead of the Royal Berkshire Regiment, had last been heard of fighting hard as our rearguard well back west of the Irrawaddy. In the area of the Mu Valley they had been repeatedly attacked by Japs.

Most of all, during those days in bivouac, I was pleased to be with Harold James again. Arthur Best, Harold and I were like a trio of schoolboys relating at the beginning of a new term our adventures during the summer holiday. Except that this was no particular picnic about which we were swapping anecdotes. Although Harold was apt to be reticent about the part he had played in one paticular engagement, he had about him that inwardly bubbling-over air of the school hero who has scored the vital try that won the match. After speaking with others in Mike Calvert's column we were able to piece together the story of Harold's bravery.

While on patrol he had spotted a large enemy force and, sending back warning to the main column, he engaged it with his platoon. After pouring a hail of fire into the surprised enemy Harold and his men had gone in with great dash and courage to give the Japs a taste of the naked steel of British bayonets and Gurkha kukris. Their sheer fierce courage and savage determination had been too much for the Japs, who, recoiling from the shock of the sudden assault, scattered into the jungle. There had been an encouraging number of enemy dead, lying twisted and bloody on the trail and in the undergrowth. The fact that Harold's courage and leadership had earned him the respect of his brother officers and men was quite obvious. You could tell by their bearing in his presence that they thought the world of him and were proud to be soldiering with him.

Our days of rest in bivouac came to an end on 19 March, when Mike Calvert led his column off thirsting for the destruction of Gokteik Viaduct. Bernard Fergusson set off with his column for Baw, some thirty miles due east of Tagaung. He was worried about Wingate and his Brigade H.Q., who now seemed somehow to have lost contact with No's 7 and 8 Columns, with which he normally operated.

Major Dunlop got us to our feet, and soon we were heading south-east towards Mogok, nearly fifty miles due south of Baw. The whittled down force that was now No. 1 Group was still under the overall command of Colonel Alexander. We lost no time in taking our next air-drop for we had an uneasy feeling the Japs, so far unseen and unheard, must be closing in upon us rapidly. This might be our last opportunity to be revictualled and rearmed from the skies. The area selected was a large natural clearing in the midst of dense bamboo jungle. It could not really have been a better place, for the cover around it and stretching away for miles and miles was so thick that we could reasonably anticipate taking a drop without any interference from the enemy.

Rapidly we set about building three large bonfires, while radio contact with base was made and the drop arranged. That night, as the crackling flames of the fires cast leaping black and red patterns in fantastic dances up and down the wall of impenetrable darkness which was the jungle, we waited with tingling anticipation for the drone of engines. To a man our eyes strained upwards into the great dome of the night, with its immense stars. Only the cicadas shrilling, the distant harsh cacophony of some angry baboons in an argument, and the cough of a hunting beast somewhere in the depths of the jungle, added background noises to the subdued murmuring of troops awaiting the drop.

Then, afar off, came the eagerly awaited droning. Soon two aircraft, one behind the other, just discernible as Dakotas by their back-swept silhouettes against the velvet glow of the night sky, came into our line of vision. Laboriously they circled our bonfires to exchange recognition signals with us, and then, one still followed by the other, they flattened out and came in low over the dropping zone. First they were making a dummy run to get a proper sight of the dropping zone and make absolutely sure it was us. Then the second time they came in confidently, and the roar of their engines had hardly passed beyond us before thuds in the darkness between the leaping flames told us that the bags of supplies were coming down right on target. There was rice and bundles of eagerly needed clothing in those bulky sacks thudding down out of the sky.

The Dakotas came in for further runs, and miraculously the sky was full of parachutes which changed rapidly from ominous dark blobs in the sky to collapsing mushrooms of white silk suffused with the crimson glow of the fires. For more than half an hour fresh supplies of ammunition, weapons and food came twirling and swinging down to us out on the end of the billowing parachutes.

While the droning of the departed Dakotas engines was still a murmuring memory in our ears, the metal canisters which had come down on the parachutes had been collected. Their contents were sorted out and distributed. For each man there was sufficient food for a full fourteen days (although we knew full well that it would have to last us at least three weeks!) and for each one of us there was also a much needed complete change of uniform. There was ammunition in abundance, and there were precious new bren-gun barrels, still gleaming stickily with their protective grease. Soon there were piles and piles of filled bren magazines, stacked ready for distribution. We all felt fitter, smarter, and more deadly as a fighting force. We were twice the men we had been before the miracle of the airdrop happened. For a rather personal reason, that supply-drop east of the Irrawaddy could not have come at a better time. It so happened that it was Kulbahadur's birthday!

Arthur and I were quite determined the Kulbaha-

Dakota C-47

dur should have a treat—whether he liked it or not! So we powdered two full mess tins of biscuits, to which we added water and slowly boiled it until it had evaporated. The resultant stodgy mess we mixed with dates and covered with a layer of grated chocolate. Then we took 19 matches and stuck them into our "birthday cake" with their phosphorous heads uppermost. Before we attacked this *pièce de résistance* of

Kulbahadur's birthday tea we began with a little specialty of dates on biscuits. Those eaten, we lit the "candles," and when all were flaring merrily Kulbahadur blew them out with one huge blow. This engaging little ceremony had the audience of most of the support group of No. 1 Column, who had gathered around our fire sensing that something out of the ordinary was taking place. Then, with the same kukri that he kept always razor sharp for the slicing off of Japanese heads, Kulbahadur, a wide grin on his face, cut the cake made in his honour. It did not take long for the three of us to eat it up, leaving us feeling really gorged for the first time for many weeks.

After our meal that night we all lay around the embers of our dying fires, sipping our rum issue from chipped and blackened tin mugs. We knew we could relax caution somewhat in this nigh impenetrable jungle. Kulbahadur was in a definite place of honour lounging between Arthur and myself. His brother Gurkhas soon made the night melodious with their haunting ballads which rose and fell with queer nostalgic undulations. Then intermittently they would break into high-pitched choruses which rose on a mounting background of merry and honest laughter to fill the night with joy.

After this came the Gurkha stories. These the merry little warriors told in their lilting, sibilant tongue with a delightful, unsophisticated abandon. They were stories of the simple and often earthy misdemeanours of their village folk back home containing many a rib-cracking anecdote of bawdy implication. Their humour was certainly simple and straight to the point, but it was full of good, honest slapstick comedy reflecting the enviable naivety of their characters. The nineteenth birthday party of that most gallant Gurkha warrior, Kulbahadur Thapa, was an event strange to the ways of the Burmese jungle, but memorable in the lives of all of us who shared in it.

The following morning was probably the happiest of the whole expedition. Mail from home was distributed! For most of us there were five or six letters, and the camp was silent for a long time as each man read and re-read longingly of his loved ones. These letters were from folk not anyone of whom had the slightest idea of the perilous undertaking upon which we were embarked in the depth of Japanese-held Burma. In consequence some sentences read strangely.

From my dear mother there was a note to say that she "had received my letter from Quetta" and she realized how the climate might trouble me because she knew "the violent extremes to be found in northern Baluchistan." Because of this she added, she was sending me "a small Christmas present by the same mail." Having read the letter it was with no inconsiderable excitement that I began to slit with my commando knife the bindings around the small cardboard box which had come in the same sack. What could it be —cigarettes, tobacco, a slab of luscious and fruity plum cake? I fumbled in my eagerness to discover what was in the box. Soon I had torn away the last wrapping of tissue paper and there, neatly folded with a loving care, were a pair of thick mittens and a balaclava helmet made of good heavy wool guaranteed to keep out the worst cold that a North Indian hill station could inflict upon me! Obviously mother was not to know that my move from Quetta would take me into the humid, suffocating oven of tropical Burmese jungle! And, for my spiritual comfort, there was the quotation that began: "I said to the man who stood at the gate of the year . . ."

As for the letter written in my father's bold, firm handwriting. He pointed out artfully that "dallying with dusky maidens" should not be a deterrent to correspondence, and he suggested that I might find time to write more frequently as he felt sure my environment was conducive to letter writing. While a girl friend in Delhi asserted that she could see no reason at all why I could not arrange with my Commanding Officer to get away for a long week-end so that I might attend her twenty-first birthday party on 20 March.

As I sat there in the jungle hundreds of miles inside Jap territory, with memories of savage fighting still unpleasantly fresh and quite aware that there was more to come, I realized that 20 March was tomorrow!

Arthur Best appeared to be having some fun with his mail. There was one pompously worded missive which informed him that unless "this final demand for repayment of over issue of allowances is answered satisfactorily and immediately your Commanding Officer will be notified forthwith." While a pal of his from back in England had written to inform Arthur that "I have just heard I am likely to be posted to that hell-hole Bombay."

From all around came snatches of conversation as the British troops digested the contents of their letters and picked on selected portions as suitable subjects for public discussion.

Near me a corporal from Liverpool said: "The wife's got a raise."

"Oh?" said the sergeant beside him, just a trace of cynicism in his voice.

"Yes, she gets five quid a week now," declared the corporal proudly.

"Oh?" again, said the sergeant, the cynicism rather more marked.

"It seems she's pretty highly regarded there and the boss is teaching her book-keeping" said the corporal.

"Ah!" declared the sergeant, with a finality and wealth of meaning such as can rarely have been put into just one monosyllable.

Yes, it certainly was a wonderful day that day they distributed the mail from home, dropped so dramatically out of the night sky by the big, dark flying machines. But that wonderful day of rest, starting with the reading of our mail and continuing with the swopping of exciting stories among friends and comrades, was obviously too good to last. Suddenly, in the middle of the afternoon, a standing patrol reported urgently that Japs were around. The result was electrifying. Within ten minutes we had changed from a cheerful chattering picnic party into a fully girded-up fighting force marching with speed and purpose deeper into the depths of the jungle.

10

KILL THOSE MEN!

Within twenty minutes half a mile of jungle separated us from our former bivouac, which suddenly behind us became a hell of fire and flying steel as Jap mortar bombs showered down upon it. The Japs, it so happened, were exactly twenty minutes late and there was nobody at home to receive their shot and shell. We pressed on, most of the time compelled to fight our way through the stubborn jungle. All through the rest of that sultry day and on into the night we forced our way forward, with hardly a respite. The Japs were close on our trail again. Then in a brief halt in the darkness Major Dunlop called his officers to him. "We are heading south-east and we are on our own," he told us. "We have been ordered to meet a small party under an officer a few miles south of Mong Mit. He is to give us our next assignment!"

To do that we men who now comprised No. 1 Column had to slog across 75 miles of waterless, burning sand and rasping elephant grass. All the way we had to drag our mules, for they liked the terrain even less than we did, and were fired with no eagerness to go into battle. The uniforms which we had changed into so gladly after they tumbled out of the skies, were soon soaked in sweat and gashed and torn by the razor-edged elephant grass and barbed scrub, as we hacked and slashed our way through it.

To assuage our raging thirst we had to exert iron will-power and take no more than hasty sips at infrequent intervals from our tepid bottles. The hot air took on an unpleasant, musty quality. The mules began to get restless and pawed the ground and snuffled at the oven-hot air each time a halt was called. On the afternoon of the third day, in this same ominous atmosphere which by now had reduced us to almost complete silence, the tension was suddenly shattered by three of the mules going berserk and tearing loose from the muleteers. Kicking up their heels and whinnying like mad things, the mules crashed through the elephant grass until they halted with a clatter somewhere in its midst.

The first Gurkha muleteer who broke through to where they had disappeared shouted back excitedly: "They have found water!" And so it was. The mules had led us to a large dust-covered pond which, for all its unappetising appearance, was nevertheless much-needed water. The animals pressed forward to drink thirstily. The men, showing a truly remarkable discipline, merely filled their water-bottles and then sipped gently until their swollen tongues became deflated and stomachs were accustomed to the liquid denied them for so many hours. Thankfully, and no longer obsessed by the atmosphere of electric tension which still persisted, we lay down to rest.

We had barely relaxed our aching limbs when there arose a startled cry: "Tiger! Tiger!" It came from one of the listening posts out in the jungle, forward of our party. Then an awful blood-chilling roar close at hand was followed by a massive crashing in the elephant grass away over to the left. We could see the grass being beaten down with amazing speed before the progress of a huge and powerful animal. Instinctively, just as though a human enemy threatened, the safety catches of half a hundred rifles clicked forward. Men looked at one another wonderingly, suddenly quite out of their element and feeling stupidly powerless to help any man who might be in danger out beyond us in the wilderness of elephant grass.

Suddenly the mysterious invisible fire that was burning its swift way through the grasses towards us laid flat the last barrier of cover standing between us and the jungle horror that had set our spines crawling in apprehension. It was a young British soldier, wild eyes and mouth agape, his clothing torn and face and hands bleeding from slashes by the razor-edged grass. He burst in among us. "I saw it!" he shouted like a man crazed. "It stood right in front of me. A tiger! I tell you it was a tiger!"

I knew enough of this particular young British soldier to know that, confronted by a platoon of Japs he would coolly have opened fire and fought them to the death. But the shock of suddenly coming face-to-face with a tiger had been too much! He had let out one horrified shout and run back towards us as fast as he could beat his way through the tall grass.

Considering the incident shortly afterwards, one of his brother soldiers commented: "Put a couple of dozen bloody great tigers behind us mate and there'd be no such thing as impenetrable jungle!"

Having slaked our thirst we set off again in single file to battle our way on through the sweltering heat in this harsh grass jungle of sand and suspense. It was with immense relief that, late that afternoon, we emerged from the elephant grass and hot sand to lurch exhausted into the comforting shade of more "normal" jungle. We had now reached the thickly covered foothills of the Northern Shan States.

Tired though we were, we pushed on a little farther until we reached a mountain stream running between banks of lush, resilient moss. It burbled and chuckled to us incessantly a beautiful fairy story of endless fresh clear water, and of deep rich vegetation cool with shadowy comfort after our frightful three days fighting through the hot hell we had just left. Only this was no fairy story, but was true. We all drank deep of the cool clear water, friendly talking water which lulled us swiftly into one of the sweetest sleeps of all the nights we had so far spent in the hostile jungle.

That idyllic night was not a taste of things to come. All too soon our march towards Mogok took us away from the pleasant and shady mountain track. Instead, because we were deliberately avoiding tracks with their threat of Japs, we had to fight our way right across the grain of the terrain. There were more days spent agonizingly hacking our way through dense bamboo jungle. First up one side of a hill, and then down the other, we struggled. Slowly we would slash and tear our way up the next hillside, hacking our way foot by foot upwards until we had reached the top.

Up there on the inhospitable ridge the world opened up before us would be a depressing vision of still more undulating jungle as far as the eye could see. Then down the other side we would have to plunge, again hacking and thrusting for our lives to force our way through.

Cut and rest, cut and rest, cut and rest. That was the inexorable order of the day. But mostly it seemed to be incessant cutting and insufficient resting. We carried on so that there was always a section of our force cutting throughout the whole 24 hours of the day and night. It was utterly soul-destroying. Before long it began to tell on everyone's spirits. The well-fed, re-armed and freshly-clothed force which had set out from the bivouc area after the air-drop had already deteriorated into an exhausted body of men of whom too many were showing signs of sickness or physical distress. Soaked through and through with perspiration, sweating so much that one was almost continuously blinded by smarting salt rivulets, we fought our way on with increasing desperation. Tough as our hands had become in the exacting weeks behind us, they now became first blistered, and then bloody and raw. The new clothes were slashed to ribbons and the cruel spikes of the chopped down bamboo not only ripped our clothing but jabbed viciously even through the leather of our boots.

Large red-raw galls began to appear under the saddles of the mules, and jungle sores and large suppurating ulcers broke out all over the bodies of the men. Curiously enough, it seemed to be the biggest and the strongest men who were hardest hit; men like Arthur Best and Eddie Edmonds, from whose strong bone structures the flesh seemed to fall away almost before one's eyes. Then they began to break out in boils and sores so that, with gritted teeth, they had to force their pain-wracked and weary bodies on and ever on.

Day after day it went on. Alarmingly, food was running low. Atebrin, vital to us as the drug with which we warded off malaria, became scarce. Increasingly men collapsed, unable to pull themselves up a slope. One after another they slumped forward to lie face downwards on the path comrades immediately in front had just slashed clear, or which they were in the act of hacking out themselves. Willing hands relieved the fainting men of equipment and weapons and laid them out as comfortably as possible until they regained consciousness. Then they would stagger to their feet and silently take their places armed with kukri or machete, to carry on again the desperate fight to break through the seemingly endless wall of jungle.

One day one of the British soldiers went completely mad. He had been cutting for about an hour at the bamboo thicket which was always before him however much he cut down. Suddenly he just could not stand it any longer. With an animal-like scream which gurgled in his throat he tore straight into the bamboo and tried to pull it apart with his bare arms. Before anyone could pull him clear or restrain him they were lacerated horribly. Soon the humid bacteria-laden jungle atmosphere caused his wounds to become infected and despite all attention he very shortly died. Now, at last, it was accepted that we had set ourselves an impossible task. The jungle really was impenetrable! Haggard, and little more than blood-streaked skeletons themselves, Colonel Alexander and George Dunlop called the officers together and told us: "We'll have to give it up. It will kill us if we go on like this. We shall have to follow the tracks after all and risk running into Japs."

We had been provided with maps which purported to indicate ways through this largely unmapped area of Burma, but those maps we had already found were far from accurate. In some places farther back on our march tracks had been encountered where our maps showed none and, more dangerous, we became aware of "non-existent" villages by the barking of dogs. These were far too close for our peace of mind. Where there were villages there were always likely to be Japs. Certain man-made landmarks printed on our maps most probably did still exist. But since the maps had been drawn up those landmarks had been swallowed up by the jungle, probably for ever. By far the greater part of the territory through which we were now advancing, however, was virgin jungle which had always defeated the progress of man and which had never been charted or mapped in any way. A plain white patch surrounding the word "uncharted" portrayed too often the obvious despair of the cartographers who had had the temerity to try and translate the whims of wild nature into the precise science of man-made maps. As quickly as possible, therefore, we cut our way back to where the maps indicated a mountain track. Accepting philosophically the increased danger of meeting enemy patrols or traitorous Burmese, our battered and tattered force took to the track. It was with an air of thankfulness that we set out to march along the undulating pathway to the rendezvous where we could expect to meet that officer who had been sent to tell us our next objective. When eventually we did reach that appointed place the unnamed officer was not there.

After a great deal of searching we discovered the almost obliterated signs of a small camp which had obviously been occupied for some time. Undoubtedly the officer had waited right up to the limit of his time. But so much time had we lost fighting through the almost solid wall of jungle that he must have presumed we had failed to slip past the Japs, and so he had left the rendezvous. This depressing fact was proved when one of the Burma riflemen in our little force donned native clothes and visited a village some miles away. There he mingled with the tribesmen and discovered from local gossip that a small party of soldiers under a white officer had been seen in the vicinity of the ren-

dezvous by some wood-cutters. This had been a few
days before our arrival. The last known of them was
that they had been seen heading north in the direction
of the Shweli river; obviously they had given us up for
lost and had headed off north to rendezvous with the
main force under Wingate.

The disguised Burma rifleman also brought back
the disturbing though hardly unexpected news that
strong Jap patrols were out along every one of the few
mountain tracks in this rugged jungle terrain. One
thing was quite certain. We had missed the briefing
party! This left Colonel Alexander only one thing to
do—to get in touch with Brigade Headquarters over the
radio and risk giving our position away.

We lay around, tense with expectancy, in the hot,
stifling afternoon while the radio operator sent out his
staccato insect noises which were our one link with the
main armed organization of the Wingate Force. The
encoded instructions that came back were quickly de-
coded to surrounding murmurs of excitement. Swiftly
and dramatically the gist of the message was told
to us. It was: "Abandon heavy equipment. Destroy
mules. Get out of Burma!" Although not the exact
words of the instructions from Brigadier Orde Wingate, this was exactly what they meant. G.H.Q. back
in Delhi had apparently decided to call the operation
off. They were satisfied that we had done our job. Now
it was up to us to extricate ourselves as quickly as
possible. The way back lay through three hundred
miles of unfriendly jungle, now furiously alive with
thousands of angry Jap soldiers. They would be sworn
to avenge their dead comrades killed by Chindit attacks, to avenge their destroyed communications, but
above all to avenge the tremendous blow to their in-
sufferable martial pride that had been dealt by this
"impossible" British rampage behind their lines.

Afterwards we were to be told that the main Japanese lines of communication had been destroyed and
that it would take six months to repair them. This had
been done on the very eve of the monsoon, when repairing blown-in gorges, shattered railway viaducts

and ripped up permanent way, would be anything but easy. The daring Wingate raid, coming as it did completely out of the blue, undoubtedly seriously dislocated the Japanese plans for an early attack into India. Some 30,000 troops they had earmarked for thrusts into Assam had been set chasing around in circles hunting after us. For all the smallness of our force we had played an important part in thwarting the German-Japanese boasts of "meeting in Persia in 1943." We were also told afterwards, those of us who did survive, that we had relieved pressure on General Stillwell's forces at that time taken up with building the Ledo Road in the north.

Most important of all, as history has now confirmed, the experiences of the men who had thrust so deeply behind the Jap lines in this raid, were to prove invaluable in the training of the newly formed Fourteenth Army, that later was to defeat the Japs at Kohima and Imphal, and then to smash them back to complete and utter defeat throughout the whole length and breadth of Burma. That was something that we, and the rest of the world, were to learn in the future. In our immediate present at that time the only question we were concerned with was: "Just how do we get out of Burma?" The news from Headquarters had been that the remainder of the Brigade was already on its way back towards the Chindwin. We had farther to go than anyone else. And farther now meant that we had longer to spend ducking and dodging the furious Japs! Every day we spent in Burma now was one more day fraught with increasing peril.

The Japanese, as soon as they realized our intention (and this they must already have done as the rest of the Brigade was heading for home) would cover every likely crossing place on the Irrawaddy and Shweli rivers, and the Mu river and Chindwin farther west. They would be there heavily guarding every mountain pass, and like packs of wolves the Japanese fighting patrols would be lying in wait all through those 200 miles (300 the way we should have to march) of jungle, escarpment and mountain which stood between us and the no-man's-land beyond the Chindwin river. We lost no time in destroying our heavy equipment. We carried out the sad and sordid task of butchering the mules. Call the mule an ugly, obstinate beast if you like, but it is a brave animal and has the stuff that heroes are made of when it comes to carrying heavy equipment on a hazardous expedition.

I paused in my work of spiking a medium machine-gun with this feeling of sadness upon me, and looked around for the survivors of my original platoon. Kulbahadur was there all right, squatting back on his haunches quite unemotionally brewing up tea over a smoky, bamboo fire. A wonderful thing, tea. It was almost a religious rite with us this brewing tea in the jungle. It raised the morale, it warmed the body, it soothed frayed nerves and, of course, it allayed thirst. I smiled quietly as I thought of the profound maxim of our column, one which had already been applied in so many frustrating or dangerous situations—"When in doubt—brew up!"

Havildar Lalbahadur was with us still. He was supervising the setting of booby traps among our abandoned stores. It was good to see the havildar. He was a fighting man who in the heat of the battle seemed to do the right thing from the sheer intuition of a warrior race. I looked from Havildar Lalbahadur to two more Gurkhas who had been with me in that bloody disaster that had shattered No. 2 Column in the ambush at Kyaikthin. They were Rifleman Lachiman Pun and his inseparable companion Rifleman Kalu Rana. At this moment they were as inseparable as ever as they worked side by side helping dispose of equipment that would slow us down too much in the fast fighting retreat on which we were about to embark. That made five of us. Just five out of the original nine who had survived Kyaikthin. Naik Premsingh had died by his own hand just after Kyaikthin. We knew what his fate had been, without a shadow of a doubt.

Exactly what had happened to Rifleman Karnabar Thapa none of us knew then, nor ever discovered afterwards. He had just vanished during those awful days of battling our way through the elephant grass. So many things could have happened to him. He could, for instance, have gone mad like the British soldier, who paid the penalty of his madness and died poisoned by his suppurating wounds. Or he could have contracted dysentery, gone off into the tall grass to ease his agony, and while there collapsed and been unable to catch up with the rest of us again. Or, of course, he could have trodden on a krait, a little black snake which can flick itself like a whiplash and inflict a bite almost instantaneously fatal. Or a tiger could have killed him, or a rogue elephant trampled him, or some other wild beast could have emerged from the thick undergrowth to savage him to swift but fearful death. Or, like one of Bernard Fergusson's Gurkhas, he might even have fallen on a sharp-pointed bamboo stump which pierced his brain. Who knows?

The fate of Rifleman Tartabsingh Thapa was equally mysterious. He just did not answer roll-call after that hurried departure when the Japs failed by only twenty minutes to destroy us with mortar bombs after the last air-drop. That could mean a number of things. But the most likely was that, like me at Tagaung, he had dozed off into the deep sleep of complete exhaustion. Then, resting in the shade probably a little beyond the rest of us, he had been forgotten in the excitement of getting away. If that were the case, and the Japs had found him, his fate was most probably worse than swift death, to say the least.

As for Rifleman Gore Pun, my other missing Gurkha, he had just collapsed and died while we were chopping our way through the jungle in the Shan foothills. Just collapsed with a gasp. He was already dead as he hit the ground, and beyond the aid of those who ran to him.

Five of my original platoon left. Only five. How many of us would live to see India again? Very few, I was certain, if we retraced our steps acting as Brigade's rearguard all the way. Thus did I meditate as I sipped the mug of scalding tea brought over to me by the grinning Kulbahadur. Still troubled by my gloomy reflections I drew my map out of my ammunition pouch. It was not for me to make any decision that would affect the fate of the party of course. After all I was only a nineteen-year-old lieutenant and very much the junior officer of the party. But there was no harm in my thinking about it, at least. Then my heart leaped with the same exhilaration that I am sure stout Cortez must have felt when he sighted the Pacific from that peak at Darien. China was the answer!

To get back to the safety of India we had to march over 300 miles, by the time we had been up and down mountains and around Jap ambushes. To reach China we had less than 100 as the crow flew. Admittedly to reach China we had to surmount the 10,000 ft. high Shan mountains which would certainly be tough, particularly as our tattered tropical clothing would give little protection against the bitter cold of the higher altitudes. But the way out through the unending jungle back to India, quite apart from the fact that it was more than three times farther, was also certain to be desperately tough. I could foresee that we would have to forsake the tracks and the known ways with the Japs so furiously hunting us. Which would mean more of that two miles per day stuff, slashing our way hopelessly through the awful agony of the elephant grass. Perhaps only to bring utter exhaustion, misery and madness in the end.

Pondering further on the China theme I told myself that, while there would be no suitable places for air-drops, we had plenty of silver rupees among us and should have little difficulty buying food and information. Still more on our side was the fact that this country was inhabited by Kachin tribesmen by repute still staunchly loyal to the British Raj. Once in China there were, of course, the American air bases we had heard so much about! It was just a matter of walking to China and thumbing a lift in a bomber or heavy transport plane to take us back to India in comfort! (My sanguine imaginings took no regard of the fact that China was quite a large place, and that those American air bases might be a long way into the interior!) I felt sure that the Japanese would never expect us to attempt the journey through the mountains to China in the cold and the wet of the coming monsoon. It seemed to me that the motto of our force: "The boldest methods are the safest!" would pay off handsomely in this instance.

My far reaching day-dream was interrupted by some hearty cursing from a cluster of trees behind me. Recognizing it as Arthur Best at his most profane, I hauled myself to my feet and pushed through the undergrowth to find him trying to attach a cluster of live grenades to a trip wire across the trail.

"You know," he suddenly said to me, in a halt between his curses, "I've just been thinking Ian. We ought to go to China!"

"In which case," I replied, "great minds think alike. I hope the Colonel feels the same way about it." Our minds were soon made up for us, so far as our next move was concerned. Shouted orders to fall in at once had us rapidly lined up in single file and then we moved off.

Our heavy equipment and everything else likely to retard us now left behind irreparably damaged, we set out a much lightened force to climb the densely forested mountain on whose lower slope we had been lying up.

We knew we were situated just south of Mong Mit, a large Jap base which had been one of our potential targets. We knew that the steep jungle-clad mountain up which we were now sweating and cursing would actually overlook Mong Mit once we had attained the summit. We were so far up the mountain that we were getting clear of the tree line, being well up into the bare rock-strewn upper slopes, when we heard the first explosions behind us. Arthur looked round and down at me, his eyebrows arched in mock surprise to call back: "Dear me! Now just what do you suppose that might have been!" We both knew full well it was the first booby traps going off as the angry Japs probed our abandoned equipment.

For all the obvious proximity of the Japs, we had to

pause for a rest. There was not a man among us who was not by now completely exhausted by the steepness of the climb and the rarefied atmosphere of these high slopes. So far up were we that we were now clear of all cover and the sun, unhindered, was beating down on us mercilessly. We seemed to be climbing upwards into a blazing inferno as arid and shrivelling as the jungle depths had been humid and sweltering.

Halt was finally called when we were nearing the summit of the barren, rock-strewn peak which had already been dubbed "Old Baldy" by the men. For days now, whenever we had briefly emerged from the thick jungle or been able to see the way ahead, this scorched height had been visible towering up above the eternal green sea of foliage. From afar we had been able to see the long, dark green spur of rising ground which ultimately rose above the tree line to shrug off its greenery and become a dominant bald mountain falling precipitously away all round except where two spur-ridges slanted steeply up to it. It was the perfect place for a "backs to the wall" fight, for the jungle-clad spurs were the only way up, and everywhere else was a sheer drop. What was more, this height directly overlooked the Mong Mit-Mandalay motor road, the only route for trucks and wheeled military traffic between the several Japanese garrisons established in the Shan States.

We had hardly flung ourselves down among the hot boulders to rest before a message was relayed by panting voices along the line of men. " 'O' Group. Pass the word along. Column Commanders 'O' Group!"

I clambered to my feet, with hardly the strength in me to lift up my tommy-gun to carry it over my shoulder. I stumbled among the rocks to the head of the column where the officers were being called up to receive the column commander's orders. I staggered into the little group of panting, dishevelled officers to find Major George Dunlop leaning on his rifle. His tattered clothes, hanging loosely upon him, not only gave him a scarecrow aspect but accentuated the slightness of his figure. Yet his protruding red beard, curling upwards at the end, gave him a buccaneer look which added strength and purpose to the over-all picture of the man. Penetrating green eyes, vitally alive in his drawn and sun-bronzed face, went well with the swashbuckling beard.

Firm and decisive though it was, George Dunlop's voice was tired. It had the underlying tone of tiredness inevitable in a man who, at this moment, had behind him more than ten long weeks of responsibility and decisions. Ten precarious weeks all the time with nerves at hair-trigger tautness with the responsibility of being a leader campaigning in the midst of the enemy. In this sort of warfare, a mistake was far more likely to result in death than in fighting on an established front.

"We will rest here, on this mountain, until moonrise tonight. We are only a few miles from Mong Mit and the motor road is very close now, almost directly down below us. Therefore there will be no fires and no unnecessary movements. Only sentries will keep a round up the spout, for I want no accidental shots to tip off the Nips." The abrupt way in which Major Dunlop concluded: "That is all gentlemen!" left us in no doubt but that there was no alternative to the decision he had made. All the officers dispersed to relay the C.O.'s orders and establish their men in good defensive positions.

The area we were occupying was little more than a pimple on the very topmost slope of the mountain. To get to this dominant position we had clambered up a slope which we could now look back on and see to be a razor-edged spur. Another spur, undulating and jungle-clad once below the tree line, ran at right angles steeply down to the motor road some 1,500 feet below. These spurs were both—like the rest of the surrounding countryside for as far as the eye could see— covered in the dark green carpet of jungle. Only the last twenty or thirty yards, where each spur climbed up to our bare pimple, were bereft of any vegetation. With the almost sheer drops of a thousand feet everywhere else falling dizzily to the dark, omnipotent jungle below, the only vulnerable sides to our position were obviously the jungle-covered spurs leading up to us. Those last twenty or thirty yards of bare rocky hillside, however, formed a deadly "killing ground" on which might be wrought the destruction of any foe who might choose to attack us out of the jungle beneath.

It was directly overlooking a sector of the spur up which we had climbed that I deployed the support group, and took up my own position. A little lower down to our left was the infantry company, commanded by Vivian Wetherall. I sent the "Heavenly Twins" (as we knew them, because they were inseparable), Riflemen Lachiman Pun and Kalu Rana, down into the jungle to act as our listening post. On them we relied for the first warning of our Japanese pursuers should they come up the mountainside through the jungle below us.

Major Dunlop came round to inspect our positions, and departed obviously satisfied. With a taut but curiously satisfied feeling within me I made my rounds of the position, chatting with the men, replying to questions both serious and facetious, and laughing at the odd humorous quip. I saw to it that a jungle sore on one man's ankle was bandaged, and I called up the doctor to give attention to the shoulder of another man grazed in a fall on the exhausting climb up. Wounds turned septic so soon in that climate.

All the time the fiery sun beat down on us like a living flame. We relaxed our toughened bodies beneath its shrivelling heat, intent on storing up as much energy as possible for the forced marching we knew to be ahead. Four days forced marching were what we had been told to expect before we gained the Chinese border. Although four days did not seem much after the exacting weeks we had spent east of the Chindwin, we knew now from experience that a forced march through the jungle could bring madness and exhaustion to the point of death.

I made the most of the scant shadow provided by a boulder, unbearably hot to the touch. At my side,

asleep, lay Kulbahadur. Premsingh's tommy-gun rested
in the crook of his arm. Despite the complete relaxa-
tion of this posture I knew that the first note of alarm
would electrify him into a fighting crouch, wits instantly alert and ready for action.

As he lay there I studied Kulbahadur's hairless face.
He looked so much younger in repose, and I wondered if indeed this youth was the nineteen years of
age he claimed. I doubted it, for the habit of most
Gurkhas of adding two years to their ages on en-
listment was a well-known military "crime" to which
several decades of recruiting officers had blandly turned
the very blind eye.

We had grown very close to one another, had Kulbahadur and I, during the two months and more we
had been together as front-line soldiers. However harrowing the experiences we had gone through since
crossing the Chindwin, we had never failed to enjoy
each other's company. Looking down on the sleeping
Gurkha youth now, on the eve of probably another
desperate and bloody battle, I thought back on an incident which had occurred soon after the ambush at
Kyaikthin. I had offered Kulbahadur the two stripes of
a naik, something I knew he desired as keenly as any
other of the Gurkhas, who were all born soldiers.

"No thank you, Sahib," Kulbahadur had replied
quietly. "I promised Premsingh that I would look after you Sahib. Have I not taken over his tommy-gun
for that very purpose?" Despite all my urgings, I
could not get Kulbahadur to deviate from his declared
intention of staying with me to fight beside me and
"look after me" throughout the war. "When we have
beaten the Japanese together, Sahib," he added with a
slow smile, "I shall transfer from the 2nd Gurkhas to
the 8th, your regiment, so that we can continue soldiering together even in peacetime."

Kulbahadur had asked me what it was really like
in Scotland. He maintained that he knew "all about
England" because his father had been there for the
coronation of the King of England. He had gone over

as a member of the Gurkha contingent and had learned about England then. I told him about Scotland, and promised him I would take him there one day.

My sturdy little Gurkha orderly was as good a servant, even under the most adverse conditions, as he was a fighter. At night he would lay my blanket in the most comfortable spot in the platoon area, and would guard it against all comers whilst I was away preparing the defence of our sector. When I came back there was always a mug of scalding tea to greet me so that, even as I write these words, Kulbahadur's softly spoken, almost tender: "Chae (tea) Sahib?" is sounding in my ears. In danger he was always at my left elbow—"One pace left-flank rear," in traditional Gurkha orderly manner. On patrols his eyes were everywhere and his tommy-gun covered my every movement. No British officer in a hostile land could have wished for a braver, kinder, and more resolute friend and bodyguard than Rifleman Kulbahadur Thapa.

As I came out of my reverie it was with a feeling of tenderness that I took the tommy-gun from his hands and laid it beside him so that he would sleep more comfortably. Then I too stretched out on the burnt and barren ground to sleep. I awoke with a start of such violence that it brought me up to a firing position, my tommy-gun instinctively at the ready. The crash of bullets and the shattering disintegration of the radio set on a rocky ledge above me were all part of the shock which had brought me from deep sleep to a pulsating wakefulness.

"Support platoon, stand to!" I shouted hoarsely, frantically pulling on my equipment as I did so. My orders were unnecessary. All around me I could hear the clattering of bolts and the clack of bullets slamming home into breeches as the men prepared to fight the enemy. I strained my eyes towards the blackness of the jungle shadows down below whence the attack must come. But for the moment nothing stirred. I threw a hasty glance over my shoulder at the shattered radio set and could see that it had been destroyed beyond repair by that burst of fire from a hidden Jap light-machine-gun. Then all at once Jap machine-guns, with their high rate of fire, fired at us again from down among the trees. Rifles joined them in a staccato chorus which swelled to a continuous clattering like the first desultory drops of a thunder shower suddenly exploding into a torrential downpour. Still I could see nothing but trees, and the silhouettes of trees and dark green shadows deepening into blackness.

"Don't fire until I give the word," I shouted.

Then, out of the corner of my eye, I saw Vivian Wetherall come bounding down the slope to join the platoon of his company nearest the enemy. It was typical that he should seek to be where the attack was likely to be strongest. Even as he flung himself down behind a boulder an inferno was upon us. Heavy mortar bombs erupted dust and rock fragments within our perimeter. Screams and yells told that we had suffered our first casualties in this new battle. The air was alive with the hum of jagged metal and the whine of razor-sharp stone fragments. I wriggled closer to my boulder. I had no more desire to be struck by a rock splinter than by a Jap bullet.

Again I peered down into the deep shadows among the trees at the jungle's fringe. Still there was no sign of any enemy. I slipped three loaded magazines out of my pouches and placed them beside me, so that I could pick them up to reload without even taking my eyes off my target if one appeared.

The thought of the wrecked radio set nagged me. That meant we were on our own now. On our own for good and all until we had fought our way clear through the rest of Japanese Burma and had attained the sanctuary of friendly China. There would be no more ammunition dropped from the skies now that the radio had gone. There would be no more food, nor medical supplies, nor any more weapons nor provisions of any sort. We were on our own from this moment on.

"Mar tio manchi! M A R !"

"Kill those men! K I L L !"

Vivian had seen the enemy. Instantly at his command bren-guns chattered and rifles cracked. Screams of stricken Japs pierced the sudden chaos of noise. Then I saw them too. Dark shadows moving among the jungle below. Moving in little darting, bobbing motions, emerging from the deeper shadows then re-merging with them. The enemy!

"Support platoon—enemy in front—FIRE!" I shouted with the full triumphant power of my lungs. And with my shout the whole of the little world around me exploded into shattering noise and flame and the acrid stench of burning cordite. I was hardly conscious that I myself was pouring hot lead down into the Japs below. The particles of burning cordite stinging my face were from my own firing. Beneath waves of shuddering sound the brown, stubby, grass flattened in front of Kulbahadur's boulder just beside me. At the end of each burst from his throbbing tommy-gun it came erect again. Our firing had been good. The enemy had felt the full effect and had suffered severely.

The Japs went to ground and the fanatical enthusi-asm of their first charge died away into sporadic firing from behind rocks and trees. Most of their bullets went over our heads but a few ricocheted from the rocks around us with a low rising whine. Then the Japs began to hurl their small grenades at us, and a light mortar started to pump bombs into our position.

As suddenly as they had started the mortar explo-sions ceased. Except for the groans of wounded, and heavy breathing, there was silence again among the rocks which were our position. The Jap machine-guns stopped. Their small calibre rifles had abruptly ceased fire. The Japs themselves were still unseen. For brazen breathless minutes the sun flung its heat down upon us. The torrid silence that ensued might have been be-cause all life was scorched out of the earth. Then suddenly something moved!

"Fix bayonets!" I shouted, conscious that my voice was high and shrill, raised almost to a scream. A little to my left with a movement that was swift and sweet, Kulbahadur slipped his kukri from its angled scab-bard. He placed the broad, curved gleaming blade at his side. Mechanically following his example I drew my long, slim razor-edged knife from its sheath which was sewn to the side of my pack. The cold steel was white and wicked. Kulbahadur flashed me a grin, as wicked as the gleam of my knife. Vivian Wetherall's voice farther down the slope suddenly pierced the silence. With beautiful accuracy a Japanese N.C.O. was picked off as he made a dash across a gap between two trees. In his death throes, he leaped high into the air to describe a perfect western roll before thudding to the earth to lie sprawled out and gushing blood.

From amidst the whining and humming splinters of metal and rock which then enveloped us a wild scream cut through. I turned swiftly towards Kulbahadur, to see that he in his turn was looking left at one of my men. The Gurkha was holding his face with blood spurting between his fingers. Already it was running down his wrists in twin rivulets to debouch on to a rain-and-sun whitened rock to form a dark and sticky pool. Then just in front of me there came a sickening thud, and a man was whipped upwards almost into a sitting position before slumping forward over a boulder. Blood trickled thickly over its rounded mass to drip down on to the baked ground.

I edged even closer to my boulder while I changed my magazine. Then the enemy came out at us again. Shadows detached themselves from the deep pool of the jungle gloom below us and suddenly emerged into the glaring sunlight to be revealed as tough, soldiers of Nippon. They were advancing slowly behind their long bayonets. Slowly and menacingly with a cold precision as though they believed themselves impervious to our fire.

A line of flashes flickered swiftly across them as they continued advancing towards us. Instantly bullets buzzed among us and above us. The Japs began to trot, the trot became a run. They came pounding up the rock-strewn slopes seeming larger than life, the sun striking burnished fire from those long-pointed bayonets which seemed to be converging towards my throat!

Terrifyingly they loomed right upon us, until the line of Jap soldiers resolved itself into just one Japanese who, with each pounding stride towards me, assumed increasingly fearful proportions. I could see his uneven black and yellow teeth bared as he panted for breath. I could see his bloodshot eyes bulging as he stared straight at me, the look of the killer glaring from them. With the next step and the next, as he pounded up, he worked his bolt back and then forward. The muzzle of his rifle droppped to become a completely round, black hole pouting at me. The sun glinted fiercely on his bayonet as it lost its elongated look and became just a fiery point directed at my heart. Six yards to go, five, four, three—the snarling Jap loomed bigger and bigger and bigger until he was as big as a barn door. The breath burst from my lungs as my finger squeezed the trigger. The Jap was jerked upwards and flung backwards by the point-blank impact of the heavy bullets from my tommy-gun tearing into his chest. Blood gushed from his mouth as he fell to the ground, his twisted face downwards. I could see his back torn out in a great gaping wound. There was nothing else in front of me.

There was not only nothing in front of me, but nothing living any more in front of anyone in our thin, scorched line of British and Gurkha soldiers. The red mist dissolved from before my eyes and I looked out more clearly into the silent world before me. A bird twittered down in the jungle afar off. It scattered its notes at random down the significant silence, and ceased. That was all.

Dropping my eyes to the bloody wreck of the Jap I had slaughtered I saw that all up the slope and all along the line of our position were dead and crumpled Japs. Then the cries of our own wounded reminded me that we, too, had had our casualties.

The sun of late afternoon was now casting longer shadows among the rocks. The battle had seemed to be but a matter of tremendous seconds in the vast sea of time of our ever present danger. But now the length of the shadows told me that the tense waiting, and the

intermittent firing which had proceeded the Japs' disastrous charge, had lasted longer than I had imagined. We lay low, each man behind his rock, sipping the warm brackish water in our bottles. We all realized that the Japs must be held off until darkness fell, when we were to make our bid to cross the motor road down by Mong Mit.

In the uneasy peace and the silence that now enveloped us I turned round to look at Arthur farther up the hillside. I waved to him cheerfully. I felt lighthearted and elated. We had killed all the men who had come to kill us.

"Look Sahib! There are Lachiman and Kalu!" It was Havildar Lal Bahadur shouting. I looked down towards where he was pointing to see Lachiman Pun carrying his wounded friend over his shoulder, making his way up from his listening-post down in the jungle. They must have been surrounded by the Japs down there as the enemy surged up through the jungle. But they had escaped into the undergrowth after Kalu had been wounded.

Even as we looked at the Gurkhas, mortar bombs started to land among us again. Lachiman dragged Kalu back into the jungle at the new outbreak of firing. Above the din of exploding bombs we heard the crack of Lachiman's rifle down there the wrong side of no-man's land. There came again the screech of a Japanese light-machine-gun. It was as I crawled cautiously up my boulder to see if we could do anything to help Lachiman and Kalu that my immediate world disintegrated in the great blast of hot air that hurled me forward and over to lie, frightened and wounded, on the mountain top above Mong Mit.

"And that," I told the Thugyi, "is how I came to be wounded so that my comrades had to leave me behind them in the jungle."

11

THE ONLY WAY OUT

I told the Thugyi of my narrow escape from the searching Jap officer, the ensuing physical agony of trying to stand and walk, and of the mental agony I had suffered during my hours alone in the jungle. I described the events up to the time when the charcoal burners came upon me, and my world of pain and fear dissolved in unconsciousness.

"What happened after that, Thugyi, you know very well yourself—even better than I do," I smiled. "For what you have done I shall never cease to be grateful all the rest of the days of my life."

During those idyllic days of complete rest in which I sat and talked long and often with the Thugyi and the chief citizens of the village, the reports from his spies out in the surrounding jungle kept coming in. From this never failing source of information he was able to inform me that there were "many British soldiers" in the Shan hills, mostly farther north. For some days the mountains around had been full of Japanese patrols, and it was from following their marches and counter-marches that his watchful tribesmen had been able to provide the facts from which he built up the full picture of what was happening. He had deduced that the survivors of the British force—who could only be my erstwhile comrades—were surrounded and were trying to fight their way out across the Shweli River, or north-eastwards through the mountains into Chinese-held Yunnan.

"Both routes are not possible for escape," the Thugyi insisted. He went on to explain how the deep, fast-flowing Shweli was not only being patrolled by armed river craft but was also simply bristling throughout its length with strong enemy patrols paying particular attention to all fords and likely crossing points. The Thugyi assured me that there were very few tracks going east or north-east. Each of the existing ones crossing the mountainous Chinese border led to one or another of four passes which were in turn heavily guarded by the Japanese.

"So you see, Sahib," he said finally, "there is only one way for your friends to get back to safety. They must forget all about trying to escape into China and must march back right across Burma into India. It is the only way. Of that I am quite sure."

Although I did not say so in as many words, I did not agree with the Thugyi's opinion. From what I had already experienced behind the Jap lines I felt sure that however many thousands of soldiers the Japs had disposed in this wild jungle country, they could not possibly watch every mile of the 200-odd-mile length of the Shweli River. Even though the Japs might reckon it to be the "impassable" barrier that would finally defeat the retreating British, the Chindits had already proved the impossible possible. There must be a way across, I told myself. I was fully prepared to accept the Thugyi's knowledge of the passes into China, but I could not accept his final assertion that the Shweli River was impassable.

Some ten idyllic days, spent mostly lazing and eating and drinking, passed by before the Thugyi would let me get up and move around. Then, on my third afternoon of being "up and about" in the village, the Thugyi and I were sitting on his veranda sipping cool rice beer in long bamboo mugs when a sentry on the palisade suddenly turned and shouted a warning. The result was spectacular! Almost with the urgency of a Chindit bivouac swarming into life at the sound of a rifle shot, the whole village suddenly boiled over into excited and dramatic movement. Men, women and children and dogs came running from huts and shady places where they had been resting in the heat

of the afternoon. There were shouts and the boisterous leaping and barking of the dogs. Then the direction
of all the bustle and alarm resolved itself into a headlong rush towards the main gate, where the crowd
halted just inside the entrance to mill around in a state
of apparently excited indecision.

"What is it?" I asked, sensing at once the urgency
of the movement.

"It is a messenger from the north," said the Thugyi
in a low voice. And he screwed his eyes up and
sucked in his lips with the air of a man expecting only
bad news.

The two of us stood up as the young Kachin messenger, looking incredibly cool despite the blazing afternoon heat, trotted up towards us from the gateway.
Without looking either to left or to right, he ran on
with the singleness of purpose of a marathon runner
heading for the finishing tape. He halted before the
Thugyi and, his broad, brown chest rising and falling
as evidence of his effort, he spoke his message in rapid,
guttural Kachin.

As the young man turned on his heels and, still
running with his loping, effortless stride, disappeared
behind a bamboo plaited hut, the Thugyi turned gravely to face me. "Your friends have had a battle trying
to cross the Shweli River," he told me, brows knitting
in the manner of a man reluctant to pass on bad news.
"Many of your friends have been killed by the Japanese, including a British officer. They were not able
to cross the river and they have now turned towards
the south. The Japanese are calling in all their patrols
with the intention of driving these British out of the
mountains and the jungle into the Irrawaddy plain.
They plan to drive them into the plain and there to kill
them all. A large Japanese force is on its way here, to
this village, now. The messenger said it is the plan of
the Japanese to stay in this village and to use it as a
base while they patrol all tracks to the east."

So grave had the Thugyi's face become, and so apparent the consternation written on it, that I found
myself feeling desperately sorry for him. At that very

moment those same Japs would be bent on tracking down and killing my friends and comrades in arms, for the British force mentioned could be none other than the No. 1 Column survivors of the battle on "Old Baldy."

"Sahib," said the Thugyi, speaking now almost in a whisper. "What will you do now?" Coming so abruptly and brutally at the very moment when I had been telling myself that the Shweli was passable, the news of the ambushing of the British force while trying to cross was now a deciding factor.

"Thugyi," I replied quietly, "I see now that you are right and that my only way out is to go back across Burma. That I will do. I will set out as soon as possible, so that I can get away from your village before the Japanese come here, and so that you do not have to pay in blood for your hospitality to a British soldier."

In my mind I was already working out that, as the Japs were not expected to reach the village until sundown, I had some hours start on them. I reckoned I could get well clear of the village in those few hours. According to the stories of the village scouts, who were now bringing in their information, the small British column which had met with the bloody repulse at the Shweli River was at that moment somewhere a few miles north of Mong Mit. I felt I could safely presume that these survivors of No. 1 Column (how many left now? I wondered) would almost certainly be turning westwards to skirt the large enemy garrison known from bitter experience to be at Mong Mit.

Maybe I could come up with them again, and this time they would not leave me behind! With them I would march westwards, heading back to India. Westwards, with all the heartbreaking 300-mile slog before us. Over the Irrawaddy, the Mu River, the soul-destroying escarpment, fighting always against the jungle, the heat, the insects, the disease, and the Japs. Until at last—if ever—we would reach the no-man's-land of the Chindwin River itself. "And once across the Chindwin we are safe," I said half aloud. "Once across the Chindwin. That's all we have to do. That's all I have to do. I must reach the Chindwin."

"But Sahib, your leg. It is much better, but you still cannot walk properly with that leg!" The Thugyi's kindly eyes were luminous with his concern for me. "Why not remain with us? We can hide you very easily. The whole village will look after you, and the Japanese will never have the chance of finding you. They could stay here for a whole year and never find you if you will let us hide you. Stay with us here, Sahib. Stay with us here and get well and fit again and be one of us."

Never had I had to face a greater temptation. After the privations of the march, the violent nervous shock of battle, the shattering impact on my mind of being left by my comrades to die, and now the vast and almost impossible task I was setting myself of walking out of Burma, the temptation was truly great. The comforts and the safety of this peaceful village were utterly seducing. Quite apart from everything else, this was the happiest, most peaceful, and beautiful community I had ever come across in my life. For the sheer stillness and loveliness of its setting I found it hard to compare it with any other scenic beauties I had known so far in my young life. As for the calm and unassuming friendliness of its inhabitants, and the untroubled and eternally friendly way of life of those who lived there, I just could not imagine there being anywhere else in the whole world that could compare with it. Yet something in me told me I had to go on. Something in me told me that I should be breaking faith with my countrymen and comrades if I did not seek somehow or other to try and make my way out of Burma. It was my undeniable duty once more to become part of a fighting force dedicated to the killing of Japs, and to the final defeat of the Jap forces in Burma.

"Thank you, Thugyi, but I must go," and in saying it I knew that the real reluctance in my voice was showing through. "You have been very kind. No man could wish to meet greater kindness anywhere. The

British Raj does not forget kindnesses and this that you have done for me will certainly never be forgotten."

"It was nothing, Sahib," the Thugyi replied quietly. He waved away the silver rupees I was offering him. He said, "No! I do not want your silver. All I want is that you come back to see us one day."

"Yes, Thugyi, I will," I said, and I really meant what I said.

So, grudgingly, the headman assented to my plan to leave his village, but not before he had seen to it that I was well equipped for my coming trials, and that a guide had been found to give me a good start on my hazardous journey. I decided it was best for me to get moving before my resolution weakened. I buckled on my revolver belt and slung the filled pack over my shoulder. The Thugyi had already seen that as much food as possible had been crammed into my pack in case any sudden crisis should cause me to go into hiding again. I picked up the stout walking-stick which one of the natives had cut for me. I had graduated from crutch to stick during my days of rest and recuperation, and some of the Thugyi's younger male relatives had helped me start walking once more. Although still limping, I could walk quite well with the aid of the stick, and now I moved off towards the main gate. The native appointed to guide me took his place silently at my side.

As if by magic the whole population of the village, men, women, children, and even dogs with tails wagging, were there to wish me farewell and God-speed. They formed a double line through which I made my way, my guide at my left hand and the Thugyi on my right. I walked down the sloping path from the headman's home on the pagoda-crowned hillock conscious of the great waves of friendship all around. I knew that the tears that expressed my gratitude at this spontaneous friendliness were in my eyes for everyone to see, but I did not care. Although I had only been among these kindly people for two weeks, and hardly knew one from the other, I felt that each and every one of them was my true and trusted friend. In their various ways, mostly unintelligible to me, they shouted out encouraging remarks to wish me good fortune on my attempt to walk through the Jap lines back across the Chindwin to British India. Most of them, I am sure, called out to me invitations to return to see them after the British had defeated the Japanese.

Then we were at the main gate. There for a moment we halted, the Thugyi, my guide and I. Looking on me with a fatherly solicitude, the Thugyi said: "Be careful of your leg, Sahib. A few more days and it will be quite well and you will not even need the stick."

"Goodbye, Thugyi, and thank you very much," I said, gripping his hand hard. I was conscious that my few words were inadequate to express the immense gratitude I felt for this kindly and upright man and the wonderful little community over which he ruled.

"Goodbye, Sahib. You have a long walk in front of you," he said, returning my grip. When I was a few paces off, he called after me: "If you don't meet your friends, Sahib, come back. We will look after you. Don't worry."

As I reached the first bend in the path which wound between the verdant growth of bushes, bamboos and trees, I turned and waved. By now the Thugyi was back on his veranda, up there at the highest point in the stockaded village. His bare arm was raised in a salute as I looked, and then he let it fall smartly to his side. He was standing stiffly to attention! Once more, in spirit, he was a naik who had carried out what he considered to be his duty in accordance with his loyalty to the British Raj. Certainly this naik had served a British officer well!

Once we were round the bend, and the blissful village with its kindly people and splendid headman was out of sight, I turned to my guide. Up to this moment I had been aware of his presence, but oblivious of his actual appearance. He was typical of the sturdy hillmen found in those parts. He was wearing a printed lungyi wrapped round his waist and tucked in at the top, extending down to just below his knees. He wore an ordinary shirt, with collar and pockets, its colour being more or less white. Over this he wore a jacket something like a battledress jacket in shape which came down only as far as the waist, in the manner of a track suit. On his head he wore a coolie hat of plaited straw, flat and rather like a lampshade. This was secured under his chin with a leather thong.

During the first few hours of our journey together my guide seemed mainly intent on pressing on to give me as good a start as possible on the Japs known to be coming up from the south. But from time to time he looked towards me and smiled reassuringly, and spoke short sentences in Gurkhali. He took me along almost invisible game trails which he followed with the uncanny skill of a hunter. Generally they followed the ridges of the long jungle-clad spurs which thrust out one after the other down into the valley. I was overjoyed to find that my wounded leg was standing up to it well, and we were getting along at quite a steady pace. I was experiencing very little pain, and most of the obstacles which confronted us I was able to overcome with the aid of my stick.

The Kachin called frequent halts, sometimes beside crystal clear mountain streams. All the time we seemed to be in a woodland world of our own, walking on quite openly and undisturbed. Until, just before the sun with all the suddenness of the East sank behind the horizon, we reached the motor road. My heart gave a leap as I realized it was practically the exact point where I had been left, wounded and desperate, to whatever fate might overtake me. I motioned to my guide that I wanted to look for something. I quickly discovered the little basin in which I had lain while the Jap officer probed among the bamboo hiding me. There I was overjoyed to find my pack, just as I had left it, together with the tommy-gun I had discarded as too heavy to carry in my desperate and wounded condition. My guide now shouldered the pack, and proudly picked up the tommy-gun to carry it over his shoulder. Thus it was in high spirits that we crossed the road cautiously to climb into the lower slope of that same "Old Baldy" spur down which Arthur and Kulbahadur had carried me after the desperate battle in which I had received my wound.

Despite the frightening memories this place aroused, I slept deeply and contentedly. Strangely but comfortingly, I felt that some great mysterious force had come to my aid, and was now a very real thing guiding and guarding me. Before dawn we were on our way again. Now we struck sharply out on a line running directly towards the north-west. We were deep in the jungle again as the sun climbed up to its zenith above us. Then, in the soft green half-light, we halted and cooked a meal over a bamboo fire. Such was my confidence in my guide that I did not even think of the possibilities of danger from Japs in the neighbourhood. I was utterly content. And in this mood of contentment I sat down and cleaned my tommy-gun, as I did so explaining in Gurkhali and by signs its mechanism and working. I could see that he was absolutely fascinated by it and, when I suddenly told him that he could have it, and also the contents of my large pack, he was so overjoyed that I thought he would burst with gratitude!

On that note of mutual regard and trust we fell asleep to let the naked heat of the day burn itself out above our jungle roof before we set off again. Most of that afternoon we slept and the green shadows were deepening to black when my guide awakened me by gently shaking me. I climbed stiffly to my feet and, having girded myself up for the march, set off once more beside him. This time the going was far more difficult. Until moonrise I was marching practically blind behind him and I continually jarred my leg on unseen roots and rocks so that I reawakened in it a stabbing pain which took a lot of the joy out of living. Dangling creepers, like sinister invisible octopi, entwined their slender tentacles around me so that I was constantly having to halt and struggle free. Strong young bamboos whipped across my body and slashed my face and stung me.

After a while I could tell by the increasing steepness of the gradient that we were in the foothills of the mountains once again. Here the hot air pressed down upon us with a humidity as though a huge hand were trying to keep us down in the stifling jungle, and deny us access to the cooler upper slopes. As I panted up a rise my guide, a few feet ahead, suddenly stiffened. I sensed that he was peering fixedly into the valley beyond as with a whisper he motioned me to be quiet. Cautiously I moved right up beside him.

"Listen, Sahib," he whispered in my ear.

I listened. But the forest was silent. Silent as a tomb.

"I hear nothing," I whispered back.

"That is what I mean, Sahib," he whispered. "Nothing heard in the jungle means that something is killing."

I shuddered. Not knowing what to expect next, I lay down on the crest beside him. There was sufficient phosphorescence from the yet unseen rising moon for me to see the direction in which he was gazing. I carefully studied the silent black silhouettes of trees and bushes in the intangible ghostly light that was really no light yet. Minutes passed, minutes of absolute silence. It was a silence completely devoid of any sense of peace or quiet. It was a silence pregnant with a brooding fear, a fear of I knew not what.

From the distance came the sound of a hoarse cough.

I started violently, and my spine prickled with horror, as another cough, as if in answer, came from the depths of the jungle immediately below us.

"Tiger!" pronounced my guide. There was no fear in his voice. In fact, he spoke with the air of triumph of someone who had known something all along, and now had the chance of proving his point to an unbelieving companion.

"Have you never heard a tiger hunting, Sahib?"

he asked me, his teeth flashing whitely in the moonlight which was now steadily invading the darkness. He turned to grin at me, and I could swear that there was an air of roguishness about him. Trying, somewhat unsuccessfully, to appear as matter of fact about the situation as he was, I admitted that I had never heard a tiger hunting. I nearly added that I had no real desire to be mixed up in any hunt conducted exclusively by tigers for tigers, when I was in such an unfavourable position as I felt myself to be in at that particular moment.

"Then I will explain to you, Sahib." Settling himself back in the undergrowth, he squatted comfortably beside me to ignore what was going on around him and tell me in halting Gurkhali: "It is a very interesting thing indeed, Sahib. Sometimes eight or ten or even more tigers combine to form a pack. Having worked out their plan of campaign, they set out through the jungle to round up the animals they intend to kill and share between them. First they send out scouts to locate a herd of young deer. A very favourite place for tigers hunting deer in this way is a valley just like the one below us now.

"Having found their prey, one of the tigers then works his way up-wind of the intended victims while the others station themselves along either side of the valley. It is what you soldiers would call an ambush. Then at the far end of the valley, closing it off to form a trap, will be two or three more tigers who are there as the killing party.

"When all is ready the tiger up-wind will frighten the herd with his scent. Having heard and sensed the evidence of fear among the deer, he will roar to frighten them more. At this the deer will try to escape in all directions, but they will be prevented from scattering outwards to either side of the valley by the tigers positioned there. These tigers cough just like the one you heard a few minutes ago. That was the cough of a hunting tiger.

"Hearing the coughs of the hungry tigers either side of them and already having been alarmed by the scent and hunting roars of the beast up-wind, the deer now panic. They stampede along the bottom of the valley, in their terror wanting only to get away from the hunting tigers behind and each side of them. Thus they rush straight into the teeth and the claws of the killing party of tigers across the end of the valley. The roars and the noise made by the killers brings the rest of the tigers in and they all sit down to eat the fresh meat. Now, just you keep listening, Sahib, and you will hear it all come about just as I have told you."

The Kachin had hardly said the words before a fearsome roar from the top of the valley announced the start of the operation. Within a space of a few minutes the valley became a turmoil of noise as the terrified deer crashed and stampeded through the jungle, scattering everywhere in their efforts to escape the killer behind them. Menacingly through this hubbub there came from time to time the hoarse cough of the ambushing tigers, some our side of the valley (the one near us was still too frighteningly close for my liking!) and the others along the far side. Then more shattering roars filled the night with a primeval horror and it became quite clear that the deer were now stampeding straight along the bottom of the valley even as my guide had said they would. The noises of the flight diminished as they fled farther and farther away from us until a culminating horror of bloodcurdling roaring and snarling from the far end of the valley told us that the climax of the hunt had been reached and the red slaughter was at its height. The law of the jungle—the law that shows no mercy and believes in only the survival of the fittest—had been put into force in its most terrifying form!

"I think we have some sleep now, Sahib?" said my guide. I agreed with him, and was heartily glad of his company. I had no particular desire to cross the valley of death below even though I knew that the tigers would show no interest in us while they were gorging themselves on the meat of the slaughtered deer. The moon rose high, and the great stars hung like green and blue jewels in the sky glimpsed through the trees above us. It was hard to believe in the soft peace that had now descended on the world, that this jungle was full of the savagery and bestiality of the Japs as well as of ravenous beasts! Nevertheless, we slept.

*   *   *

The next day, as soon as the sun had surmounted the horizon, and was piercing the morning jungle mists, my guide and I set off again. He led me down a gradual spur through forest now so thinned that it was almost like a pleasant woodland walk in England. The spur led us down to a sandy plain in which grew little but the razor-edged elephant grass, and I knew we must be near the scene of our dreadful outward struggle. Here we rested to talk over a plan we hoped would lead us to the trail of the rest of the column. My guide assured me that from the information which had come into the village, the British soldiers who had fought the Japs on the banks of the Shweli River were now trying to make their way out of Burma in this direction.

As I saw it at that time, there were two disadvantages to me trying to catch up with the survivors of No. 1 Column. First, the Japs would almost certainly have exactly the same idea! Second, it could be that the column was travelling more slowly than I had anticipated, so that we would cut across in front of them and thus stand little chance of finding them. The first I knew to be a continual risk as long as we were in Jap-held Burma. It was a risk I expected to have to take. As for the second, I did not feel somehow that this would be very likely. I could imagine all too clearly how they would be desperately forcing themselves on through jungle or elephant grass, in their efforts to get out of Burma before the Japs closed their trap. And also (an increasing danger now) before the monsoon broke.

For one man on his own to cross the 30-mile belt of elephant grass I knew now to be before me, I realized it would be quite impossible except by following a known track. The business of hacking one's way through was quite impossible single-handed. It had, I knew too well, ultimately proved impossible for close on 250 men working in relays to the point of exhaustion as they battered and slashed, tore and hacked their way into this seemingly endless heart-breaking barrier. But what track would I follow? I knew very well that game tracks, which often looked so inviting, led almost anywhere. The likelihood of me chancing on a game track which would lead straight to the Irrawaddy river, my immediate goal, was highly unlikely. Thus my only sure hope of crossing both the grass belt, and later the mighty Irrawaddy, was to catch up with the column.

Waiting at the jungle's fringe until the sun had passed its zenith, my guide and I set out in the late afternoon to march towards the north. He advised a route which took us along the edge of the elephant grass belt, so that on one side we had elephant grass and on the other the shadowy jungle. Our eyes were constantly alert for any sign of marching men, but we walked on until nightfall without seeing a single sign. Somewhat disheartened, we crept into the jungle for the night and bedded down in a little hollow hidden by clumps of bamboo and thick undergrowth.

The next day we started earlier and pressed on with a growing urgency. We did not wait for the sun to lose its fiercest heat, and it beat down on us without mercy. The new strength which had been built up in me during my two weeks stay in the hill village was already beginning to be sapped. Even more worrying, my limp was becoming more pronounced. I was having to lean more heavily on my stout stick. The pain of my healing wounds nagged disagreeably. My spirits had started to dwindle.

It was about noon, and I was as dully silent as the panting jungle beside us, when my guide suddenly ran forward with an excited cry. He dropped to his knees, to study marks on the ground. A flame of excitement flared in me and stirred my tired body so that I started forward expectantly and joined him where he was kneeling. Despite the efforts to cover up, there was evidence before us that a track had been cut through the grass! Further investigation showed the unmistakable imprint of British boots. We had struck the tracks of the column I was seeking, and they were heading westwards!

Wildly excited, I shouted: "It's them! This is it! Let's get cracking after them!"

But my guide stood up and shook his head sorrowfully. He started forward, heading northwards still. "That trail is about three weeks old, Sahib," he said ruefully. "I am afraid we must keep going."

I did not want to believe what he said although I knew that he, with his inborn native skill at tracking and jungle craft, must be right. I bade him wait while I inspected the footprints more closely. Their edges were crumbling, and some had almost been obliterated by animal tracks. Much had obviously happened along this trail since the troops passed that way. So much that my guide knew that those boot marks had been made at least three weeks earlier. The trail must have been that of another column of Wingate's force, one of whose plans I had no knowledge. Another column which, in any case, was most probably safely out of Burma by now. (Later I learned it was the trail of Mike Calvert's column, by now well on the way back to India.)

Dejectedly, I followed my guide and we tramped on. We trudged on through the heat of the afternoon, with the sun striking back cruelly from the burning sand of the elephant-grass country on our left, and on our right the leaves of the outer jungle hanging limp and lifeless beneath the pulsating fierceness of the sun's heat.

Suddenly, we found it! From the depths of my depression which was accompanied by gradually overpowering physical weakness, my spirits soared gloriously. I dropped on my hands and knees beside my Kachin guide. There was no doubt about it, this trail was definitely warm! The earth had been pounded and torn up by the feet of dozens of men crossing over from the jungle to the elephant grass country. There was little doubt but that this was the trail of the column with which I was trying to catch up. The column in which I hoped to find Arthur Best and Kulbahadur, and others of my friends.

"Come and look, Sahib!" called my guide excitedly. I knelt down beside him to examine in detail a set of footprints close to the elephant grass. There was no doubt about it, they were quite firm and stiff in the soft soil. The edges were clear cut because the sun had not yet had time to crumble them with its full pulverizing heat. Admittedly, they were still under the shadow cast by the tall elephant grass, but there could be no doubt at all but that they were freshly made.

"They were probably made early morning today," declared the Kachin.

We examined more closely the evidence of soldiers passing by, and found many more boot-prints a little farther along. There was no sign of any mules, nothing but boot-prints. Best of all, all the prints were British ones and there was no sign of rubber-soled Japanese jungle boots having followed on the same trail. It seemed that I was in luck at last! I had found my comrades' trail and for the moment they were free of Japs! My gamble had come off!

I had been confident that sooner or later I must pick up the trail of one of Wingate's columns, if not that of No. 1 Column, for we had all been operating in an area within twenty or thirty miles of each other. At the end of our separate marches in we had converged to deal with our various objectives in a strip of Upper Burma about thirty miles across at the most. This meant that there had been some 3,000 British troops operating over that mere thirty miles, and I felt there was a reasonable chance of me striking one trail or another if I kept at it. The fact that the trail we had found was very "hot" convinced me it was my own column. I knew, from operations orders we had received before our last battle, that the others must already be on the way out and that we would definitely be the last to leave the area.

The complete absence of the unmistakable sign of Japanese jungle boots was very heartening. These were rather like a British rubber-soled hockey boot, but left an unmistakable print because the big toe on each foot was separated from the rest of the foot. Only a basic knowledge of tracking was required to tell when there were any Japs about!

My guide reckoned that the column had crossed from the jungle into the arid thirty-mile-strip of elephant grass something like six hours earlier. They had done so somewhat farther north than I had anticipated they would. The length of their strides, the depth of their boot-prints in the sandy soil, the slashing down here and there of the elephant grass, were all evidence that the column was moving fast. Speed was the order of the day, with no time for deception. Obviously they intended getting through the elephant-grass country, and to the Irrawaddy at its other side, as fast as possible.

Without doubt, No. 1 Column was pushing on in forced marches, intent on getting to the Irrawaddy and across before the Japs could forestall it. I calculated that they would be heading back towards Tagaung, where we had crossed on our way out and had found the natives so friendly. They wanted to get back to those friendly people while there was still a likelihood of getting boats across.

This meant that I would have to move fast indeed if I were to catch up with them before they crossed the river. I knew I *had* to catch the rest of the column if I were to cross the Irrawaddy. Nearly a mile wide and fast-flowing, although not yet swollen by the monsoon rains, it was a formidable barrier. Any chance of one man crossing, without a boat or the help of friends and comrades, I realized would be absolutely nil. But we had found the trail, which was what we had set out to do. I had a definite objective and I was once more full of enthusiasm and strength that were both physical and mental.

I turned to my friendly guide for this, we both knew, was as far as he had undertaken to accompany me. He had served me well and I was deeply grateful to him. I pressed two silver rupees into the sturdy Kachin's hand and thanked him with great feeling. I could sense that he did not want to leave me, even though he had nobly fulfilled his side of the bargain. I felt that had I asked him he would have gone on with me until I caught up with my comrades. But I was determined he should run no further risk on my account.

"You have led me well, my friend," I said, gripping his hand. "Now everything is all right and soon I shall be with my comrades. Goodbye and good luck."

I turned my back on him and limped purposefully off to follow the trail I felt sure would take me to the column. Within the next twenty-four hours I should be with Arthur Best and Kulbahadur once again!

12

HAUNTED HOURS

As I set out, alone again for the first time since that awful delirious moment when I had fired on the friendly charcoal burners, I began to turn over in my mind any possible alternative plan in case I did not catch up with the column. I soon realized there was little I could do in such an eventuality. The Irrawaddy was about a mile wide, and, although there were many sandbanks in it at this time of year, it was likely to prove an impassable barrier for me. I felt I was still not strong enough to attempt to swim a mile in a fast current, because I should most likely have to swim nearly three miles by the time the stream had had its play with me.

The only plan I could think of, if I did not catch up with the column, was to endeavour to slip into a village under cover of darkness and locate a boat. I would then have to try to drag it to the river and paddle it across without being detected. This in itself was likely to be a formidable task, because the dug-out canoes the natives used on the Irrawaddy were heavy, unwieldly craft rarely less than 16 feet in length. To drag one of these down into the water would almost certainly have been beyond my strength. Anyway, how I would paddle it across singlehanded I could not imagine. Nevertheless, it seemed the only alternative plan.

I decided to think only on the bright side of things, and so I kept in my mind a picture of the column ahead of me. In that mind picture I was all the time steadily overhauling them, despite my limp. I imagined them as a straggling, forward-straining column, moving ever westwards through the sandy Irrawaddy desert strip with its maddening elephant grass. I visualized them, heads down, sweat streaming from faces and chests and down their backs, their tattered bush shirts and trousers stained almost black by the constant soak and drip of it. On some there would be blood, oozing from hands and arms cut as they forced their way on and ever on past the wicked razor-edged elephant grass. . . .

Kulbahadur would certainly be there, I told myself. I could not imagine any column with which I identified myself without Kulbahadur being in it!

*   *   *

I could not possibly have been confronted with worse terrain over which to carry out such a march against time as was now required of me. The thirty or so miles of elephant grass covered wilderness of hot sand between the jungle and the Irrawaddy was an absolute inferno. As the sun climbed higher and higher through the day it burned out the whole wide sky into a pulsating white heat. From amidst it the blazing orb of the sun beat down on me with such a savage heat that it completely numbed my senses. During much of the ensuing time through those dreadful days crossing the Irrawaddy desert I was barely conscious. Often I was delirious. I was vaguely aware that I shouted aloud, and sometimes screamed and cackled with laughter, as the sun continued mercilessly to play on me. Somehow, for hour after hour, I staggered on. I staggered on despite the fact that my wound awakened to a new throbbing agony and my new-found strength was burned out of me.

Only the knowledge that ahead of me, somewhere, my friends steadily marched towards the Chindwin, kept me lurching and swaying onwards. Only that, and the insistent faith—persisting in the spasms of clear-headedness which interspersed waves of near-delirium—that I had put my hand into the hand of God, and this awful way I was now following would in the end, somehow, prove to be safer than a known way. In my periods of clear-headedness this feeling was very strong upon me. While it persisted I could not give up.

It was soon quite evident that I had badly over-estimated both the speed with which I could overtake the column, and my chances of living off the land while pushing on through the elephant grass belt. Otherwise I would have paid more heed to the Thugyi when he sought to press upon me additional gifts of food for my journey. I had insisted on taking only the bare minimum so that I should travel as lightly as possible and so be enabled to make the utmost speed. Consequently, when I took leave of the guide from the village I had only a few handfuls of rice left.

Later that day, my first day, in this dreadful wilderness of six-foot high elephant grass, I came across a small tree on which grew small apples about the size of ping-pong balls. They were not really apples, I found, because they contained a single stone. They were very bitter to the taste, but this was an advantage under conditions of such fierce heat. During the day I discovered more of them, and whenever possible I picked them so that I had a small store with me to chew. They lasted me almost to the end of the time I took crossing the hell-on-earth of the Irrawaddy sand belt. As the sun started to go down at the end of my first day in the desert, I was able to focus my eyes a little better with the lessening of the vicious white light. Thus I was able to surprise a small hare which was lying panting and apparently exhausted beside a dried-up water-hole. I swooped on it exultantly—but grabbed only a handful of dust and stones . . .

I stumbled to my feet and frantically gave chase, oblivious at first of the cuts I sustained as I lurched through the rasping barrier of elephant grass. But, of course, I could not catch it. I stopped, and picked up stones and started to throw them after a hare, which had already disappeared completely. Then giving up hurling stones, I hurled invective!—"Blast you!" I shouted furiously. "Come back at once!" But the hare did no such thing. It never occurred to me the whole episode had been ridiculous. In my heat-crazed state it was high tragedy.

I discovered many game tracks through the wilderness of grass. During my first day I followed one or two in the hope that they would lead me to water. But every time it was the same answer—a dried-up water hole. Among the spoor marks I recognized on these tracks were those of both tiger and buffalo. Fortunately I never met either. Sinisterly, however, there were from time to time piles of bleached bones which told of kills made by carnivorous beasts out in this waste of sand and razor-edged grass. Once I came across the remnants of a carcass of a mule. But from its advanced state of decomposition it was obvious the beast had died on the way out.

Later, during that first afternoon, I saw a large flock of kite-hawks circling away to my left, probably a mile and a half away. Without any doubt they were waiting for some wretched animal, or human being, to sink down and die out there in the desert beneath the flaying sun. It would be time enough for me to worry when the kite-hawks began to trail me!

*　　*　　*

By far the worst thing during those awful hours in that savage inferno were the flies. They attacked me from the moment I left the shade of the jungle to strike out across the hot sand. Before noon on that first day a persistent jungle sore which I had had for some time on my left arm, but which had lately lain dormant, began to suppurate. The whining, buzzing flies which had been incessantly and maddeningly around my head descended on it in droves. Unable to bear this loathsome invasion, I ripped the pugri from my Gurkha hat and bound it around the sore. But this did not daunt the flies, which returned as soon as the bandage was in place and settled along the whole of my forearm. Their place around my head was swiftly taken by thousands more flies which encompassed me in a perpetual misery.

Ultimately, I gave up all attempts at beating them from my face and my bandaged arm and I resigned myself to their torture. I let my arm hang loosely at my side with the flies clustering on it. Soon more settled and pushed in among the disgusting throng already there, so that my arm was completely covered and alive with flies from wrist to shoulder. I ignored them, and stumbled on.

Night brought relief from the insects, at least, from the flies. But lying out there among the elephant grass I was haunted continuously by the shrilling of a million cicadas. Sounding like a ceaseless surf washing a haunted shore, their deafening sibilance completely surrounded me. And through their maddening chorus there came the deeper drone of other insects whose origin I could not even guess, while occasionally I heard the ominous movements of heavy beasts going through the grass. But at least I was free of the flies! As the sun rose up on the second day, burning and parching already although hardly clear of the horizon, I climbed to my feet and stumbled on again. Surely, before the sun reached its zenith today, I should catch up with my comrades? I had travelled barely a quarter of a mile before the pain returned to my wounded leg with a nagging, throbbing insistence. Now I had to lean heavily on my stick. Thus early in the day I was already soaked with sweat—and my loathsome hordes of flies were around me and clustering on my arm once again. As I became weaker with the exertions of my painful journey, I realized more than ever that to cross the Irrawaddy river would be absolutely impossible now unless I had the aid of friends.

Within half an hour the sun was once more beating down in the fullness of its ferocity, and the sky and the glare reflected from the sand all around me beat again on my eyes in waves of hot and blinding whiteness. Then, suddenly, through the intense stillness of this inferno, there came a great rumbling noise. It was as if a mighty avalanche had started. But from where could an avalanche come in the endless flat and sandy waste which lay all around me? The rumbling grew louder and more and more ominous. I expected any minute that a cascade of stones and earth and great boulders would descend upon me and obliterate me completely. But from where?

I realized that the ground all around me was actually shaking. My body literally trembled with fear of the great unknown in unison with the trembling of the earth beneath my feet. Death in some unknown form was very near, I felt. But in what form would it come?

The rumbling swelled up to such an intensity that now it was a thunderous roar, like the sound of a huge tidal wave curling over to swoop down and engulf me. I felt that the earth any minute would split asunder at my feet, and that I would be swallowed up. Instinctively I threw myself over backwards, into the tall elephant grass. I was overwhelmed by an urge for concealment despite the fact that whatever the danger which was descending to overwhelm me, it could not possibly be confined just to the very narrow track along which I had been making my way.

Then, as I lay there gasping and sweating with fear, the elephant grass along the track in front of me was suddenly flattened at a tremendous speed as if a huge blast of hot air was hurling it down. The thundering reached such a climax that I was completely swallowed up in its noise and my senses no longer functioned. Momentarily I was conscious of the huge mass of a herd of wild elephants looming up above me, and then away from me, to vanish as abruptly and terrifyingly as they had come!

As I collected my scattered wits, and stared into the rolling cloud of dust left behind by the charging herd, I realized that the nearest of those mighty beasts had passed less than ten yards from me! Indeed, I had been near to death!

Throughout that second day I somehow managed to keep going. At one period during those haunted hours of awful physical and mental agony, I remember standing on a sand dune which raised me head high above the unending sea of parched elephant grass. The grass extended all around me, as far as my eyes could see, in the blinding, quivering air of the noonday heat. As I stood there, I imagined all sorts of noises, sinister and clamorous, rising from the infinite wilderness of that scorched-up dry-grass desert. I put my hands over my ears to shut out the horrid sounds, for in my fevered imagination they welled up to a threatening crescendo. Crazily I sought to shout it down, with a stream of curses which came to my lips without sequence or reason. I shouted and cursed until my parched throat would utter no more sounds.

Down among the elephant grass, almost at my feet, I surprised a large lizard dozing beside a dried-up

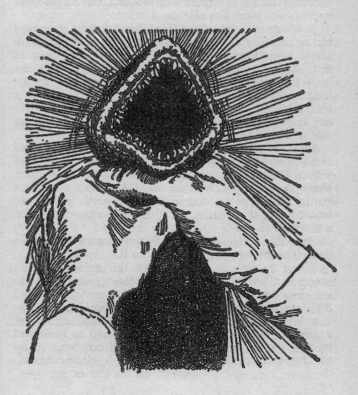

water-hole. With an exultant shout I flung myself upon it and strangled it. It was about eighteen inches long, of a sandy-green colour with red markings on its head, somewhat like a miniature dragon. Whatever it was or whatever it looked like, it was food! Eagerly I slit it open with my knife and gouged out its entrails to hang its gutted corpse by the tail at my belt. The heat of the afternoon sun would dry it swiftly. Disgusting food that it was, I was hard put to it not to wolf its slimy flesh there and then. But I managed to be patient until I slumped down just before nightfall for my final halt. Then I ravenously devoured its dried-up flesh. It probably tasted like muddy cardboard, but to me then its flesh was more like pheasant!

Towards the end of the third day I finally staggered out of the belt of elephant grass. I found myself in a sandy waste devoid of anything at all. At the sight of this barren desert my resolution evaporated and my body collapsed. I slumped down exhausted on to the hot, crumbling soil. I felt I could go no farther. For a time I lapsed into unconsciousness, for how long I do not know, but when I opened my eyes again the sun was still beating down upon me.

Now too feeble to move, I became aware of a small red ant making its way across my immediate field of vision. On its back was a piece of earth at least three times its size, which must have been an enormous burden. The ant seemed to have set itself the task of transporting it across a crack in the parched soil. To the ant that crack must have been an awe-inspring chasm. Its bridge over this frightening ravine was a dead stalk of grass which lay across it.

When it was halfway across the dried up stalk snapped. The ant went tumbling down into the yawning chasm beneath it. It lay still for a second, its load beside it, and I was sure that it was dead. But it was not. Wearily hoisting the piece of earth on to its back again, the little red ant set off once more and climbed up the half of the broken stalk which now slanted up the far side of the chasm. Slowly it climbed until, eventually, it reached the top. After some precarious manoeuvrings the ant carried its piece of earth over the lip of the crack to safety the other side. There it halted and rested a while, slowly twitching its antennae as though sharpening up its will to press on. Suddenly it seemed to have made up its mind and briskly hoisted its load on its back. Then, with an air of almost cheerful abandon, it set off jauntily into the vastness of the desert ahead. I realized that little ant did know where it was going, although there appeared to be no future at all for anything in all that burnt-up wilderness ahead.

I watched the brave little red ant until it was beyond my vision. Then, no longer distracted by its adventures, I switched my attention to my own immediate predicament. I realized with some amazement that the future did not seem so hopeless! I had seen a parable enacted there on the sand below me, and it had had a heartening effect on my willpower.

I raised myself laboriously to my feet and set off once more to limp off into the shimmering distance ahead. Eventually, the desert began to give place to scrub. As the sun began to lose its fiercest heat I saw ahead of me the inviting sight of a teak forest. All traces of my recent despair vanished completely. Calling on a reserve of strength I had not imagined I possessed, I stepped up my pace to head straight for its blissful shade and cover. Soon I came across a cool stream running among the trees, and tumbled into it to drink my fill of it and soothe my scorched and aching limbs. Thinking coherently once more, I guessed that the column must have halted somewhere near. It was far too pleasant a place to leave behind without a second thought. My bathe finished and my water bottle replenished, I searched around until I found ample evidence that the men I hoped were my comrades had, in fact, bivouacked farther along the stream beneath the trees. The ashes of numerous cooking fires were scattered around the area, and though they were all cold, I could tell that they had been used only the

night before. This implied, of course, assuming that
the column had moved off promptly at dawn as was
the usual practice, I was at that moment only some
twelve hours behind them!

Pleasant as it was in the teak forest, I could not
afford to dally there if I were to get out of Burma and
escape the Japs. I had to press on. Hurriedly I
buckled my equipment about me once more and, supporting myself on my stick, I set off still westwards at
a pace that was now almost a trot. Spurred on by both
hope and fear that I might be too late, I maintained
this pace for a full hour. At the end of that hour,
waves of dizziness began to come upon me, so that the
ground before me seemed to rise and fall. I limped
forward, gasping, conscious that my mouth was open
yet not able to close it. Then the rising of the ground
before me became something real, and not just an
hallucination. Desperately I set myself at the slope,
aware of only one thing—that I had to get to the top.

It was because of the very desperation of my effort
that I was suddenly confronted with the village of
Tagaung. One moment there was only the rising forest
track before me, the next Tagaung lay sprawling
among its trees ahead! Such was my exultation that
I barely restrained myself from staggering down to
the village shouting with joy. But jungle wisdom came
uppermost and I flung myself down on the crest of the
rise to study the village. Not a single inhabitant was
visible. Could it be that they were asleep? If no Burmese was visible, neither was any Brisith. I asked
myself: "Am I too late? Have they already crossed
the river?" I tried to keep calm and work out exactly
what had happened, according to the evidence around
me. Without a doubt the trail I could plainly see leading down to the village was that of No. 1 Column, or
some other scattered column of the Chindit force. The
marks of numerous British boots went down to min-
gle with the many footprints of the villagers among
the bamboo bashas and the open-fronted village shops
of split bamboo.

Why all the stillness now? Could that mean that the Japs had been there in Tagaung waiting for them? Yes, that could be one reason why there were neither Burmese nor British to be seen or heard. It could have been that the British had all been killed or captured, and that the villagers had fled in terror from the fighting that had broken out among them. But where were the signs of battle? Where was the wreckage, and the blasted and burned out bashas and huts? Where were the smashed weapons and spent cartridge cases? I made a decision. I had to take a chance. Climbing to my feet, I half-ran, half-staggered down the sandy track through the trees leading to the village.

I had entered the outskirts of the village, and had passed a few of the bamboo houses, when I was aware of the excited chattering of a group of villagers whom I had not seen among the huts. Before I could assess what it all meant, a lungyi-clad Burmese rushed out from the shadows and seized my arm. He dragged me into some bushes beside the road. I had just no idea at all what was happening, but I went without a struggle. With his hand still tugging at my tattered sleeve, I stumbled along a narrow footpath close behind him and lurched between two closely set lines of houses. From their shadows we plunged directly into a clump of bushes in which I was momentarily completely lost and bewildered. In the midst of my bewilderment I realized that he had let go of my sleeve and was no longer pulling me. Instead, he put a hand in the middle of my back and pushed me!

I half fell, half-staggered out from the bushes on to a sandy beach. Dark-leaved banana trees and upthrusting bamboos on the bank above cast shadows over it, so that I was in a sort of half-light. But there was light enough for me instantly to realize (and it came like an electric shock) that I had been abruptly thrust out into the open on a sandbank directly behind a group of armed men. Their faces showed yellow-green in the shadows as they turned towards me. Galvanized into action beyond my real strength, I flung myself down, drawing my revolver. Reacting with equal speed, some of the men flung themselves flat, others dropped to one knee, and the muzzles of a dozen rifles and tommy guns menaced me.

Then—"By all that's holy! Look who's here!" Doc Lusk's voice broke the silence. A dozen fingers relaxed from triggers. I breathed an audible gasp of relief. Then I literally wept with joy at the realization that I had, after all, caught up with the column!

"You're just in the nick of time, my boy!" declared Doc Lusk, whose instant recognition, despite my wild appearance, had undoubtedly saved my life. "How on earth did you get here? We all thought you were a goner at Mong Mit." The burly genial Irish doctor slapped me on the back, and propelled me towards the river's edge where the other soldiers were waiting. "No. Don't answer, Ian," he said. "I guess I can wait until we get to the other side before you tell me your story."

I had been lucky in arriving when I did. The last two boatloads of the column were about to set out across the Irrawaddy. One craft was already filled, and the other was even now filling up. Both were very ancient and leaky boats which somehow or other had been successfully hidden by the villagers from the vigilant Japs. I noticed there was a Burmese boatman in charge of the craft which was not yet completely filled.

Doc Lusk said: "Those are the best boats we could get. You get in now, Ian. There's plenty of room for one more, I guess." There were eleven men in already, apparently dangerously overloading the ramshackle native boat. It looked so unlikely that this leaky half-rotten dug-out would make the journey even as it was, that I felt its occupants might legitimately grumble at having to take yet another one. But I could not have wished for a better welcome. "Didn't expect to see you again, sir!" It was a young, bearded corporal, his face the colour of mahogany, who spoke. "Just like a regular bad penny, ain't you, sir? Except that now you're a penny with a hole in it!" Everyone aboard laughed at this sally, including myself.

The corporal and another man grabbed me and yanked me into the boat.

13

CALAMITOUS CROSSING

I had no sooner wriggled myself into some semblance of comfortable squatting when the leaky dug-out pushed off. It slip-slopped precariously out on to the dancing blue waters of the Irrawaddy, propelled forward by a couple of half-rotten paddles and an assortment of improvised ones made from pieces of driftwood.

The motion of the boat out on the water was soothing. The sun, now more kindly bright as it poised on the verge of sunset, played sparklingly on the swiftly moving Irrawaddy. Pale shadows flickered out from the long humped yellow sandbanks which at various points in the main stream emerged to form long, soft islands. In not many days time now, when the monsoon would burst upon this parched land, they would be submerged beneath the boiling turgid torrent that the Irrawaddy would soon become.

The corporal began to fill in for me the story of what had become of the rest of No. 1 Column after they had left me behind helpless and wounded. He was a likeable character, but I had not remembered seeing him before and presumed that he was one of the original members of No. 1 Column. Yet although he had not been in No. 2, he seemed to know me. Probably I had acquired some measure of "fame" in both columns by now by the doubtful virtue of being the first wounded British officer they had left behind to the tender mercies of the Japs.

"Corporal," was how he seemed to be known to everyone, except to those who just called him "Corp." The skin of his face and neck and arms, and of every part of his body that could be seen through the many rents in his tattered uniform, was burned so black by the sun that he was darker even than a native Burmese. His battered felt hat had all, and more, of the quality of "batteredness" so much courted by the British soldier wearing the coveted bush-hat of the Burma campaign. But although the bush-hat was designed specifically for keeping the sun out of the eyes, the corporal insisted on wearing his so far back on his head that it was difficult to see how it remained there at all.

He was made for the sunshine was that corporal. That was how he seemed to me.

From this slight and smiling corporal I learned, as we crossed the Irrawaddy, that the column had only arrived on the east bank that morning. They had soon learned that the Japs had commandeered all the boats for miles up and down the river, having towed them away behind motor-boats to put them under guard far away from our reach. Despite the depressing news, Major Dunlop had refused to be beaten. He had personally unearthed the two discarded half-rotten craft which we were now using to cross the mile-wide Irrawaddy. In a series of patient and laborious ferryings, all the rest of No. 1 Column had crossed the Irrawaddy during the course of the day.

Doc Lusk and his party were paddling over behind us, little more than thirty yards astern. "There must be Japs about," declared the corporal with breezy disdain. "Mr. Wormwell took over a section to the bridgehead this morning and about an hour after that we heard a burst of bren-gun firing. After that there was nothing but silence. In fact, Mr. Wormwell and the section haven't been seen or heard of since. We just can't understand what's happened. Eerie, ain't it, sir?" To change the subject, I asked the corporal why it was the column had not been able to cross the Shweli River, as they had first planned.

"We tried to, two or three times, sir," he replied. "But it was always the same. The natives got wind of our coming long before we turned up, and the dirty bastards went and warned the Japs. Whenever we got near the river, there were the Japs. We had some pretty near-goes. At one place we did manage to creep up through the jungle without seeming to be noticed. At any rate there was no one there to greet us, and shoot at us and scream at us. The river really was running fast at that point.

"We made a rope of rifle-slings and three men tied themselves to it and swam across. We had got it fixed to a couple of trees our side, and they had just managed to fix it lightly at the other side, when the Japs turned up. The little bastards opened up at once with rifles and machine-guns. They got three or four of the boys in the water and, of course, they scuppered the three who had got over. We knew we had had our lot, but at the same time the Japs knew they couldn't cross to get at us. We could mow 'em down just as well as they could mow us down. The only good thing about that show was that we did manage to pull our rifle-slings back without the Japs getting hold of them.

"After that we tried to make a raft, but we hadn't even collected half of the timber we needed when the blasted Japs came at us through the jungle our side of the river. It was altogether too hot for us and there were too many of them. We killed a lot but they killed too many of our chaps. So we had to push off into the hills and lie low to lick our wounds and think what we would do next.

"They got Captain Wetherall there, the dirty little sods!" the corporal added reflectively. "He was leading a charge that tore right into them. It set the little bastards running fit to bust. But some little sod of a machine-gunner hidden in the undergrowth got him. Bloody shame that! He was a good officer, was Captain Wetherall."

So Vivian was dead! No British officer could be paid a higher compliment by a British other rank than he had just been paid by the corporal. "He was a good officer!" I could think of no more fitting epitaph for a brave and inspiring leader such as Vivian had been. I learned later that many of the Gurkhas and British soldiers broke down and wept unashamedly when told of Vivan Wetherall's death. Such was the tremendous affection and admiration with which he was regarded. I could not get out of my mind that memory of his mother, and her sad and worried eyes, when she was telling fortunes at the party in the officers' club. Was she now, at this very moment, consumed with the deep dread of the knowledge that her son was dead?

The corporal had finished his narration, and was quiet for a while. To change my train of thought I turned to look at the other boat. It seemed to be going very slowly and had dropped behind us still farther so that it was barely a quarter of the way across while we were by now over half-way. The flashing of mess-tins in the evening sunlight told all too clearly what was going on back there in the second ramshackle craft.

"Leaks like a sieve, sir," the corporal broke in, as if reading my thoughts. "We've expected her to sink all day long. But so far it hasn't. Bloody miracle, I call it."

Another of the bearded sun-shrivelled scarecrows spoke up. "How long do you think it will take us to get back to India, sir?" he asked.

"How long? Oh, I don't know. Perhaps a fortnight," was the best answer I could give him. Even as I said it, I realized that time was no longer an ally. Three weeks was the absolute maximum time ahead before the monsoon would break upon Burma with all its fury of lashing rain and rising, raging rivers. As far as I could estimate we still had something like 200 miles to cover, much of it through heartbreaking jungle, quite apart from the fact that everywhere there were Japs hunting us so that we could not march straight out of Burma.

The Irrawaddy was only the first of the big river barriers in this frightening obstacle race in which the booby prize was death! The Mu river, and the Chind-win would be increasingly watched. At every likely crossing place there would be Japs, and all the boats would be taken away. The natives in the villages would be bribed or bullied into betraying us at every step we took near likely crossing-places. To add to that, the railway line would be patrolled constantly, and there would be standing patrols of Jap soldiers in all the villages along our probable route. The enemy would undoubtedly endeavour with all his savage energy to deny us both a way through and the food and drink to keep us alive in this inhospitable land.

Now nearly three-quarters of the way across the Irrawaddy, it did not help me to imagine the scene when the Japs ambushed the party trying to cross the Shweli on the rope of rifle-slings. I could imagine the men trying to get across that fast-flowing river, each with one hand grimly grasping the rifle-sling rope, and the other used to half-swim, half-drag himself across. Their rifles, slung across their shoulders over their heavy packs, would encumber them. I imagined the abrupt turnabout and mad struggle to get back to their own bank when the screams of the attacking Japs suddenly rang from the jungle towards which they had been heading. The Jap bullets would come whining and whipping among them then.

"Does anyone know the date today?" I suddenly asked, shaking my head to clear it of the gloomy thoughts that had been oppressing me. There was a confused murmuring all around as these men, who, for so many weeks had been in a jungle world, tried to say what day of the week it was. "I think it's 13 April, Sir" replied one of the British soldiers. "But I may have missed crossing off a few days in my diary."

April the 13th! That meant that for 66 days we had been behind the enemy's lines. That meant that for more than two months we had been marching and fighting the Japs and the jungle too. That meant that for over two months we had existed on food that at its best was no more than half hard rations. Two months! It did not sound too long said that way. But developed to its true length of 66 days it became much more like it. Developed a little farther it became 1,584 hours of sweat and pain, fear and death, jungle and Japs and hunger and thirst.

Oh God! How much more of this was there to be!

Then an idea struck me. If it were in fact 13 April*
then today was my twentieth birthday. A year ago
almost to the very day I had arrived in India, after a
voyage half around the globe. I had been an eager
schoolboy then. Eager to be trained in the latest and
most effective methods of fighting and killing the
hated Japs. But I was an eager schoolboy no longer.
Now I was a battle-weary soldier. Tired, oh, so
tired . . .

"Come on sir! Wakey! Wakey! We've only a hundred yards to go now, sir and it's all ashore!" It was
the corporal's voice, cutting through the deep sleep I
had fallen into in the completeness of my exhaustion
out there on the wide Irrawaddy.

It was as though the corporal's cheery call for me to
wake up had been a signal for the Japs to open fire
from their hiding-place on the bank among the undergrowth ahead of us. A Jap machine-gun fired at us
so close that it seemed almost on top of me. The water
all around frothed as the bullets poured in. Some
ploughed down into the depths leaving streams of bub-
bles, and others richocheted to whine away across the
river. Of all this I was vividly conscious in a moment
of fear timeless and terrible in its detail. In their sudden attack men became frantic animals. The young
boy who had told me the date was slumped limply
over the side, his long hair floating on the water.
Blood gushed from his mouth. Another man, up forward, his body riddled with bullets, had been hurled
backwards by the force of their impact and had collapsed on to his comrades. Blood was spurting from
his wounds.

Then the boat capsized. The water was suddenly
full of desperate men. Frantically I clung on to the
upturned hulk, into which bullets were thudding
within inches of my head. Providentially the boat began to swing round, so that I was completely shielded

---

*Actually the date was more like 23 April. The soldier had lost
count of some ten days in his reckonings.

from the enemy guns by its bulk. The safest thing to
do was to stay where I was. Quite apart from the
murderous hail of bullets still pouring into the river, I
did not feel that my wounded leg would stand up to the
swim of a hundred yards still remaining.

My boots and heavy belt began to weigh me down.
But I was loath to part with them, especially when I
realized my pack had already gone to the bottom. The
boat was drifting downstream, and I noticed the current was steadily taking it in towards the shore. I
held on with all the strength I had, seeking to fight
against the swift stream. The weight of my waterlogged boots was becoming greater. They threatened
to drag me under.

Then bullets ceased to whip and whine around me.
I was invisible from the west bank, and no doubt by
now the Japs believed all in the river to have been
killed. A confused battle was raging along the shore
within the screen of the jungle. Bren- and tommy-
guns were barking their answers to the screaming of
the Japanese automatics. I saw three men crawl out
from the undergrowth on to a mudbank farther upstream to help drag survivors from our boat into the
cover of the darkening jungle. The mud bank itself
was stained red, but not with the blood of the men.
The redness came from the last rays of the setting sun.

The men still on the mudbank seemed to be im-
mune from the Japanese fire, which was directed at
them. Somehow all struggled clear and clambered up
to merge with the black shadows of the jungle. Doc
Lusk's boat I now saw, turning my head as I drifted
on, had been little more than half-way across when
the shooting started. They had obviously turned
round straight away and were now well on the way
back to Tagaung. They, at least, would get out of this
safely, I told myself. (I was not to know that I should
never see gallant Doc Lusk again. He was to die as a
prisoner of the Japs.)

When within ten yards of the narrow, muddy beach
on the west bank of the Irrawaddy, and well down-

Bren-gun

steam of the ambush, I decided I could risk leaving the waterlogged boat. I pushed off and struck out laboriously through the swirling waters. A great pain shot through my hip at the strain imposed upon it, but somehow I managed to keep going. I reached the muddy bank and crawled across it, and then up the steeper bank of the river to draw myself into the jungle's cover. I was conscious of two things at that moment, of a feeling of complete exhaustion, and of the peculiar sensation caused by the water in my boots pouring out through the eyelet holes.

With the soldier's instinct for self-preservation I ripped off the sealing tape on a waterproof box of cartridges that I still had with me and re-loaded my revolver. I threw the six wet rounds that had been in it into the river. As I rose, staggering drunkenly to my feet, a voice suddenly hailed me from out among the shadows.

"Hey!" it proclaimed insistently, "Wait for me, sir!"

It was the corporal. He was swimming towards the bank, his rifle showing safely above his head where it was slung across his shoulders. As he grounded on the mud I reached down to help drag him ashore. Instantly he slipped the sling of his rifle over his head, flicked open the bolt, and in a twinkling had loaded it with ten rounds.

"What do we do now, sir?" he asked, shaking his wet hair out of his eyes. Even in the growing darkness I noticed, with a feeling of relief, that those eyes were still laughing.

"We'll stick together my lad, that's what we'll do," I replied. "We've got no food, we've got no money, we've got no maps and we've got about a couple of hundred miles to go. But if we stick together, I reckon somehow we'll make it."

"Wait a bit, sir. Wait a bit. Don't be so ruddy depressing," the corporal cajoled me. "I've got all of five rupees and an escape map. I traded it with a sergeant for a packet of biscuits at Mong Mit. He said he didn't want to die hungry. I reckon I did a good deal."

"We're O.K. then, because I've got a compass," I said. "Come on, let's get cracking!"

The battle had now developed into a running fight which appeared to be around and before us. Behind us lay the now sinister quiet of the racing Irrawaddy. The column had obviously dispersed into groups, and groups had dispersed into twos and threes, or even into single men seeking to fight their way out of the trap. It was certainly a case of every man for himself from now on! To get out alive was the order of the day, and Jap take the hindmost!

We doubled westwards through the jungle, clawing our way through clumps of bamboo, and charging headlong through thickets of banana and palm trees. Creepers lashed our faces and keen-edged leaves

cut flesh almost to the bone. None of this we noticed
in our desperation to force our way out of the trap the
Jap soldiers had obviously set for us in the jungle
facing our river crossing. We ran on for a full ten
minutes until we came to a small hillock in the depths
of the forest. It was covered more thickly with undergrowth than the surrounding area. We crawled into the
middle of its dense cover and lay there gasping for
breath. When we could talk again we set about making a definite plan of escape.

The plan we agreed on was that we would wait until moonrise. By then we estimated the Japs would be
well out of the area chasing the rest of the column
survivors. We would then have a better chance of getting through the jungle to the railway, which would be
our next obstacle.

A loud crashing in the jungle, which I calculated instinctively to be something like 200 yards away,
caused us to keep quiet. I slipped my revolver from
its holster. I heard the click as the corporal pushed
forward the safety catch on his rifle. The crashing
came nearer. A few seconds later I saw a British
soldier, his left arm swinging grotesquely, stagger into
the clearing below us. As he did so, the moon rose and
bathed the scene with white light.

I called softly. The soldier, unsteady as a drunken
man, reeled to a stop directly beneath our hide-out.
He was a frightful sight. Sometimes I still shudder at
the sight. He had a long, gangling body, and he had
lurched in little inane leaps into the clearing. His
wounded arm hung loosely, flapping like the partly-
severed wing of a hen. His beard, broad and shaggy,
framed his wide-open mouth, so that the inside of his
lips showed almost coral pink against the blackness of
beard and moustache. He had the crazed look of a
man screaming soundlessly. His eyes were wide open
and stared so intensely that they were all white, and
there appeared to be no iris and no pupil. He had no
hat, and his hair was matted and blood clotted. He
looked straight at me, but did not see me. I had a
violently sickening impression of colour that was at

once a mixture of dark red and brown and khaki. His clothing, I realized, was almost completely saturated with blood.

Before I could recover from the shock of this man's appearance, the corporal had jumped up and run down to him. Then he guided him to our refuge. A machine-gun bullet had shattered his left arm below the elbow and one bullet, I found, had passed through his body striking the bottom rib. There was a jagged hole a few inches below his right shoulder blade where the bullet had burst out of him. He was obviously in a bad way.

I jabbed the morphine needle into his arm while the corporal gave him a drink of water. He stopped moaning and gurgling and appeared to have recovered a little. He spoke, in a painful way, rasping from somewhere back in his throat: "There are others back there, wounded." Then he slumped into a drugged sleep.

The corporal looked at me quizzically. I looked at him. Each of us knew what the other was thinking. Should we leave this wounded soldier, for he was obviously far gone, and go on by ourselves? The two of us together might stand a fair chance of getting through while the Japs busied themselves about looking for larger groups of British stragglers. Or should we go back to where the soldier had indicated there were other wounded survivors?

Ultimately, I suppose, it was my bitter experience of being left behind wounded that decided the issue in my mind. I had to go through the motions, at least, of seeing whether there was anything I could do for the wounded men.

"Come on, corporal. Let's go and look for the others!" I said.

"O.K. sir, Off we go then!" and without the slightest hesitation he turned in the direction the wounded man had indicated.

The corporal and I left the wounded soldier hidden in the cover on our little hill. Then we set out to look for other survivors, following the trail he had left. His trail was all too easy to follow. Besides the broken twigs and snapped creepers there were the blood splashes quite visible in the moonlight. Suddenly we heard the murmur of voices. Forgetting all my need for caution I said in a loud voice: "They are British!"

"Not so loud! I'm not so sure!" whispered the corporal. "We'd better go carefully, sir."

We dropped to our hands and knees and crawled forward, with the utmost caution. The murmur of voices became louder, but was only just audible above the chuckling of water where a little stream obviously wound through a jungle clearing ahead. Then we came to the edge of the clearing, and peered through the thick undergrowth at the men who were gathered beside the stream.

A tall, powerfully built man was standing in the centre of a group of men. His attitude was belligerent and obviously he was haranguing them. It was equally obvious that he was British, and that his companions were a mixture of British and Gurkha soldiers. The big man carried his left arm in a blood-soiled sling. He had a mop of shaggy, unruly hair thrusting out from beneath his battered bush hat. A slightly aquiline nose and a full and jutting beard added to the over-all impression of great strength, both of physique and character. He was talking in low but authoritative tones to the rest of the little company as we crept up. Some of them were squatting at his feet while others were stretched out as though in a state of advanced exhaustion.

"I tell you, you've got to bloody well march and march now!" This snatch of what he was saying to the men drifted to me.

"I'm not leaving any of you bastards behind. We're going to get out of this God-damned, awful country, and we're going to go out on our own bloody feet. So get on them and get going, every one of you!"

As he said this, the big man bent aggressively over a soldier who was lying at his feet and, with his sound arm, caught at his shirt. He gave it a wrench as though to pull the man to his feet. But the soldier held out against him truculently and the sweat-rotten fabric tore to leave a tattered strip in the big man's hand.

"Leave me alone, blast you! I'm bloody well not going back any farther! I've had enough of this bloody do. I'm all for being a P.O.W. Whatever the Japs do to me nothing can be worse than this."

"He's dead right Sarge!" another voice joined in, rebelliously. "The column's left us. They couldn't care less whether we live or die. So I say we surrender."

For a moment a cajoling voice within me told me this was none of my business, and the sensible thing was for the corporal and me to leave this wretched and mutinous band to their own devices. After all, if they chose to give themselves up to the Japs, and risk all that went with surrender, then that was their own look out.

I suppose it was at that moment that I became a man. Suddenly I knew I had to intervene; had to assume the command that my officer's rank required of me. I gripped the corporal's arm and said: "Come on. This is where we step in!" Together we rose to our feet and thrust our way abruptly into the moonlit clearing. All eyes turned towards us in consternation, and hands hastily slid to the triggers of rifles and tommy-guns. But I had reckoned on the moonlight being bright enough to show the tattered and war-weary little band of soldiers that we were British. And so it did. The tension vanished and gave place to expectancy.

I walked straight up to the sergeant. As much as possible I strove to hide my limp and make my entry an authoritative one. I could not remember ever having seen the sergeant before, but apparently he recognized me. He straightened up, almost as if he were going to salute me, which would have been contrary to Chindits' battle regulation. He checked his instinctive move in time and said: "Hullo, sir!"

"The corporal and I have been sent back for you!" I lied. "I am your Commanding Officer now. We are going back to India and should catch the rest of the column up soon!" I could sense at once that my ready lie had had the desired effect on the men, even though the wary look in the sergeant's eyes told me he had not been taken in by my subterfuge. But his momentary suspicion gave place to a ready gratitude, which twinkled in his eyes although he said nothing. The rebellion had been quelled and the pathetic little band of wounded, almost at the end of their endurance, were once again a body of Wingate's Chindits, determined to carry out to the last letter his instructions that killing the enemy was the main object of the raid. Heaven knows, they had already been through enough to weaken their morale. They could readily be forgiven losing their will to go on at this point.

I looked around the little group of battle-stained and weary men. Above the stench of their sweat-sodden clothing, by now little more than rags, the air was rancid with the sweet-sour smell of dried blood and suppurating sores. Every one of them was wounded, or had fearful sores, that had eaten almost down to the very bone. Yes, they could be forgiven.

"What is your name, Sergeant!" I asked.

"Hayes, sir. Of the R.A.F. section," he replied briskly.

"How many men have you got with you?" I enquired.

"Fourteen, sir. That includes the four Johnny Gurkhas."

"Right then!" I ordered: "Let's get them sorted out so that we can get on our way." Quite apart from my personal eagerness to get moving westwards, I could see that these men had to be got going quickly.

The burly R.A.F. sergeant then took me on a brief conducted tour of his little party. We found that two of the Gurkhas, and one British soldier lying on the ground in the moonlight, had died even as they rested there. The British soldier, his sightless eyes glistening in the moonlight, was grinning horribly at us. It was as though in his very last conscious moment, he had seen in my terse assertion that we would march to India some quite ridiculous and impossible joke. I had never before experienced dumb insolence from a dead man.

Of the rest, two were very badly wounded in the chest and could not walk in any circumstances. The remaining nine men, although all hit by Jap bullets, could at least hobble along. Sergeant Hayes was probably the worst wounded of all the "walking cases," although he had neither said anything about his wounds nor had anything but scorn for suggestions of giving in. The arm which was supported in the sling had been almost smashed by a burst of Jap machine-gun fire. A long bloody gash which had split his face cruelly told of the savage close-combat fighting in which he had been embroiled. He never flinched nor murmured, although he must have been in continuous pain.

"How did you all get here, Sergeant?" I asked him.

"Well, sir," he replied: "I just got them together at the river crossing after we were fired on, and I brought 'em here."

The full story of Sergeant Hayes's "just getting them together" I learned later. Instead of heading westwards, during the first lull in the battle, he had quite deliberately wandered all around the whole battle area, seeking out wounded British and Gurkha soldiers. One by one he had dragged them to the safety of the clearing in which I had found them. With great dash and bravery he had personally charged into a number of running fights going on in the jungle, and had pulled out wounded to save them from almost certain bayoneting, or capture and torture, by the Japs. It was while he was thus heroically engaged that he had been hit in the arm. He had carried on.

I told Sergeant Hayes about the wounded man we had left on the hillock.

"The poor devil!" said the sergeant with feeling. "He just went mad with the pain of his wounds and screamed out that he was going to go home. Then he rushed away into the jungle and that was the last I saw of him. I guessed the poor devil hadn't long to live so I let him go. I felt sure he would drop dead trying to fight his way through the jungle. It would be the kindest way out for him."

Then, in an undertone although we were out of earshot of the others, he added: "Thanks, sir, for stepping in then. I know you were only kidding about being sent back, but the others didn't tumble. It did the trick all right. Thanks a million."

With speed, remarkable considering its condition, the battered little band now organized itself for the march to India that I had promised them. Some of the men set to work to make two stretchers from bamboo poles and creepers. Sergeant Hayes and I set about sorting out the arms and ammunition and allocating them, so that each one of us could be as effective a fighting man as wounds and physical weakness permitted. Excepting for the two stretcher cases, there was a rifle for everyone. The ammunition worked out at 30 rounds per man. I swapped my revolver with Sergeant Hayes's rifle because it was obviously better that a man with two hands should have a rifle.

Then we set about rationing out the food. Our total provisions amounted to something like four pounds of rice, sufficient for one cupped handful to each man. We shared out the silver rupees with which we had been provided for buying provisions from friendly villagers. This gave each one of us 8 rupees. To point us the way ahead there was still my compass, while the corporal had his handkerchief map. The two together were quite ample for our purpose.

As soon as we were ready I told Sergeant Hayes to get his squad to their feet. Then I led off my new command—one R.A.F. sergeant, one corporal, and nine other ranks, including two Gurkhas, all who could walk. We stepped from the moonlit glade with its little sparkling stream out into the deepening darkness of the jungle. Once again we were on our way to the Chindwin river, and the safety of India beyond!

14

THE MAIMED LEAD THE MAIMED

We all took turns carrying the stretchers bearing the two wounded men. I led the little band back along the path taken by the wounded British soldier whom we had left hidden in the thicket. At the foot of the slope I gave the order to halt, and, accompanied by the corporal, pushed my way through the undergrowth to where we had left the wounded soldier. It was our intention to cut down some bamboos and make another stretcher to carry him, but he had died before we came upon him. We closed his staring eyes and folded his hands across his chest. We pulled grasses and ferns and creepers over him. So we left him to become just one of many another unidentified skeleton deep in the Burmese jungle.

When the corporal and I returned, he giving a silent thumbs-down to the others, I took my place at the head of the column. The stretcher bearers picked up their wounded companions and we set off marching due west. The luminous needle of my compass was our guide through the darkness of the night. Occasionally during that night we heard scattered shots around us, as the Japs caught up with other survivors, but none was really near us. At dawn, we saw a village ahead of us. It stood in a clearing with a checkerboard of paddy-fields surrounding it. Nothing moved but the slow drifting spectres of the dawn mist.

I looked at Sergeant Hayes, and he looked at me. Each knew what was in the other's mind. "This will do Sergeant, I think," I said. "I don't think we shall find a better place to leave the stretcher cases than here." This was something I could handle, this leaving of the wounded.

So the two wounded men on the stretchers, unbelievably cheerful and without any malice in them at all, were carried forward to the jungle's edge. There, in full sight of the village, they were placed under a prominent tree. They would be shaded from the sun even if no one came to them before its burning rays beat down their way later. Despite my own experience, I found myself hating every moment of this act. True, the two men appeared to be comfortable and were being given as reasonable a chance as any Chindit could expect. But we all knew that their fate was entirely dependent upon the tender mercies of the Japanese. If a Jap officer had not enjoyed his breakfast, or if a Jap soldier had missed a promised visit back to the comforts platoon, on just such things as that could depend whether or not the two British boys would live or be bayoneted to death. In the end my eyes stung with held-back tears and my throat swelled with emotion as I turned my back on those two cheerful British soldiers and left them there. I had been through it myself. I knew all about it.

Then we slipped back into the jungle and, carefully camouflaging our trail, we skirted around the northern edge of the clearing about the village. It was still dark back in the jungle, and into its depths we vanished from any inquisitive eyes that might have spied on us from the silent bashas.

I decided we would go to ground that day, firstly in case the villagers set the Japs on our trail early, and secondly because the physical condition of nearly all of us demanded the rest. Within an hour's march of the clearing we were fortunate enough to come across a cave which plunged back, deep and dark, into a jungle-clad hill in the midst of the great forest. We lay up there all day, sleeping practically the whole time.

When night came once more we emerged and pressed on through the jungle. After a little while the ground beneath our feet levelled out and we could sense that we were marching over a plain beneath all the thick cover of the jungle. The air was sultry and hot in the darkness and there was a sense of oppression everywhere. We staggered along, with myself and Sergeant Hays still at the head of our short column. We knew we were all getting steadily weaker as we grew hungrier and hungrier. Lack of food was already becoming a desperate problem.

Later, the moon rode high above our jungle roof and spread its eerie whiteness in patches along our trail. But spirits did not lighten with it.

There came a hoarse shout from behind. As if jerked to a standstill by a pull on the same string, we all stopped. The British soldier at the very end of the line had collapsed. I limped back, but the corporal had reached him before me. While I was still six feet away the fallen man suddenly convulsed as if in a tortured effort to get to his feet. Then he sprawled out flat again on the jungle trail.

The corporal knelt beside him, near to his chest. Then he felt his pulse.

"He is dead, sir!" he said softly, looking up.

The soldier, a private in the King's Liverpool Regiment, lay there on the track as if bereft of all his muscles. He was just a crumpled-up form. As reverently as I could I closed his eyes and mouth. Then the corporal and I pulled him into the jungle some ten yards off the track and covered him with sticks and leaves. So we left another British soldier. After what seemed a thousand miles, but was more likely three, I gave an order to halt. We slumped down in the undergrowth beside the track, too weak and weary even to post the necessary sentries. Sergeant Hayes went back along the line and then returned to where, bent almost double with weakness, I was leaning on my rifle.

"We are two short, sir" he reported: "A couple of them have just disappeared, sir. I reckon they must be deserters."

"No, Sergeant," I replied. "I wouldn't call them deserters. I would say they are just a couple of fools."

We never saw those two men again. So we were nine.

Three times more during that night of agony we pulled ourselves to our feet, formed into our ragged single column and lurched away westwards again. Three times more we slumped down in the undergrowth at the track side, not caring whether we slept or awakened, lived or died. The moon-haunted jungle had never seemed more vast or menacing; never in its overpowering humidity more like an oven sapping and sweating out our strength until we were drained of every vital spark within us.

Just before dawn I realized from the thinning of the jungle and the greyness of the light ahead, that we were approaching open country. In a croaking voice I ordered the column to halt and hide themselves just off the track while I went forward with the corporal to scout what lay ahead. In less than fifty yards we came to the edge of the jungle. Ahead of us lay paddy-fields for some two hundred yards. At their far end was a Burmese village. The inhabitants were already astir. The men were gathering together their implements for the day's work in the fields, and the women were getting out their brass pans and bowls and starting to clean them by polishing them in the sand of the main street. As we watched a young girl, flaunting her swelling womanhood in a purple lungyi, made her way with delicious grace towards the village well, a gleaming pitcher balanced on her head. In each of her hands also she held a pitcher.

It was now time to be moving. "I think it's safe, come on corporal, let's go," I said. And we got to our feet and together strode boldly out of the jungle on to the sandy track which led across the paddy-fields to the village. Side by side we walked up the track, our rifles slung over our shoulders. It was a risk we had to take, we were going forward in a patently non-belligerent manner on the assumption that the villagers would be friendly and would appreciate a friendly approach from us.

"Nice bit of stuff over by the well there!" observed the corporal. He rolled his eyes speculatively towards where the Burmese girl, the voluptuous moulding of her figure even more apparent as she straightened up from drawing water from the well, now stood in profile before us. I glanced towards her, allowing my gaze to be distracted from the main cluster of huts in which I felt any danger in the village would lie. In that moment she turned her head and saw us. Without a sound she dropped the pitcher she was holding and fled for the cover of the village as though pursued by all the devils in hell.

"It's this bloody beard that does it," grumbled the corporal. "Really I'm quite a handsome-looking bloke, you know."

Before we had advanced many more paces I became aware that something was happening in the village.

"Wait a moment! There's something I don't like going on there!" I exclaimed, seizing the corporal's arm and halting him in his tracks. We both stood there, absolute sitting ducks out in the middle of the flat paddy, gazing towards the village. Had the girl's precipitate flight been a warning for Jap soldiers lying up in the village? Out there in the open we could almost sense a wave of consternation running through the village.

"Get down!" I gasped. We dived from the broad, flat track to the inadequate cover of the six-inch earth wall which divided it from the nearest paddy-field. The corporal hit the dust a split second after me.

"What's up, sir?" asked the corporal. "Japs, is it?"

"I suppose so," I said, aware of the resigned tone in my voice. Somehow it always seemed to be Japs. We slid our rifles forward ready for action. The menace of our action was not lost on the excited group of Burmese who had started to scatter outwards from the shadows of the village towards us. They dispersed immediately.

Then something else happened. A little knot of some ten or twelve men of the village, carrying spades and hoes, were now advancing along the track towards us.

"Keep your head down, sir," laughed the corporal. He was in high spirits now that action seemed imminent. "Say when, and we'll let 'em have it!"

I sensed the corporal's finger tightening on his trigger. "Hold it," I said. "There's something funny about this that I don't quite understand. If the Japs are in the village why didn't those people tell them? How is it they are coming out like that just carrying their working tools and not even a single dah between them? If the Japs had been there, I'm sure they would have come out after us."

"Yes, but these characters can do a helluva lot of damage to a bloke's head with a shovel!" the corporal answered.

The little knot of Burmese men, still walking out as though bound for their daily work in the fields, were now only a few yards from us. They were under the very muzzles of our rifles and were so close that they must have been able to see the glint of the lighter ridges of the rifling in the black maw of each muzzle. All the time they kept on gabbling and chattering among themselves. Almost on top of us, the leader suddenly started miming and making signs which I felt sure I understood. My understanding left me gasping with surprise.

"He wants us to take our hats off and join up with them," I told the corporal. "There's obviously something up. We've just got to trust them, that's all."

"If it's O.K. with you, sir, it's O.K. with me," grinned the corporal.

And as the party of men from the village came abreast of us, the corporal and I whipped off our hats, rose to our feet and mingled with them to walk along among them without their party even pausing. We did not stop until we were all within the cover of the jungle. Sergeant Hayes rose from the undergrowth and stepped towards us. "What's up sir? We jolly nearly let this bunch have it when we saw them coming for you with shovels and things," he said.

The villagers now all crowded round us in the jungle and all seemed to be shouting and jabbering at the same time in high-pitched, shrill voices. But there was no hostility in their voices or expressions, just excitement and eagerness. For a few moments it was like the Tower of Babel until eventually we managed to single out one man, obviously their leader, to act as spokesman. I called up one of the Gurkhas to help me and managed to get some sense out of the villagers.

The spokesman explained that a Jap patrol had spent the night in their village. Even as we had lain there at sunrise watching from the verge of the jungle the patrol had marched off into the forests the other side of the village. They were heading north, losing no time in hunting down the "despicable British soldiers."

Peace and order were now fully restored among the villagers, who squatted back in the dust of the jungle track while their spokesman talked to us. We learned more about the way ahead of us. The headman told us that we were very near the railway line and that it was patrolled night and day from a small Jap garrison based in the neighbourhood. He agreed to provide us with a guide who would take us through the jungle that night to a point within sight of the track, but he did not dare lead us any farther.

I asked our new-found friends if they could provide us with food. Readily they agreed and, again with grins all over their faces, the little band of native workmen stood up and tramped off back along the track out into the open across the paddy-fields, and returned to their village.

Something like an hour later the hearts of nine hungry British and Gurkha soldiers bounded with unspeakable joy at the sight of a dozen women from the village walking out on to the wide dusty track across the paddy-fields. We could see that they were carrying large bowls, and our imaginations ran riot at the thoughts of the hot rice and delicious curry contained within them. The native women made a wonderful sight as, with their delightful straight-backed carriage, they walked gracefully towards us across the open ground. They were all well formed and the brilliance of their lungyis vied one with the other, in mauves, purples and reds.

"Do you know, sir," declared the irrepressible corporal, "it's only what's in those bowls I want after all. Even if that smashing piece by the well were to come out empty-handed and a come-hither look on her face, I would go for one of those with a bowl full of grub!"

The women all smiled at us as we rose again from among the bushes and undergrowth to stand around them in the green twilight of the jungle track. Graciously they handed us the bowls of food, which we discovered to be full of delicious rice with strands of tough meat. We found the meat to be strips of hide, one of the Gurkhas explaining that it was elephant hide. He said the idea was not that we should eat it now but that we should keep chewing it as we marched.

The village women had also brought with them strips of clean cloth and hot water which had been rendered antiseptic with herbs picked in the jungle and known and used by the Burmese villagers for centuries. The women soon busied themselves among our wounded, cleaning and bathing ugly gashes and bullet holes, plying them with antiseptic herbal ointments, and finally binding them skilfully with the clean, white linen bandages.

I watched my wounded companions as they were treated thus. My heart swelled with pride at their magnificent bearing and guts. Although I saw several wince as their matted, filthy wounds were cleaned, there was never a sound of pain from any. Truly this little band of maimed, exhausted soldiers of whom I had assumed command so unexpectedly were splendid men. They had plodded on and on and on with their backs bent with fatigue and their bodies and limbs racked with pain. On and on, with their eyes glued to the ground, possibly not even daring to look ahead but just driven forward by indomitable will.

But we were weakening fast. How long dare I keep up this marching? Would short distances and long rests be the answer? I knew the sands of time were fast running out now, for according to the rule of things the monsoon was barely two weeks away. Once that burst upon us streams would become rushing rivers and rivers would become tumbling torrents. Even if the Japs couldn't stop us, the elements would. Meanwhile all the time the Jap net was getting tighter as more and more of them poured into the area in which the Chindits were now known to have been operating.

I reckoned we had still 150 miles to go: 150 miles in two weeks, with all the Japs, and hunger and thirst, and the monsoon only two weeks away! The only way, I decided, was to force on at maximum speed and hope for the best.

Our guide from the village was as good as the headman's word. Quietly and efficiently he took us through the jungle by little-known tracks until we reached the edge of the hundred-yard-wide avenue hacked clear and flat where the railway line cut between the high walls of the forest. It was exactly 2000 hours by the sergeant's watch when we arrived at that point and, according to plan, our guide took his leave and vanished into the shadows whence he had brought us.

We lay tense and breathing quietly among the thickly clustering leaves and saplings on the edge of the jungle. Before us the single railway track gleamed dully in the light of the stars. The moon had not yet risen high enough to flood its ghostly white light into this broad avenue between the jungle walls. There was no embankment as there had been at Kyaikthin, just a single-tracked line running straight from end to end of our immediate field of vision.

At 20 minutes past 20 hours we heard suspicious sounds along the track to the north. It could be a Japanese patrol. At 2025 we knew that it was a Jap patrol. There were eight of them, their domed helmets coldly gleaming, their flat faces inscrutably evil as they stopped in front of us. And they sat down on the rails right opposite us! They sat there with the purposeful deliberation of men who were waiting for something.

"Do you think those Burmese have given us away, sir?" Sergeant Hayes whispered in my ear.

"I shouldn't think so," I whispered back. "But why are they waiting like that?"

"Could it be a ten minute halt for a rest, sir?" suggested the corporal on my other side.

"It could be," I admitted.

"Let's knock the little yellow bastards off, sir. We can get the whole bunch of them all in one go!" Sergeant Hayes whispered back unable to disguise the enthusiasm even in his hushed voice.

"We may have to yet, but we must not fire unless there is no other way out," I replied.

The minutes ticked on. Silent, breathless, frightening minutes in which the Japs, the starlight gleaming on their thin bayonets and the black steel of their butt plates, chattered softly and menacingly among themselves. Then, at 2032 hours another patrol came in sight, coming up the railway line from the south. Were they reinforcements? Were they the reinforcements the patrol before us was awaiting before charging down into the jungle to destroy us where we lay? Was it after all a trap? Had the guide who had led us to this spot done so with the complete knowledge of the Japs who had been in the village? When they were right abreast of us the second patrol halted. Then they sat down on the rails beside the Japs already there and began to chat with their comrades. We could hear their voices quite clearly, in the high-pitched, unintelligible gabble of the Japanese.

At 2037 by the watch the men of the first patrol stood suddenly to their feet on the sharp order of the N.C.O. Then the patrol formed up and instead of making any move towards us set off marching back along the track, towards the north from whence they had come. Almost simultaneously the patrol from the south turned about and set off marching back the way they had come. Within a few minutes both parties were out of earshot and visible only because we knew where they were, and by peering we could sense them receding in the starlight along the railway. We had been fantastically lucky. The guide had left us at the very point where two patrols met, the most vulnerable point in any patrol system!

As soon as the Japs were completely out of sight and earshot, we slid from the shadows and, bent low, made a dash across the hundred yards of open space to dive into the jungle the other side. Carefully on my orders we avoided touching the rails as we crossed the track for I had learned to my cost at Kyaikthin that noise along a railway line carries for many miles. We had made yet another dangerous crossing on our way back to the Chindwin and salvation. Now we had to face up to the next one—the River Mu.

For the rest of that night we continued to march westwards along the track through the jungle. The going was not hard here, but it was as much as my wounded men could do to keep up the pace I was setting. My wounded leg was paining again now and I was limping badly, which I suppose was a good psychological point for a leader of the lame and maimed! I was conscious that I was forcing the pace and that every man was having to strain both his body and his willpower to the utmost to keep going. But keep going they did, for hour after hour, with only small rests, all through the hot night and right on till dawn broke again. With the coming of day, we abandoned the track and melted once more into the jungle's deep shadows. There we mostly slept through the hot sultry hours while the relentless sun poured its white heat upon the towering jungle roof above us.

During the next night's march I realized that I would have to cut the pace. The men were cracking, and I was having to call halts more and more frequently. In the end I decided that the only thing to do was to march as long as all of the men could stand it, and then to rest whenever anyone fell out. I decided that, marching this way, we would have to keep moving both by night and by day. This would spread out the physical activity over a full 24 hours while increasing the necessary rests. At the back of my mind the threat of the imminent monsoon was now looming as large as the danger of being caught by the Japs.

It was during the morning of the following day that we were lurching and staggering forward in single column when we suddenly came upon a village. I rounded a sharp bend in the track, and there it was! In the heart of the jungle, as neat a little Burmese village as one could wish to find. Instinctively we ducked out of sight into the jungle. I lay down at the head of the column with Sergeant Hayes to study the problem. Undoubtedly we could slip around the little village unnoticed by making a wide detour through the jungle if we so wished. But we had eaten no food for two days, and things were getting desperate.

"What do you think, Sergeant Hayes?" I asked quietly: "Do you think we should risk it?"

The sergeant was staring at the village, his eyes screwed up as he peered from beneath the wide battered brim of his bush hat.

"The dogs seem to be barking a lot, sir," he said. "There's definitely somebody there that they're not used to."

"You mean it could be somebody unpleasant?" I queried.

"Yes, Japs or B.T.A.," he replied.

I took another long look at the village. "We've got to get some food, Sergeant," I decided.

"Do you want to have a look, sir?" asked Sergeant Hayes. "We'd better, hadn't we?"

"We've got to I'm afraid. We can't miss a chance of food now with the escarpment ahead of us," I said.

"O.K., sir." When there was work to do or risks to be taken, Sergeant Hayes never hung back. "You cover me while I make for the back of the first house!"

"Right, Sergeant," I said. "I'll keep you covered all the way."

Sergeant Hayes slipped across the track, and it was

surprising the speed and the silence of so powerful a man moving through the undergrowth and trees. He held my revolver firmly before him in his right hand, his badly wounded left arm bandaged firmly to his side. I saw him reach the rear of the nearest bamboo hut, and then crouching make his way to its corner. He took off his bush hat and cautiously edged his face up to the corner to peer round.

The suspense of the moment was with me as it must have been with him. I sensed everything that would be going through his brain at this moment, all the tautness and the apprehension, all that innermost fear of the sniper you can't see but who you know is, with slow and deeply relished deliberation, taking aim. It is a sense of apprehension that no amount of experience can quell entirely. It is a moment that could lead you to friends and salvation, or could end forever in the obliterating explosion of a bullet through the brain. Suddenly I saw Sergeant Hayes drew back his head. He turned in my direction and signalled for me to follow.

"Come on, Corporal!" I whispered to the corporal, who was beside me.

Our six wounded comrades covered our advance as best they could with their rifles while the corporal and I made our way towards Sergeant Hayes. We reached the rear of the house.

"There's someone here all right. There's a bren-gun outside a house at the other end of the street," he said urgently.

I crawled forward to have a look. A man was squatting behind the light-machine-gun in the shadow of the house. Because of the depth of the shadows I could not see him clearly. He could have been of any nationality. He could for instance, have been a Jap sitting behind a captured British bren.

I turned to Sergeant Hayes. "He's probably B.T.A." I said. "We can't take the chance after all. Let's pull out and make a detour."

We started to crawl back through the trees towards the others. Then: "Wait a bit," said the corporal, who was bringing up the rear. "I can see someone coming out of the house!"

The corporal crawled back to the corner of the nearest basha to have a look for himself. Then he looked back grinning all over his face. "Yes, sir! Just come up here and look! I'm sure it is! I'm sure it's Mr. Best, sir!" he chuckled.

"What!" My voice seemed to boom through the jungle. I crawled back hastily—making no attempt to keep silent.

I was in time to see a tall, gaunt figure wearing a floppy Gurkha hat descending the steps of one of the huts. As he emerged from the shadows around the building and out into the sunlight he turned his head to call to the man behind the bren-gun. I could see it was quite definitely Arthur Best! Without any further attempt to weigh up the situation I leapt to my feet and ran out into the village shouting his name. "Arthur! Arthur! You old devil! What on earth are you doing here?"

If I was overjoyed, Arthur was doubly joyful. Arthur Best and I ran into one another's arms and beat each other enthusiastically on the back. Our hands remained clasped for a long time.

"I saw you coming across the Irrawaddy, but you did not come ashore after the shooting," said Arthur. "I thought you had been killed and had gone down with the boat. I've just been paying for some rice we got here, come along with me up to the main body."

The corporal had already gone back for the rest of the party so, leaving Sergeant Hayes to bring them on, I joined Arthur and walked with him into the jungle. We chatted happily, in a few minutes reliving many hectic hours on our way to rejoin the column. Suddenly I was face to face again with Colonel Alexander! My last glimpse of him had been when he said goodbye and turned away to leave me in the jungle alone, wounded and unable to walk, beside the motor road to Mong Mit. Colonel Alexander greeted me with a wide and genuine smile. "So glad you made it old chap!" he said.

Then Major Dunlop came up with extended hand and wrung my right hand enthusiastically. "Jolly good show, Ian!" he laughed. "I don't know how you did it, but you have done splendidly."

Then Eddie Edmonds, John Griffiths, Captain Dicky Clarke, and John Fowler were all there as well. I was wringing hands enthusiastically without any pause. People seemed to be slapping my back from all angles. It was a magnificent reunion!

Then Arthur Best was in the forefront again. "As soon as the rice is issued we are going to cross the Mu river, Ian" he said. "That will be in a very few minutes time."

So we had reached that barrier now!—"What about my party, Arthur?" I asked. "Do you think there will be enough rice to spare some for them?"

"How many have you got with you?", asked John Fowler, who was in charge of rationing, among these surviviors of No. 1 and No. 2 Columns.

"There are nine of us now," I told him.

"Oh, yes, we can manage you a mess-tin of raw rice each," he said. "That'll keep you going for a couple of days, anyway."

Seargent Hayes marched my tattered little band of wounded warriors up. We might have been just about to enjoy the most magnificent meal imaginable from the exuberant gratefulness with which we watched the rice grains pouring into our pockets or army socks used as store bags. As soon as I had received mine I crammed a handful into my mouth and happily munched the brittle grains.

The boisterous greetings over, and food issued to my men, I lay back in a sheltered hollow in the jungle immediately behind the village. The whole party were lying up there. I began to search the pale brown faces of the Gurkhas around me. The tough little men were talking in subdued tones, reminiscing about their immediate past and filling in gaps in each other's lives with the two Gurkhas who had been with me. But I searched in vain, and for all my joy at being among all these friends again there was still someone missing. I was looking for Kulbahadur.

Arthur, who had been watching me without me realizing it, said quietly: "You are looking for Kulbahadur, aren't you, Ian."

"Yes I am, Arthur. Have you any idea what happened to him?" I replied. "Is he still alive?" It meant a lot to me, that Kulbahadur should still be alive.

"When I last saw him he had gone back for you at the Irrawaddy crossing," Arthur said. "He was still on the beach searching for you when the Japs got in among us. We had to run for it pretty fast and I don't really know what happened."

"Have you no idea at all, Arthur, what could have happened to him?" I asked anxiously.

"I just don't know, Ian. I did not see him again. I was far too busy getting my platoon out of the trouble," Arthur said. "But Doc. Stocks has got a party somewhere. John Fowler saw him with about twenty men, heading towards the south. It is most likely that Kulbahadur is with his party."

"Yes, Arthur. As you say, it's quite possible," I replied. But the disappointment and disbelief in my voice was evident even to myself.

"Don't you worry about him, Ian," said Arthur Best, pressing my arm consolingly: "Your Kulbahadur is plenty tough. If anybody ever gets through this show, Kulbahadur will. After all, most of us here were in small parties until we ran into each other yesterday and the day before. It is very likely that he's in another small party making their way out."

Arthur grinned and stood up. "It'll be O.K., Ian you'll see. After all it's not far to go now and we'll all have a grand reunion. We have only got to get over the escarpment and then we are as good as home, Ian old boy. We'll be back in a week, just you watch!"

Now I began to view Kulbahadur's absence in a more favourable light. Arthur was talking sense. Kulbahadur was "plenty tough," and if I were still in the running for the home stakes, then I saw no reason why Kulbahadur should not be as well. And when last seen he hadn't even been wounded. So Arthur and I got round to talking of more pleasant things. We began to discuss at some length and with high spirits the immense meal we would order as soon as we got back to Calcutta.

"Load up!" Our pleasant imaginings were rudely cut short by that hated order. "Load up!" had been the goad which seemed now to have been forcing us forward, always under almost unbearable physical stress, for the major portion of our lives. Slowly and methodically men everywhere got to their feet. They began to wriggle into their equipment and take anew the strain of their packs.

"Well, bye-bye for now," called Arthur with a grin. "I'm the advance guard today. So I guess I'll be seeing you tonight. We'll have a nice cosy chat, somewhere in the jungle!"

"Bye-bye Arthur. Keep your head down and don't do anything I wouldn't do," I grinned.

With a lighthearted wave Arthur Best turned and was gone. Gone forever—gone amidst the sudden vicious hail of bullets which tore into us at that moment from the Jap fighting patrol who had sneaked up on us through the jungle. (Gone, I was to learn years later, to be murdered as a prisoner-of-war by the bayonets of the brutal little Jap animals who had been set to guard him.)

The bullets zipped and screeched into us through the trees. Men leaped in the uncanny contortions of their death-throes; men screamed and fell writhing; men slumped silently, coughing blood and twitching. A giant creeper, severed somewhere high up in the jungle roof by wildly fired machine-gun bullets, came coiling down upon us like a huge snake. I fought and struggled through its coils and plunged onwards desperately. Suddenly I was in the shadows of the trees which overhung the Mu river. I lurched forward and plunged down the bank, down into the cool water. It was water which stretched away ahead of me, swift-flowing but shallow, for some 200 yards.

Most of the rest of the force were already crossing. From the number of them I could see forcing their way through the shallow, bullet-spattered waters, there had not been so many hit in this latest ambush as I had at first feared. The leading sections of the column were, in fact, already over halfway across. Some of them, by their flagging progress through the swift running river, were badly wounded although still on their feet.

I was both amazed and heartened to see that the separate formations of the column were still holding together in the best military traditions. This was no panic flight, despite the hail of machine-gun and rifle bullets that were enfilading them. This was an orderly, if rather precipitate, crossing with surviving officers and N.C.O.s still in command of their formations. Somehow the fact that before my very eyes a man here and a man there threw up his arms and slipped down beneath the fast-flowing stream did not strike the terror into me that it should have done. Undoubtedly the order and discipline of the troops at that time was good for the morale of all of us.

"Extended order!" I shouted instinctively to my men, all of whom by some miracle, were still with me.

They fanned out into a line. On my left was the powerful and comforting presence of Sergeant Hayes, on my right was the corporal, still chirpy and nonchalant despite the seething lead that swept amongst us.

We ploughed on waist deep through the waters of the Mu, our firearms held above our heads to keep them ready for the fighting we would have to do the moment we landed on the other side. As the leading troops ahead of us reached the far shore another concealed Jap machine-gun opened up and bullets tore into them. Men went down on all sides. Horrified, I heard yet another machine-gun hidden in the jungle open up. More men fell directly ahead of me.

I turned to see if we could go back. But now the Jap forces on the east bank behind us had obviously been reinforced. Firing from behind was rising to a new crescendo. Gasping for breath, so that my lungs were stabbed through with pain, I shouted above the battle: "Keep going! It's our only way!" Then, as the bullet-torn waters began to become shallower as we neared the west bank, I managed to break into a splashing run. The soldiers on either side of me took it up.

Like driftwood tossed ashore by a turbulent flood stream two British soldiers appeared abruptly on the bank dead in front of us. They shouted to us frantically, and waved their arms. I could not make out what they were trying to say or to signify, so I kept going. The two British soldiers disappeared as suddenly, turning and diving into the deep green of the jungle behind them.

The moment they had gone I realized what they had been shouting. Half a dozen Japs burst through the trees and took aim at us from the narrow strip of flat ground between the jungle and the river bank.

In the same breath Sergeant Hayes and I both shouted: "Keep going!" The corporal was shouting abuse at the Japs with an almost gay abandon.

The water was now only knee deep. Less and less it was retarding our frantic movements forward. The zip and whine of bullets from behind spurred us on. From ahead came the screech and crack of the Jap machine-guns and rifles which were cutting us down. The body of a British soldier swirled past me on the swift current, the water around him pink with his blood. The Gurkha in front of me slipped quietly into the water without a sound as though playing a gentle game of hide-and-seek, except that he did not come up. On we lurched in spite of the bullets and miraculously, none of my section was hit.

Suddenly we were clear of the water and belting hell-for-leather up the sandy beach. Vaguely I realized the Japs on the bank were wavering. "Charge! kill the little bastards!" I hardly recognized the voice as mine. The corporal, less than six feet ahead of me, suddenly screamed in agony and somersaulted forward to lie kicking on the sand. Even had I had the will to do so, I had no time to stop. I took a flying leap over his body.

I snatched one look at him before I continued my charge up the sandy slope. What I saw impelled me to keep going. A burst of light automatic fire had torn into him leaving blood gushing from chest and throat. He was dead.

Then I was under the shelter of the steep bank of the river, in a sort of little bay curving in from the line of the bank. In there the angry bullets hummed above me but could not hit me. Even as I slumped down Sergeant Hayes barged sideways over the last few yards of the beach to tumble down beside me. In quick succession three men dropped down alongside of us. We were the sole survivors of my little band.

"Run for it. It's our only chance!" I shouted above the hellish noise of the battle still going on above us and all around us. "Come on. Follow me!"

I jumped up and half-scrambled, half-flung myself over the ledge of the river bank, with every ounce of strength I possessed. I knew all too well that speed of movement was now the only difference between life and death. Head down, I bounded towards the screening jungle. My third bound took me into the first low undergrowth of the jungle wall. I cannoned straight into two Japanese machine-gunners lying crossways in firing position working their fiendish little gun, so intent in putting down enfilading fire across the beach they did not notice me in the heat of the battle. There was not even time for any one of us to be surprised.

I tripped over the body of the nearest Jap and flew literally head-on through the air, my rifle cartwheeling after me. I crashed into a low bush, conscious that my rifle had landed farther ahead in denser jungle. Instinctively I whipped out my long hunting knife and turned at bay to meet the hand-to-hand attack of the Jap machine-gunners. Even as I did so a revolver exploded so close behind me that its detonation was a roar rather than a crack. Immediately there followed the sickening crunching thuds which I knew was a rifle butt smashing into flesh and bone. Then through the smoke Sergeant Hayes loomed, grinning ferociously, his revolver muzzle still smoking from the point-blank shot that had killed one Jap gunner. A British soldier charged through close on his heels, blood and a mess of flesh and hair on the butt of his rifle telling how the other Jap gunner had died.

There was no really deep cover immediately around us. We were in open teak forest with low bushes dotting the sandy soil. We raced on. Through the trees I caught a glimpse of Eddie Edmonds dashing across a clearing with the inert figure of Colonel Alexander hanging limply over his shoulder. The Colonel was mottled red with his own blood and flopped about lifelessly over the powerful frame of Edmonds. Another figure—who it was I never made out clearly—running desperately behind him, suddenly slumped down in his tracks and rolled over and over. Eddie stopped for a moment, turning to look round, then carried on galloping through the trees with his load.

"This way!" Eddie shouted, and I went lurching after him. Sergeant Hayes passed me, lumbering through the teak trees like a young bull elephant. All of us were going flat out! I gulped for breath. For no reason that I could discover I suddenly hit the ground with a thud. I sprawled there, gasping. From where I lay, all the wind knocked out of me, I saw the backs of Sergeant Hayes and another soldier disappear into a thicker clump of bushes into which Eddie Edmonds had forced his way, still carrying Colonel Alexander.

I started to crawl after them. I tried to shout "Wait!" —but couldn't. I gave up trying to fathom why I could only crawl. Suddenly an excruciating pain shot through my right knee. I felt my body twitch but did not feel it was me. Then a piercing pain came as a sheet of blinding light through body and mind and soul. Then there was only the most utter blackness, peaceful, timeless, and painless.

15

"PRISONER—PRESUMED DEAD"

An unknown number of hours later I awoke beneath a setting sun. The sweet, cloying taste of blood was in my mouth. With a conscious effort I forced my eyes open. The pain in my head doubled and redoubled. Shakily I put my fingers to my face. They revealed that it was covered with congealed blood and that my beard was stiff with it as well. I shut my eyes, first one and then the other, and the searing headache was reduced to a dull throb. I had to have a drink! Whatever the cost!

With an effort of will I persuaded my right hand to move up as far as my belt. But my belt was not there! The horror of this realization forced both my eyes open again to fill my brain once more with pulsating pain. Despite it, I tried to look around. Gradually my immediate surrounding came into focus. There were tall, dark trees looming up all around me, fringed with the red glowerings of the brief sunset. At the foot of the tree under which I lay was a bush. The bush was just by me, its shadow, in which I lay, already dark. I could see my Gurkha hat and my water bottle lying by my other side. The prospect of a drink increased my strength and I reached for the metal bottle. I greedily gulped down the warm, rank water. It was nectar.

In my great physical weakness my mind wandered. But the water brought me a measure of contentment. I raised myself slightly from the ground and looked around. Vaguely I expected to see the yellow-robed priest, or the Thugyi of my Shangrila village in the

Shan hills. Would I see them now approaching me with smiles and presents of food?

I did not. I heard instead the clink of metal on metal. A wave of pain almost engulfed me at that moment, but through it I saw that I was lying behind a rock which was at the edge of a road. On the rock sat a man, a man who was obviously a soldier. He appeared to be dressed in khaki and there was a rifle across his knees. With an effort of concentration I tried to force my tired, befuddled brain to register something more about him. He was looking at me passively but without moving. He was wearing a soft, peaked cap which was not familiar. His eyes were not the eyes of British, Indian, Burmese or Gurkha, they were the impassive slant eyes of a Jap!

"Oh God! No!" I cried out loud. "Not a prisoner!"

After that, in the desperate weakness induced by semi-starvation and my wounds, my mind did not register much that followed, except in flashes. Two things emerged as dominant factors in the confusion of mind that overwhelmed me through most of the ensuing days (how many days I never knew). The first was the fact that I had been wounded again. I discovered that a Jap bullet had seared my right leg an inch below the knee. The wound, which appeared to be only a flesh one, must have poured blood because my trousers were soaked from thigh to calf. But if—as it seemed—the bullet had only gouged the bone, the worst damage I had suffered was my weakness from loss of blood. Another bullet must have missed my head by a fraction of an inch and exploded into a hundred splinters on striking a nearby stone. There was a neat round hole through the brim of my hat where the bullet had entered, and my face was scored with innumerable cuts where the splinters from the disintegrating bullet had ricocheted into my face. The largest cut, like a razor slash, ran diagonally across my right temple. I had not been badly damaged by this either, but it had bled profusely and I must have looked ghastly.

My hair and beard were long and matted and caked with blood, my face was almost a mask of dried blood, and one trouser leg was black with dried blood from thigh to ankle. To the Jap who guarded me I must have looked almost at death's door. The privations and semi-starvation I had endured for so many days had reduced me to the semblance of a shaggy, blood-stained spectre of a man. I had reached the utmost depths of my despair. I could plumb no deeper depths. Either death must now, after all, claim me, or some miracle must intervene.

I slept the sleep of exhaustion for a long while. How long I do not know. I next awoke in a canvas-covered truck which was bouncing along a rough road through the jungle. I dragged myself painfully up into a sitting position. As I did so the Jap soldier guarding me turned to look at me and his uneven teeth gleamed as he laughed at me. In so featureless a face I could not decide whether it was a laugh of derision or amuse-ment. I guessed that it was not one of friendship. Then he turned his head, and once more sat watching the roadway flashing past below as the truck sped on.

Unexpectedly the truck came to a halt in a cloud of choking dust. The Jap soldier let the tailboard down with a clang and half a dozen Japanese soldiers clam-bered aboard. They did not see me at first, but my guard pointed towards where I lay huddled and miser-able in the far corner under the canopy. One of the newcomers pointed and laughed. Then like a jungle chorus of hyenas all the Japs joined in and laughed at me in brutal scorn.

The Japs crowded round me. Their laughter was high-pitched and raucous. Without understanding them I knew that they were jeering at the scarecrow British soldier they had chanced on. In my dulled mind their jeering did not rankle. It was their laughter I could not stand. I had never before heard Jap soldiers laugh. It was hateful. With that laughter ringing in my ears I sank once more into unconsciousness. The next thing of which I was really conscious was the movement of my sentry as he stood up at the approach of an officer. The officer stood in front of me and seemed to be studying every inch of me. His seemingly lifeless eyes moved over me to take in everything from my blood-matted hair and tattered shirt, to the wasted condition of my frame on which my blood-stained rags of clothing were hanging like the jacket on a scarecrow. His scrutiny over, the officer took a step back and rapped out an order to the sentry. The sentry laid his rifle smartly on the ground and stepped over to where I half lay, half-crouched on the floor. As he loomed above me I flinched back from the expected blow, but the Jap only placed his arms around my body and pulled me easily to my feet. A hot pain stabbed through my leg and I swayed as I stood there before the officer. He reached out to touch the solitary black cloth "pip" which he could now see on my shoulder.

"Officer?" he asked in English. I nodded.

The Jap officer turned away and started to walk off. As if suddenly remembering something, he turned round and shouted an order to the soldier. Then he went. The stocky Jap sentry came back and planted his feet firmly in the dust to stand over me where I had slumped once more to the ground. With a flourish he crossed his right arm over his body and whipped his bayonet from its scabbard. It gleamed long, and cruel in the sunlight before me. When he stooped quickly towards me I had no feeling. No feeling of anything at all as the wicked blade plunged down towards me. I saw just the flash of the sun on the bayonet and then my hands fell apart to drop back one each side of my limp body. He had cut the ropes that bound them! The Jap sentry grinned again, having enjoyed his little joke. Then he passed me a water bottle and looked on indulgently as I gulped ravenously at the tepid water.

I slept again. I had many more hours of deep sleep. Hours in which I was barely conscious of waking up from time to time to eat some sort of food and gulp at some sort of warm liquid. How much food I had—or did not have—and how much of the putrescent water I drank, I do not know. I was aware that it happened from time to time during those hours which are a just dim memory within the twilight of my mind.

It was broad daylight when eventually I returned to

full consciousness. I was bouncing about in the back of the truck, which I now realized was a captured British 15 cwt. vehicle. It was probably the third day after my capture. Now there was only my guard in the back with me. All through the heat of that day the truck was driven on and on. In the beginning the track we were following was obviously difficult, for the truck lurched a lot, and the driver often changed his gears right down. Sometimes the speed dropped to little more than a crawl, and the sturdy vehicle shuddered as the wheels skidded in soft mud or yielding sand. Yet for me whatever route it was following. the truck must be taking the wrong way. My anguish was almost unbearable.

During the afternoon we halted for a meal. For me it was a handful of sour rice and a couple of swigs at my water-bottle. Then shortly after that the truck pulled onto a flat, sandy road and the going became much easier. Still we went on, speeding past small villages nestling in secluded re-entrants.

During one of the longer halts my guard showed signs of humanity. By signs and repetition of the one word he managed to indicate that we were on our way to Kalewa. This I knew to be a riverside town on the east bank of the Chindwin, some fifty miles south of where I had hoped to cross the river. From Kalewa, as far as I could make out from more signs and the repeated words, I was to be transported by sampan to Rangoon and lodged in its infamous jail.

I relapsed into a state of utter quiescence, content to remain slumped in the corner of the truck drowsily watching the road run out under the wheels away from me. Mile after mile streaming away behind me, taking me always towards captivity or worse, even if towards the Chindwin and not away as I had at first feared. Before the last glow of day drained out of the sky, I saw that the dust road was being replaced by a deep-rutted track as we swung off abruptly to the right. The truck bounced and slithered along the track until it pulled up in a cloud of dust that rose around us. We were beside a bamboo-walled shack which I could see was isolated by a strip of paddy from a small village whose lights gleamed guardedly farther along the track.

Two Burmese villagers walked into the rectangle of my vision. They were carrying cans of petrol on their heads to refuel the truck. While this was being done I was half-carried and half-dragged from the truck by my guard. Water-bottle clutched in my arms, I was hauled over to the shack. Once within the evil-smelling blackness of the hut the sentry laid me down quite gently on the rancid, mud floor and threw a blanket over me. Obviously the truck was going to remain the whole night at this re-fuelling point. Again I dozed.

When I awoke the bright moonlight was streaming through the open doorway, silvering the prostrate forms of my two guards, for both the sentry and the truck driver lay across the threshold. Everywhere was pervaded by an uncanny almost phosporescent silver glow, and the whole world seemed poised in utter stillness. I had the curious feeling that I was not of this world, but was part of that glow. If I could merge with it, and rise in a silver mist to escape up a moon-beam, I would be clean again and safe forever. Then my spirit seemed to rise to the moon's soft beckoning. My imagination took over completely, and in my imagination I stood up. With the lithe strength with which I was suddenly imbued I noiselessly and easily jumped over the bodies of both the Japs. I found myself standing in the doorway wondering at the magnificence of the dappled blue-and-silver night.

I gripped my water-bottle tightly and turned to look once more at the two soundly-sleeping Japs over whom I had passed with such light-footed ease. It gave me a flippant pleasure to note that their rifles were both loaded and cocked, and that the slings were wrapped tightly around their wrists, so that they would awake fully prepared to kill on the instant of alarm. They had not even bothered to take turns at sentry-go. Obviously they did not fear me in any way for they knew that at my slightest movement towards them they would wake. Jungle-sharp, they would respond to the slightest sound, and to fire would be instinctive. Perhaps, maybe, they thought to themselves that even if I were to escape I would soon die in the mountainous jungle which bulked huge, black and ominous. Emaciated and weakened by wounds and privations as I was, the Japs knew that I was no longer a force to reckon with.

I have heard it said that people who have nearly died, but have recovered, sometimes tell of strange near-psychic experiences while deeply unconscious. Whether I was near death at this time I do not know, but I do know that in this strange experience I felt as though my spirit had completely left my body. I saw myself lying down there asleep in the corner. I saw myself there with all hope abandoned but, in that abandonment, resigned completely to the will of God. From outside in the cool cleanness of the moonlight, where my spirit stood, I looked in to where a slanting moonbeam fell upon my recumbent form, crumpled and pathetic. If only I could depart now, leaving this torn, blood-stained bundle behind me, a voice whispered to me. Without that useless, battered body I could soar like a mountain spirit and cross the looming jungle and span the mountain effortlessly. And thus, light and free and splendid, untroubled by heavy pack or equipment, I could swoop down from the skies and land among my joyous and welcoming comrades in safety the other side of the Chindwin.

Out there in the moonlight I was not hungry any more. I felt young and strong in body and soul. I felt sorry for that pain-racked creature that I knew was me back there in the hut. Then, abruptly, I was back in that body. And my body opened its eyes and a flood of determination and strength welled up within me: "I am not dead. I will live!" I said: "I will cross the Chindwin. Nothing shall stop me now!"

I must have said it aloud, for the Japanese sentry stirred. He opened his eyes and looked at me, and then shut them and continued his sleep. He saw only

my shrunken, battered body. He knew I did not even
require guarding. I slept.

*　　*　　*

The approaching roar of an engine being revved fast
in low gear was the noise that awakened me. At first
it penetrated my consciousness slowly, but then I knew
what it was. I was awake. I sat up. It was to find that
my guards were both already well awake sitting up in
the moonlight and craning out, their rifles firmly
gripped, to see what was happening outside. The truck
stopped in the village just across the paddy from our
hut. Immediate with its stopping there came an outburst of shouting, and clattering as rifles and equipment were flung aboard the truck.

Away up the valley a burst of machine-gun fire
abruptly startled the night. It echoed down with crackling reverberations, flung back from side to side by the
dark black jungle walls. At once a rattle of rifle fire
answered it. I realized that it was not as close as I had
at first imagined, because the stillness of the night and
the walling in by the jungle on the sides of the valley
had canalized the sounds of battle towards us.

From somewhere there rang a command in an authoritative Jap voice. It was the officer. My guards
jumped to their feet at the sound of it, and ran towards
the voice. Left alone, I crawled to the door and
watched. Out there in the moonlight I could see at
least a platoon of the enemy had arrived crammed
into a three-ton truck. They had debussed in the little
village and were forming up in four ranks.

My guards were now talking to the officer, who was
very excited and kept pointing up the valley in the
direction of the firing. One of the Jap soldiers who had
been guarding me turned and pointed at the shack.
The officer looked briefly my way, made a deprecating
gesture with his hands, and said something to the soldier. Then he shouted more orders, and one of my
guards ran to the 15-cwt. truck with several other Japs.
As he vanished around the dark bulk of the truck the
Jap officer led the rest of the men away in single file.

They disappeared running hard into the jungle, towards the sounds of the firing. As they did so I realized that the squad that had vanished behind the truck with my guard, had converged to join them.

Not a soul was now in sight and the whole world about me was just one of moonlight and black shadows. Beyond lay the deep black depths of the jungle. Should I make a dash for it? Had I the strength to get clear of this Jap refuelling point before my disappearance was noticed? I knew that there must still be Japs in the village, including my remaining guard. Obviously I was considered too weak for there to be any chance of my escape. But could I get to the jungle's cover fast enough to have made myself invisible by the time they did find I had gone? I decided to take the risk. Between my hut and the blackness of the jungle lay only twenty-five yards of open moonlit ground.

I knew exactly what to do, and strength welled up in me anew at the joy of it. I slipped out of the hut, weaved unsteadily across the open ground, and ducked into the jungle following in the wake of the enemy platoon. New strength, both of body and of purpose, flooded through me so that I sped on light-footed and seemingly inexhaustible. I was doubtless light-headed as well! I passed a succession of paths shooting off the main track, both to right and to left. Eventually I came to a fork where a steep track ran up the side of that same mountain which had bulked so huge and black above me when I was lying a prisoner back in the hut.

Up and up and up I went, clawing at rocks and trees and undergrowth to add speed to my flight. All alone in this world of deep black nothingness and moon-dappled shadows, my feet seemed hardly to touch the ground. I began to be conscious of my newly wounded leg aching abominably, too badly for me not to notice even in my new-found but light-headed strength. It ached until I felt something snap. Then a seductive warm feeling creeping down my leg told me that the wound had opened and that the blood was flowing. The ache ceased. I kept on going. I came to the top of a ridge. I had climbed the first hill. How I had managed this I could not really remember, but I was there. Below me I saw the headlights of a lone truck moving south, obviously on its way to warn other garrisons that a party of British stragglers was trying to force its way through the hills towards the Chindwin. The warning given by the men in that truck would set even more Japs swarming out to guard all the river crossings, and watch all the villages, in the immediate neighbourhood.

I wondered, in a rather abstract manner, if my sentry was in that truck. Had he, in fact, yet discovered my escape and alerted the other Japs remaining in the village? I dismissed the thought from my mind. That was their problem. Mine was to press on to the Chindwin. I climbed on, immersed in the blackness of the jungle and beckoned onwards by the glittering Southern Cross, poised magnificent and triumphant in the black velvet sky ahead of me. Oblivion came down on me again. But it was an oblivion only of the mind, in which my body kept working, impelled by the burning spirit urge from within my subconscious. I was not even aware of which way I was going. But I knew deep within me that I was heading for the Chindwin river. For me I believed the Chindwin would mean safety at last.

"I must reach the Chindwin! I must reach the Chindwin!"—I remember startling myself by saying it out loud. Furiously, I forced my emaciated body onwards. The Chindwin had to be attained—and crossed! Some time during that night, somewhere even higher up in those jungle clad hills, I wandered off the track into a thicket of clustering bamboo and undergrowth. And I slept deeply from the moment I lay down.

When I awakened the sun was already up, although not yet hot enough to be unpleasant. I was conscious that my awakening had been coincident with the final mutterings of some distant reverberation. I lay there for some minutes, the jungle disturbing, tense and hushed around me. The reverberation came again—a heavy rumbling in the near distance. I realized, with a feeling of foreboding, that it was the rolling thunder

that heralded the monsoon. How many days off now was the monsoon? I wondered. I had lost count of days since my capture by the Japs. Were there enough days and nights left for me to reach the Chindwin before the onslaught of the rains whipped it up and set it boiling into a raging torrent that would prove to be the final, impassable barrier? I was sweating, with apprehension, as I set off once more; set off due west, to march with all the remaining strength in my gaunt, sick body. Marching desperately for the Chindwin, unarmed now, and without food, drink, map or compass.

In the ferocity of the sun's heat that day I became increasingly aware of the maddening notes of the Brain Fever Bird. Over and over again, high in the jungle here, high in the jungle there, never in any one place that was definable, it scattered its random shrillness on the stupor of the day. After a time I caught myself listening for it. Listening with the fatal fascination of a lost soul which knows it cannot resist the haunted music of the dance of death. Then, when I believed I was beyond the sound orbit of the invisible bird, its song that was not a song, that was nothing, yet was madness in the end, would be in my fevered senses again. Was it really the Brain Fever Bird I heard, or was its tuneless song now in my head forever, so that I would never be without it any more? I know now how it drove white men mad.

Late in the afternoon, as the full fierceness was beginning to go out of the sun, I walked over the brow of the mountain track to be confronted by a most beautiful valley. I was feeling very tired, but so delightful did this valley appear that I had to force myself onward until I reached it. The mountain wall rose steeply on one side of me, and from the other side of the track the jungle-clad hillside sloped down to be lost in green depths shimmering beneath the heat haze. The valley came as a complete surprise because the track was just as it had been for many miles along the side of the mountain, and I had no inkling at all that this valley lay anywhere near.

When I arrived at the near end of the valley it was

to find that the trail I had been following swung away so sharply that it might have been deliberately seeking to avoid the valley. It disappeared over the shoulder of another rise climbing ever upwards into the mountain's higher levels. But I was so taken with the beauty of the place, that I decided that I would walk off the track and thread my way down through the trees until I reached the valley. Immediately I was off the track I noticed the wonderful resilience of the grass. I walked on until I had threaded my way right through the maze of beautiful trees to enter into the valley itself. It was quite small, being about a hundred yards long. I now saw that it was threaded by a brook, which sparkled and gurgled between bright, shining stones and tumbled down over a series of crystal-clear cascades. Overjoyed, I flung myself down and gulped up the water eagerly. It was bitter to the taste and I could not take many mouthfuls without finding it so unpalatable that I had to spit it out. I was so tired that I lay back and slept. And I must have slept for a long time because I awoke quite naturally and feeling that I had had sufficient sleep.

It was some time in the early hours of the morning, but even in the darkness the valley retained its peculiar beauty. The stars glittered and glistened with a greater brilliance than I had ever seen before. I could even see the greenness of the grass by night, so rich was it and so bright was the moonlight. Then a feeling that there was something uncanny about it came strongly upon me. I felt almost as though I were sitting alone in the centre of the Albert Hall and that in all the seats rising in tiers around and about me there were nameless indescribable human beings staring down at me. I felt that I was not alone, although everywhere was complete stillness and silence. I felt that I was being watched by the unknown.

Any remaining sense of happiness at being in this valley vanished, to be replaced by a rising fear of something intangible yet horrible. I fought against it for a few minutes and tried to get back to sleep, but my contentment was gone. With every second of time there grew within me the feeling that I was not alone and that some malevolent force was gathering to strike at me in an unpredictably frightful manner. My feelings reached a pitch where I could stand it no longer and I jumped to my feet. As fast as I could go I fought my way back until I had left the valley and had climbed to the track again. Gasping for breath, but thankful to have escaped I knew not exactly what, I set off following the way I should have gone in the first place. It was only thinking about it later that I realized there had been a complete absence of any tracks leading to the valley. Both man and beast must have had a very strong reason for shunning completely such a delectable looking place, but I never discovered what it was.

16

DEATH OF A HERO

How many hours, or even days, later it was that I came up on the escarpment I do not know, for often now I lurched onwards in a state of complete mental blackout. At last, quite suddenly, in a spasm of clearheadedness, I realized that I was on the escarpment. I knew that across the other side of this vast savage wilderness, riven by innumerable chaungs and ravines, was the mighty Chindwin itself. My heart gave a leap as I recognized the terrain of that escarpment. With any luck I had another twenty miles or so to go before I reached the Chindwin! Once I had crossed the river I would be within the orbit of British patrols, and there friends would find me and take me back to safety and good food, and sound sleep once more. At last it seemed my travelling was very nearly over. All I had to do was to keep going! I was very conscious at that moment that the hand of God was with me and would see me safely through. I calculated that the Japanese must have transported me something like fifty miles away from the point on the Mu river where I had been captured, but fortunately they had taken me nearer to the Chindwin instead of away from it. I had no idea how far south they had taken me on the road to Kalewa, but it was a point that did not particularly trouble me at that moment. As long as I was near the Chindwin, that was all that mattered!

Through the day that followed I fought my way on beneath the broiling sun, clambering from rock to rock, and up and down parched and baking chaungs. Everything I touched or saw was dried up and brittle.

Bamboos were bone dry from the lack of moisture. Thorns and grasses were utterly parched and sharp. No living thing was to be seen anywhere, neither was there any water. Everything that grew was now dead beneath the blistering ferocity of the sun, and the rocks and the stones were burning hot to the touch.

Despite all the prevailings of the spirit, buoyed up by the knowledge that the Chindwin was now so near, my body began to wilt beneath the savage heat of the sun. My head throbbed and spun and was shot through and through with vivid pains. My mouth and my throat dried up until I found it difficult to swallow. I tried the old trick of putting a smooth round pebble in my mouth, but it seemed to bite into the roof of my mouth and felt like a coal of fire. I had to exert actual physical force to extract it from where it became pitted into my swollen tongue. Weakness and tiredness began to claim me again. My initial energy, induced entirely by spiritual urge, was being burned out of me by the pitiless sun. My body and brain were crying out for water, sugar and food.

Then there came a period in which I just had no thought at all. I had no time to think for my brain became fully occupied in the single repetitive effort of making one foot go forward, and in then persuading the other to follow it. I came to counting each step, one after one. I came to talking to myself and discussing aloud the problems each fresh obstacle which arose before me presented. Talking to myself, I would arrive at the solution to the problem, and then lurch forward, overcome the obstacle and stagger on. I must have been getting very near my end. Ultimately, I called on the Almighty to intervene. Gasping in little painful breaths I turned my face up to the sky, aloud I called: "God! Make the monsoon early. Let it be now. Please God!"

I had to have water, or die.

I never even saw the rocky depression into which I ultimately slithered. It stood in a patch of shadow between an oasis of parched and lifeless jungle and an outcrop of scalding rocks. If the monsoon arrived

at the normal time this depression would soon be the
foot of a tumbling cataract of water plunging down
on its way to the river. As I slumped into it, there was
nothing. Nothing except a green slime where once
there had been water which had stagnated. With all
the speed I could manage I lowered myself down to
the level of the nauseating slime. I scooped away layer
after layer of stinking, green crust and rotten twigs,
until, flat on my stomach, I was able to suck up from
the midst of this putrescence a little moisture. There
was sufficient to deflate my swollen tongue and as it
deflated I was able to taste again. The rank liquid was
absolutely filthy. But foul as it was, it had undoubtedly
saved my life.

Once more I set out on my way across the waste of
the escarpment, and again there followed recurring
waves of unconsciousness during which I still lurched
on, driven forward by the mysterious force within me;
on and on, towards where instinct told me the River
Chindwin lay.

I next came to my senses in a sandy clearing among
the wilderness of brittle thorn and parched vegetation.
I followed it because it was easier under foot than the
terrain around it, and after a while it widened suddenly. As it widened the hot sand under foot became
more firm and the jungle that flanked it showed faint
signs of green life. Soon it was all a dusty green, ahead
I could see that it was luxuriant. I stopped. Above the
rustling of the forest into which I was now about to
enter there came a more positive sound. I listened intently. It seemed to my tortured brain to be the sound
of running water! With every ounce of my remaining
strength I forced myself into a tottering run. I lurched
to the right around a thicket and then gave a shout
of unspeakable joy at what lay before me. Flickering
in the sunlight was an expanse of water! The last few
yards seemed to take me an hour to cover.

At last I had flung myself down and felt the comforting coolness of water upon my face. "Don't lie in it!" I
said aloud to myself. Chindit training had taught me
that when suffering from extremes of thirst and star-

vation the stomach shrinks considerably and to drink
a large quantity of water with the stomach like this
causes rapid swelling and sometimes loss of consciousness. If you are lying in the water when you become
unconscious you drown. It took all my self-discipline
to compel myself not to gulp down great draughts of
water and to force myself up into a kneeling position
to fill my water bottle. Still kneeling in the water, I
took frequent sips from the bottle that eased both throat
and brain. The book said that a man dying of thirst
should always sip water very slowly so as to condition
his throat, tongue and stomach to the liquid. I looked
with delight on the water now flowing past me. It could
be going only towards the Chindwin. At last my route
was signposted clearly and without a shadow of a doubt!
I washed in it and rolled in it. The joy of a cleanliness
gave me an immense pleasure and I ripped the tattered
legs off my trousers to convert them into shorts. Then I
bound the wound in my leg with a piece of the discarded
material. I tied a narrow strip of the soaked cloth
around my head to keep my long wet hair out of my
eyes, for by now it almost reached to my shoulders.
Then I set off splashing downstream revelling in the
water lapping at my knees.

This new turn of events seemed too good to be true.
But the danger of the situation was quite clear to me.
This chaung obviously was one of the few in the area
which remained wet all the year round. It was getting
wider and wider, and before long it would develop into
a river with flat, sloping banks. This meant that soon
the rich jungle that would flank it would give way to
clearings, and in those clearings would be villages;
villages meant frequent Japanese patrols, if not garrisons. It was for this reason that I resolved to leave
this wonderful water and take to the jungle just as soon
as I saw or heard any signs of civilization.

I had waded almost three-quarters of a mile downstream when I came to a sandbank which split it in two.
I was glad to step up out of the water and to walk on
the sandbank's firm surface. It stretched away before
me for something like a hundred yards before being

lost to view where the river turned sharply to the left and a promontory of jungle jutting out to hide what lay beyond.

Almost before I realized it I was round this promontory. It was no more than a very narrow tongue of jungle jutting out into the river bend. The sun was just going down, and the whole immediate world before me was suffused in soft, crimson light, edged with the deep greens and blacks of jungle and jungle shadow.

Resting on the sandbank just round the promotory was a small group of officers and men from No. 1 Column. I recognized Major Dunlop and John Griffiths, and Douggie Quayle, who had been at the Officers Training School with me; Dicky Clarke and also John Fowler, No. 1 Column's quartermaster and animal transport officer. I staggered towards them with all the speed I could muster. There were about a dozen men with the five officers. No rifle was raised, nor did any hands fly to hip-holsters at my unexpected appearance. There was an air of lethargy about them, the air of men who had had almost as much as human beings could stand. As I reached them I could see that they, too, were all terribly weak from lack of food. Like me they had reached the pitch where their stomachs were so shrunken that they no longer cried out for food. There was no demonstration of pleasure at my appearance. There were just a few slow smiles as they all turned to watch my approach.

"Hullo, Ian. You again," said John Griffiths, the first I reached.

John was sitting beside a large man whose prostate body seemed still well covered with flesh. The man was panting and the sweat stood out on his brow in great beads. One arm was swollen terribly and was supported in a sling. I now saw that his apparent bulk was nothing to do with the flesh on his bones. His whole body was bloated with the loathsome dropsy of beri-beri.

"He's got beri-beri," said John in a quiet voice, as if to confirm. With a shock I realized that it was Sergeant Hayes. We exchanged meaning glances. It was quite obvious that Sergeant Hayes was dying. Then the sergeant opened his eyes. As he saw me they lighted up bravely and he grinned. Even so near the end, I would not have expected anything but a grin from Sergeant Hayes.

"They can't kill you, can they, sir?" he said in a broken voice. Then, as if the effort had been too much, he closed his eyes. Soon I could see that Sergeant Hayes had dozed off. Out there on the sandbank in the middle of the little river we decided we would all rest for the night. John and I lay down one on each side of the sergeant, this brave man who had done so many magnificent deeds all through this expedition.

Almost at the end of the night Sergeant Hayes woke. Both John and I sensed it immediately. He was struggling to do something. I saw that he was pulling his small pack up towards him and I helped him to get it. "Will you take this for me" he asked, his voice now soft and low. "You will see that my wife gets it, won't you sir?" I saw that what he was struggling to get out of his pack was a photograph album. John took the book from him and said: "Of course we will Sergeant, of course we will."

As the sun rose the life of the gallant Sergeant Hayes came to an end. Sadly I picked up his belt with my pistol, still in its holster, clipped to it, and buckled it on myself. John Griffiths was flicking through the pages of the battered photograph album.

"Photographs—all photographs of his wife," he said with a sob in his voice.

To my mind the most bitter thing of the whole Chindit expedition was the fact that John Griffiths and I were never able to carry out our promise to Sergeant Hayes. At that point we were all so weak that to carry even that small extra weight would have been unbearable. It must have become unbearable to the sergeant himself as the beri-beri overwhelmed him, yet he had insisted on carrying it to the end. John buried it with the sergeant's body in the jungle undergrowth. Then George Dunlop called the party to their feet, and we moved off.

Suddenly some bushes farther downstream began to wave alarmingly. One after the other every firearm our little party possessed was raised to point that way. Then a great clumsy, grey-skinned water buffalo came lumbering out to slummock its way into the languid shallows at the river's edge.

"This is where we eat!" exclaimed George Dunlop. "Take him, Sergeant. Just one shot is all we want." The sergeant fired and the water buffalo keeled over and flopped into the shallow water. As fast as we could we waded across the wide chaung. Then we fell upon the carcass of the buffalo like a pack of emaciated savages, with knives, kukris and bare finger-nails. We hacked and clawed the warm meat and with horrible sounds drank the hot blood as it flowed from the carcass.

We were standing there, quite oblivious of caution or of anything but our savage desire to eat, when a

high-pitched shout from the other side of the chaung suddenly startled us all into turning round. There, at the edge of the clearing, we saw a Burmese waving a white flag on a stick. The flag looked ill-omened as it fluttered there raggedly against the deep green wall of the jungle.

"All of you stay where you are!" said George Dunlop. Then he stepped out into the water and waded across to where the Burmese had now been joined by two others. The man waving the white flag was wearing the typical Burmese lungyi, but his head was crowned with a Western bowler hat. This dignified headgear no doubt signified he was the headman.

"Just keep still and don't move," John Griffiths ordered. "If they are enemies and we scare them they might shoot the Major."

We all stood there too obsessed by the possible danger of the situation even to chew the red meat which we still held in our hands. Then we noticed with apprehension that George Dunlop's lips, as he turned and began to wade back, showed no sign of a smile of relief. They were set in a tight, grim line.

"They are Burmese Traitor Army," he said in a low voice, as he came up. "They have just given me a surrender ultimatum. And there are Japs there behind them in the jungle."

"The filthy swine!" said John.

"That headman with the flag told me that they had informed the Japs of our presence," George Dunlop continued. "Apparently they heard our shot and did not even wait to come and see who we were. They had an idea that there would be British troops in the area and sent word to the Japs at once. They have armed men just behind them in the jungle. They have given us three minutes to surrender. The alternative is death."

The utter despair which we all felt at this latest turn in our fortunes showed clearly on every face. We were now so near the Chindwin and safety, and yet here we were caught in this trap with armed, traitor Burmese and Japs on one side, and more Japs undoubtedly working up the other side. Surrender or death were our alternatives, at a moment when we knew that safety was probably only a few miles farther west.

"Every man has a right to decide for himself," Major Dunlop was speaking quickly and earnestly. "We have just one minute left. Those who intend to stay and surrender get down behind that buffalo. Those who do not, follow me!" And even as he finished speaking, he turned and made a dash through the shallow water towards the opposite steep bank which was thick with undergrowth right down to the water's edge. Immediately bullets were whipping and whining about us. I heard them crash into the foliage beyond us and thud into the sand by our feet. With every ounce of strength left in me I lurched desperately towards the high bank. I never looked back. Once again it was every man for himself, and perhaps by now I was more experienced than any of them at this kind of survival!

As I reached the bank I realized that John Griffiths was in front of me. He scrambled up first and lying on his stomach, twisted round and pulled me up after him. On our feet, we lurched on, crashing and careering through bamboo thicket. I realized that my pistol was in my right hand, bucking powerfully from time to time as I fired. Who or what I fired at I still do not know. On and on I went until ultimately I crashed headlong into a tree. When I regained consciousness I loaded my revolver with my last six rounds, and lapsed once more into unconsciousness. The sun was high when I awoke. In a kind of delirium I staggered to my feet and limped through the undergrowth until I was confronted by a track. For no apparent reason I turned to the right and stumbled on. A few yards along the track I stopped, my eyes drawn to a tree beside the track. On it had been nailed a large white notice which read:

"SURRENDER.
You will drown if you try to cross the Chindwin!
You will die in the mountains of Manipur!
The British have been driven back to India!
Surrender! It is your only chance to live!"

I spat feebly at the notice and lurched on along the track deeper into the jungle. I barged straight into a clearing in which were sitting and lying, in a state of complete exhaustion, George Dunlop, Dicky Clarke, John Griffiths, Douggie Quayle, John Fowler and at least nine of the party who had fled when the Japs and Burmese traitors had opened fire upon us.

"Good God!" exclaimed George. "It's Ian again."

When they asked me where I had been I explained I did not know much about my immediate past, because I had been unconscious. They told me that the Japs who had come up on this side of the chaung seemed to have lost them in the jungle and gone off on the wrong track. Or possibly they had gone for reinforcements believing that there were more British soldiers than they cared to cope with.

We lay there in the jungle throughout the day, barely talking to each other in our exhaustion. As the gloom deepened towards darkness, George Dunlop stood up propped against a tree and told us of his plan. He said that he did not think we stood a chance by sticking together as a military formation. We were too weak (every one of us had been wounded at least once), and were now too short of ammunition, for us any longer to constitute a fighting force.

"From this point on it will be every man for himself," he said gravely, the jut of his red beard testifying to the dominant courage that would still drive him on, come what may. "The Chindwin can only be a few miles away to the west, and we might make it if we slip through singly or in twos and threes. But moving as one party I'm afraid the Japs will get us."

As we lay or crouched there in the gathering night, one British soldier suddenly croaked: "I reckon surrender is the only way."

"It's surrender for me, too. I just can't go on any more," said a gaunt young soldier with a look of terrible sickness about him. Several others said that they too were going out under the sign of the white flag as soon as it was light, to give themselves up to the Burmese villagers.

"The decision is up to you," said George Dunlop, the desperate tiredness in his voice telling of the relentless straining of both body and nerve to which he had been subjected for so long. "I want each one of you in the morning to let me know what he is going to do."

Major Dunlop's ordeal in the Wingate expedition had been more severe and protracted than that of any other column commander. When the order came to get out of Burma his force had been the last to receive it, and he had had to lead No. 1 Column, with its survivors from No. 2, back some 300 miles.

At the head of his men George Dunlop, always setting a magnificent example, had fought, hacked, crawled and torn his way through terrible jungle country, across mountains and over rivers, and through the awful desert of elephant grass. He had commanded in a succession of bloody battles. Always, in addition to sharing every peril that confronted his men, he had also been constantly subjected to the mental strain that is the additional burden of the man who makes the decisions—decisions becoming increasingly ones of life and death.

The mental strain to which George Dunlop was subjected became even more acute in the closing stages of the march out. Soon after the column reached the escarpment a very jittery Gurkha sentry reported that he had seen a native, wearing a bush hat, standing with a dog beside him silently watching from the jungle shadows. Major Dunlop decided to say nothing about this, because some of the men were by now very jumpy. Instead, he laughed the Ghurka to scorn, told him he was imagining things, and then quietly slipped away and erased the tell-tale footprints of man and dog, which were there right enough! After this incident George Dunlop confided his worst fears to Lieut. Chet Khin, a splendid young Karen officer with the column. The two of them then took it in turns to go on ahead continually wiping out all traces of the man and dog, whose footprints sure enough preceded them all along the trail. In this way, all the time that they were crossing the hell of the escarpment, the two of them hid from the rest of the column the unnerving knowledge that they were undoubtedly being shadowed.

No sooner were they over the escarpment than the Japs did try to ambush them, but George Dunlop had been prepared for this. Shortly before he had found footprint evidence that the man and his dog had met a Jap patrol, with whom the native had obviously stopped and talked. The Japs, therefore, lacked the necessary element of complete surprise, and their ambush failed. The enemy had scattered before the fierce fire they immediately encountered. A little later a larger scale battle developed with the Jap reinforcements which were brought up. George Dunlop had had to give the order to disperse.

With the dispersal rapidly effected according to plan, Chet Khin brilliantly led a large group of Chindits clear of the pursuing Japs, and got them safely through and back over the Chindwin (as we learned later). Another party was not so lucky, and was compelled to surrender to a superior Jap force which brought them to battle in a village whence extreme hunger had driven them. George Dunlop himself had emerged from the battle at the head of the handful of officers and men with whom I had found him when I overtook them on the sandbank. All were very obviously at the end of their tether, even as I was.

For all his indomitable will, Major Dunlop realized he could not now make his men go forward any farther, however much he had inspired them, ordered them, cajoled them or forced them ever onwards during the past terrible weeks. Now, at last, he had from sheer humanity to give them the option of surrendering or still further pressing on.

My own resolution was firm. Nothing, no one, would dissuade me from going on to the Chindwin. Not because I had any more courage than any of the rest of them, but because I was so completely obsessed with my burning desire to reach the river. More strongly than ever my fevered brain conjured up the picture of that great river across which I was sure was salvation.

Through that hot and perilous night we all slept the sleep of utter exhaustion. When the next day dawned, George Dunlop called us all together again. He said he was standing by his word of the night before and if any man wanted to surrender he would not prevent him. Some hesitant discussion followed, with those who had overnight decided on surrender now not so sure that they wanted to give themselves up. Although their leader through so many dangers had at last offered every man freedom to decide his own fate, the waverers found his resolute presence among them still to be the dominant factor. "It's O.K., sir. We won't give up. We'll have a go at getting over the Chindwin," the sick-looking young soldier who had been the chief advocate of surrender now rather shamefacedly told Major Dunlop.

A smile, tight-lipped but approving, came to George Dunlop's haggard face, and a little of the tiredness seemed to ebb from his steady eyes. He then quickly outlined his plan for us to split up into small groups to try to steal through the many Jap patrols scouring those last few miles of jungle which separated us from the Chindwin. I was to go with John Fowler and four of the British soldiers. All of us were nearly at our last gasp.

Of those last few miles from our hiding place to the banks of the Chindwin I can recollect little. With dwindling strength, but unabated determination, I bent aside one screen of foliage after another, clawed away snares of creeper and vine, lurched through bamboo thickets, pushed from my path great flaccid leaves that left their slimy sap on my hands—then, suddenly, there was the Chindwin!

Overwhelmed with a vast pride of achievement I slumped down in the undergrowth on the river's east bank, and gazed westwards at the wide water as it slid past. Here, at last, was the end, the culminating point of my obsession! I had reached the Chindwin, my symbol of safety. Now all I had to do was to cross it! Just to cross the Chindwin. Only 800 yards of warm, muddy water sliding by sluggishly with hardly a chuckle in its last few lazy days before the monsoon broke to transform it into a raging torrent. There before me were the last 800 yards of my trek of more than 300 miles achieved since that fateful hour of dusk at Mong Mit when I had been left behind too badly wounded to walk! Left behind to die.

I had achieved my goal. I lay there consumed by my pride, gazing at the Chindwin, quite oblivious of my companions near me. Still oblivious of them I raised myself to my knees. I slipped off my tattered shirt to tie it tightly around a bundle of dry bamboo which I now broke off and arranged together. This was to be my life belt, and on this I would be supported during my long swim across the strong current of the Chindwin. Vaguely I realized that George Dunlop and Dicky Clarke were in the water, and swimming steadily. With equal vagueness I saw John Fowler struggling in their wake for a short distance, and then turning back. I did not know or care—or want to know or care—about any of them. This was my moment. I was going to swim the Chindwin.

I tightened my belt. With the cool-headed precision that had come to me in this significant time, I balanced the weight of my revolver on one side of my belt with that of my water bottle on the other. Then I tied my boots to the strap of my Gurkha hat and slung them over my improvised "life-belt." In this last stage of my journey back to safety I had no intention of leaving any detail overlooked, I was half aware that John Fowler was back on land again. Despite his presence and that of the four soldiers on the bank beside me I was in a world of my own. They were comparatively new companions on my journey from Mong Mit. I dropped my "life-belt" into the water and slid in after it. A shout came from the shore behind me. Laboriously I turned to see that John Fowler was waving to me. He was motioning me to return. Why I should have done so I do not know, but I turned about and kicked my way back to the east bank again. Aided by two of the men John pulled me out of the water. I sat panting on the jungle-shrouded bank, not

really knowing why I had come back, and not understanding what it was all about. I barely understood
what John was saying to me.

"You'll never make it, Ian," he said earnestly. "The
current will be too strong for you farther out. Come
with us, we are heading north to Auktaung. We should
be able to get boats there."

"No," I replied, "I am going on now. You see that
river?" and I pointed to the Chindwin. "I'm going to
cross it. What's more, I'm going to do it now!"

I lurched to my feet once more.

"But look at it, man! You'll never make it! You are
not strong enough with that stream running," reasoned
John.

"I tell you, I am going to cross the Chindwin!"

John Fowler stood up and began to unbuckle his
pack. "We are going upstream to Auktaung as I told
you," he said quietly. "We shall cross there." With a
wry grin he added: "You see, Ian, most of my chaps
can't swim. Here's a present for you," and as he said it
he pulled a battered pair of water-wings from his pack.
He had carried them for fully a thousand miles, ever
since Wingate's expedition first set out from the mountains of Assam, so very long ago. For a thousand miles
he had carried them against just such an eventuality as
this. Now he was offering to give them to me!

"You see, Ian," he continued simply. "I can't swim
much either, so maybe they will be of more use to
you."

I thanked John, hardly realizing how great was his
sacrifice. I inflated the water-wings with considerable
difficulty because I was almost too weak to force my
breath into them. Methodically once more I hung my
hat and boots over my support in the water and I slid
down into the Chindwin again.

Before I waded out into the deeper water I turned
and called to John on the bank above me: "John! You
might need this!" and I unclipped my gun belt and
threw it up to him, heavy with its loaded revolver.

"Thanks," he replied. "We ran out of ammunition

some time ago. Now I can at least take care of half a dozen Japs!"

"Good luck John," I called, and I slipped out into deeper water and let my new "life-belt" take my weight. I swam slowly from the bank followed by calls of "Good luck." The last one I heard was John Fowler shouting: "Good luck, Ian. See you some time." Then he and his party disappeared into the jungle.

I was all alone, out in the Chindwin, and less than 800 yards now between me and safety. Out in the warm river water I moved my arms in a few sluggish strokes, then rested on the water-wings as the current caught me. I was lulled into a feeling of deep safety and satisfaction. I was crossing my last river and my goal was as good as won.

When I had still something like 200 yards more to go the water-wings started to collapse. The sweltering heat of the jungle had obviously been too much for them. Now they had deflated beyond the point where they could hold me up any longer and so, bobbing and gasping as I did so, I had to transfer my boots to hang them round my neck, and stick my Gurkha hat on my head.

Somehow I was not worried at losing my support for I felt it was inevitable that I should cross the Chindwin. I had come so far, and been through so much, that now I must not fail! I felt borne up, as if my starved body was too light to sink. It never occurred to me that I could sink. Pulling through the water with my arms in a painfully slow breast stroke, and maintaining slow but regular kicks with my legs, I drew steadily closer and closer to the west bank. Slowly, so slowly, but always steadily closer. Until, well over a mile south of where I originally entered, I suddenly realized I could see the bottom of the river just ahead of me. A small promontory was thrusting out here, where the Chindwin took a right bend, and with it the river's shallows were reaching out as though to help me.

George Dunlop and Dicky Clarke had vanished long

ago, having presumably swum over far upstream where they had set out. John Fowler and his little band had long disappeared in the jungle on the eastern bank. So I was all alone in this, the moment of my triumph. Joyfully I dragged myself out on to a mudbank and I lay there panting and tired, but very, very happy. The whole world seemed at peace. The sun seemed to smile now, rather than to flame with ferocity, and the Chindwin rolled on southwards in a bright world. Even the distant thunder of the approaching monsoon was no more than a good-humoured grumbling in the hills.

17

SHOT BY A TRAITOR

For a long while I lay there in the sun on the mudbank. At last, physically strengthened, with the tremendous morale boost of my achievement, I sat up and started to pull on my boots. I tied each one with its scrappy piece of lace that was just sufficient to go through the two holes halfway up my instep. Then I slipped and stumbled along the mudbank towards the bank of the Chindwin proper. The mud sucked at my feet, but I could brook no restraint now. Even when it sucked off first my left boot and then my right I could not be held back, and I left my boots where they were in my eagerness to reach the bank. It was only when I had actually touched the bank triumphantly with both hands that I realized my stupidity, and I went back for my boots and put them on again. When I came up to the bank of the Chindwin the second time I pulled myself up, and sat exulting on a flat piece of bare ground between two bushes. Now, at last, I had finally done it. I was over the Chindwin and out of Japanese territory. I was safe!

As the joyousness of my situation rose up within me I climbed to my feet and threw out my arms and said aloud: "Thank God I've done it! I've done it!" I set my face towards the jungle and the mountains which lay west of me. In that jungle, and in those mountains, there were British patrols. Farther back there were many British troops and installations. Behind me, at last, lay the Chindwin river!

Consumed with joy and pride in my achievement I stepped boldly into the jungle. I had gone only a few yards before I emerged into a wide clearing of flat paddy, and set out light-heartedly across it in the direction where I knew there must be British patrols. The smack of a bullet into my right foot synchronized with the crack of the rifle of the unseen foe who shot me at that moment. As though hurled there by some invisible force I crashed over backwards and spreadeagled into the midst of a large bush! I lay there clawing the earth in the harsh undergrowth, my breath coming in great gulps. Pain from my injured foot shot up my leg like stabs of fire. But, unarmed though I was, unaccountably I knew no fear. Instead I was overwhelmed with a rage which was both brutal and uncontrollable in its violence. There was I, my great and desperate journey over, shot down by some treacherous enemy despite the fact that I had crossed the Chindwin! Once you've crossed the Chindwin you will be safe! rang mockingly through my mind. Cross the Chindwin! Cross the Chindwin! Do that and all your troubles will end!

There came the whine and whip-crack of another bullet. It swept past me and plunged into the undergrowth beyond. Aware that I had been cursing aloud with such fury that I must have made noises almost like a wild beast, I peered round through the foliage that covered me. For the first time I saw my enemy. He was not a Jap. He was a Sikh! A Sikh civilian, the tail of his turban streaming behind him, charging across the flat paddy towards the thin belt of trees in which I lay. His white teeth were flashing in the midst of his great black beard. He was heading straight for me!

To be shot by a civilian—and a traitor at that— was even worse than being brought down by a hidden Jap sniper. The Sikh was running as a trained soldier would run, his rifle held high in front of his chest and his eyes fixed on the undergrowth in which I crouched, searching for any movement. I felt certain he must be an Indian domiciled in Burma who was now a member of the B.T.A. Great would be the reward for this Sikh when he dragged my body back to his Japanese masters. Great would be his glory for shooting down a

British officer, who was, moreover, an escaped prisoner.

But I was not dead yet. With a feeling of overwhelming hate I determined that this traitorous Sikh would die under the sights of my revolver. My hand went to my belt. But I had forgotten! My pistol had gone, I had given it to John Fowler. I was unarmed, and this murderous Silkh was closing the gap between us with every galloping stride. There was only one thing for me to do. I had to run for it. I jumped to my feet, but as I did so I stumbled and fell. The bullet that had hit me had struck my right boot and ripped off the heel and part of the leather upper. Although the bullet had not penetrated my foot the force with which that leather had been wrenched away had torn the flesh on my heel, and gashed my Achilles tendon. I could feel my ankle was badly wrenched and already swollen painfully. But if I were to escape I had to get away from the meagre cover provided by the belt of trees in which I was at the moment hidden. They were little more than a single line of trunks, lying just back from the river bank, and running parallel with it as far as a dried-up chaung some twenty yards away.

Ignoring the pain in my foot and ankle I rose up once more, forcing myself to run, crouching low, along the line of trees to the chaung. Soon I could run no farther, the fury that had driven me having momentarily expended itself. So I flung myself into a nearby clump of bushes and hid as best I could. The crashing of the Sikh charging after me through the trees was almost upon me. I wished I had had the strength to make a thicket farther up the chaung, but knew I could not. Then I heard the crackle of tinder-dry twigs and underbrush as the Sikh jumped down into the chaung.

The ease with which I could see the Sikh, as he made his way up the far side of the chaung, filled me with fear that he must be able to see me as easily. But he was not looking at my clump of bushes. He was looking intently at the thicket up the chaung, his nostrils dilating with anticipation. He obviously thought I was in that thicket. His eyes were still fixed upon it as he crossed over the rubbish-strewn bed of the chaung to come right up close to my hiding place. He had only to glance once to his left, and he must see me!

When he was almost upon me I could hear his panting breath as he stooped to look for my trail. Obviously farther back he had found the blood splashes from my gashed foot and was intent on following them until he ran me to earth. I heard the jingle of his steel bracelet on the metal of his rifle as he leaned forward to peer more intently at the thicket ahead. I glanced down to take another look at my throbbing wounded foot, and as I did so I saw that I was almost kneeling upon a large piece of driftwood. It must have been flung up there the year before, when the Chindwin had been last in spate. I grasped it with both hands and found it was part of a bough torn from a teak tree. And being teak, it was so heavy and hard that it would require all my weakened strength to wield it.

The Sikh's rifle was now down at the ready, and one finger I could see was crooked around the trigger. I could see his dark eyes flashing as they caught the light slanting down into the chaung. He looked neither to left nor to right, for his eyes remained fixed on the thicket. Purposefully, he came on, his eyes still glued to the cover in which he obviously felt certain I was hiding. Because his attention was so riveted ahead, and he was hunching forward, moving soft-footed as he stalked past me, he never knew what happened to him. With the almost superhuman strength that welled up within me in a fresh surge of fury, I suddenly rose to my feet and swung my heavy club down on to his skull. It crunched home horribly as I expended all my hate in that one tremendous, savage blow.

The Sikh went down without even a groan. I shuddered with horror as I saw what I had done to his skull with my crude weapon. I had never killed a man in this way before and to me it was the most horrible of all the ways of killing. I shuddered, and suddenly found it all so loathsome that I could not bring myself even to touch him to pull away from his dead hands the rifle I so badly needed. To avoid touching him,

I took instead his curved Sikh's knife. I stooped and drew it from his cummerbund, its razor-sharp blade flashing in the sun as I did so. I thrust it in my belt and lurched off, heading for the deeper cover of the jungle beyond.

All that day I stumbled along, going ever westwards away from the Chindwin and onwards to where I knew I must ultimately meet my friends. All that day I tried somehow to cleanse my mind of the vision of the twisted body of that Sikh, his head smashed so brutally, sprawled in his own blood in the clearing at the jungle's edge. Even though it had had to be either the Sikh or me who died, I hated the very thought of what I had done.

On and on I went, sometimes through thick jungle and sometimes across welcome paddy-fields, deserted by the natives since war had swept across their land. For this, although the British side of the Chindwin, was the no-man's land where British and Jap patrols were always likely to clash. My hand still gripped the curved knife, my only weapon against whatever dangers might lurk. The only definite thing I could think about was the Yu river, the next river I would reach. The Yu, I knew, was considered to be in friendly territory, and I would have only to follow its course upstream to come to the advance British H.Q. at Tamu. What if it *were* true that the British had been driven back right out of Assam, beyond Imphal, back into India itself? What if Tamu were now a Jap H.Q., and no longer British?

On and on I lurched, often delirious, but always moving forward. Sometimes in the jungle I flopped down among the undergrowth to rest, but never did I let myself stay for very long. I had reached my goal. I had crossed the Chindwin. No one, nothing, was going to prevent me getting right back to safety now!

Suddenly I saw a flash through the trees, like the flash of sunlight striking up from running water. I stopped. Yes, it was water! I pressed on, and saw now that it was indeed a wide expanse of water. My spirits soared and I broke into a lumbering painful gallop, thanking God that at last I had arrived at the Yu river!

I was running hard now, heedless of the uneven parched paddy and of the pain it was causing my torn and swollen foot. Then I was there. On the banks of the river itself. I arrived so suddenly that I slipped on the muddy shore and landed sitting down in the mud with the swirling waters sliding silently just below me. I strained my eyes to see the other side, but the other side was a good half-mile away and already hazy in the gathering darkness. Slowly the awful truth dawned upon me. This was not the Yu river. Only one river, besides the Irrawaddy, could be as wide as this. In my demented, delirious state, unconsciously I had used the sun as my guide all day, but because I had started the day with it behind me, I had crazily kept re-orientating myself to keep it behind me. So at the end of my tormented journey I had the west behind me. I was back on the west bank of the Chindwin! Slowly the tears of frustration ran down my cheeks. I flung myself down and sobbed unrestrainedly, overcome with misery at the thought of all that painful, wasted effort.

The wave of hysterical grief passed and with its passing came the deep sleep of utter exhaustion. I slept where I lay, sprawled at the jungle's edge on the west bank of the Chindwin river. I awoke in that brief greyness that presages the rising of the sun over Burma. My sleep had done me good, for my despair at my own incompetence had vanished overnight. Although weak and light headed, I awoke refreshed and resolved to set out once again for the British lines and safety.

Slinging my water bottle over my shoulder and cramming my battered Gurkha hat over my shaggy tangle of hair, I set off westward once again, stepping out as strongly as I could across the flat paddy. The rising sun behind me pointed my way ahead with my own shadow, a way which I knew must lead through scores more miles of inhospitable jungle to where the mist-shrouded Chin hills arose in the near distance. Somewhere between the west bank of the Chindwin and those hills I would fall in with a British patrol if I were lucky. But if that last Jap surrender notice had been telling the truth and if I were unlucky, it would be a Jap patrol. But now I was determined not to be taken alive and was prepared to fight to the death, even though my only weapon was the curved Sikh's knife. Things were not as bad as they might have been, I told myself. My foot which had been damaged by the Sikh's rifle shot throbbed no longer, and the swelling of ankle and tendon had gone down. My worst worry was the gnawing hunger I now felt, a hunger which threatened to make me throw aside all caution in my overwhelming desire for some sort of food. Any food.

As I neared the far side of the stretch of paddy I came across a deserted village. From experience I knew that if one scavenged very carefully in one of these deserted villages one could sometimes find cultivated fruit and vegetables, even a few grains of sour, mildewed rice.

Hugging the most deeply shaded side of the track I crept cautiously onward. I could see that already creepers had descended from the trees above and were weaving their leafy shroud over some of the houses. Quite sure now that the village was completely deserted, I threw all caution aside. I lurched forward at the fastest pace I could muster, and went into the first hut I came to. The steps up to it nearly collapsed beneath me as I mounted them, and in the patchwork of light that struggled through the disintegrating thatched roof I saw only mouldering household rubbish. From house to house I went, not needing even to enter many of them because of the great gaping holes in their sides. But not one grain of rice could I find, nor any kind of food. A depression fell upon me as I continued to walk on, and such physical strength as I had left was draining away fast. I had to eat something or I would collapse and never rise again! Yet this village offered me nothing.

When the sun was at its zenith, and the jungle sweltering almost beyond endurance, I sighted another village. This time I was too far gone to care about caution. I staggered forward in a drunken weaving run until I had reached it. My heart sank again as I realized that it was as deserted and derelict as the one I had searched earlier. I saw one bigger building which had obviously been a storage barn. Thinking I might at least find some grains of rice there, I lurched into its inner darkness but had barely time to see that there could be nothing here of use to me when a flock of bats, disturbed by my entry, fluttered about my head with a horrid rustle of skinny wings. I fled.

Once more, overwhelmed by weakness and depression, I slumped down and decided I could go no farther. I sat on the ground with my back against a fallen tree. I sat hunched there, almost too weak and dejected to want to live any longer.

A sound of heavy rustling came from the hitherto silent jungle immediately opposite me and a spark of life leaped again within me. The Sikh's knife was in my hand as I crouched there. I was determined to sell my life dearly. There emerged from the jungle opposite me a young python about ten feet long. With sinister undulations it wove its way between trees and bushes, its large flat head only a few inches above the ground. My hatred of reptiles became almost fear when confronted by a snake. Yet for all my loathing of snakes, I knew that I had to kill this python if I were to live. It was a snake, but it was food. I felt with my hand along the wall of the house beside me to see if I could find any implement with which to attack the python. My luck was in. In a tangle of weeds just behind me was a rusty spade-like implement which some Burmese villager must have used for tilling the paddy-fields.

With all the strength left in me I lurched out into the open and, with one desperate slash of my spade, I severed the python's head from its body. Hastily I gathered slivers of dry bamboo and built them up into a fire. I ignited them by the old forester's trick of revolving a sharpened stick in a hole in another dry stick. I heaped larger pieces of broken boughs on the fire so that it flared up hotly. While the fire's heat was building up I poked around among the weeds and creepers enshrouding the village to find some sort of vessel in which to boil water. Again I was lucky, for I succeeded in finding a rusty can. Just through the jungle behind the village there was flowing a silent little stream, and I realized now that it was towards this that the python had been crawling. I filled the can with water and set it on the fire which had now produced a heap of red hot glowing embers.

While the water in the rusty can was coming to the boil I cut slices off the python with my knife. My revulsion for the reptile had vanished before my urgent need to eat. The first thick slice I dropped into the bubbling water, and sat impatiently waiting for it to be cooked. I prodded it repeatedly with the point of the Sikh's knife until I felt it was tender enough to eat. I bit into the python steak without any feeling other than the necessity to assuage my hunger. I was surprised how pleasant it tasted. I dropped a second thick slice of python into the water while I attacked the first with relish.

By now I was certain that it tasted like chicken, with probably just a small flavour of tender veal about it! The next python steak tasted just as nice, and so did the next! Then I cut off another slab, thicker than the others, and when my knife-point probings showed it was done to my liking I collected some banana leaves and wrapped it in them. I tied around it the loose end of the parachute cord which was supporting my tattered trousers and was able to walk from the clearing not only strengthened and satisfied but carrying a reserve of food with me.

From that point I kept to the jungle track, stepping out as purposefully as I could in my new found strength. The terrain now seemed to repeat itself over and over again with patches of jungle and stretches of deserted paddy field. By nightfall I was once again in jungle and I fought my way through thick undergrowth to lie up some twenty yards off the track. This time I had made no mistake with my directions. Each time I emerged into paddy fields I was able to reorientate myself, certain that my way ahead was now ever onwards towards the distant Chin hills. These hills be-

yond which lay the plain of Imphal and the area
where the British forces would be building up their
strength. I slept deeply right through that night to
awake again in the hour before dawn. As light welled
through once more into my world of weird green gloom
I ate half of my python steak, re-wrapped the remaining half, and set off again westwards. This day was
like the day before and the day before that. I kept on
and on. But although I now had food in my stomach
my weakness was recurring. And worse than weakness,
I realized that I was becoming delirious again. As I
staggered on, I sometimes laughed aloud shrilly, and
was momentarily alarmed at the inhuman noise I
made, only half aware that I had made it myself.
Sometimes tears of anger and frustration filled my eyes
and trickled down my shrunken cheeks in my agony at
not being able to walk faster in my weakness. For
much of the time I was either unconscious on my feet,
or, increasingly, unconscious where I fell sprawled out
on the track or in the undergrowth beside it. As the
sun went down and the heat drained from the day I
entered into a brief period in which I was completely
sane and rational. I dragged myself under cover and
away from the track and ate my remaining half of the
python steak. Then I slept again, curiously strengthened by a feeling that I was within the protection of
some undefinable power.

he whole mud-shrouded waste of mud, water and
ng vegetation seemed trackless. Here and there
appeared opaque ... and had no swervus
... ... rope, to the ... ... that the
... ...
... ...

18

THE MIRACLE OF THE SWAMP

How and why I set off next day I have never discovered. Even though my mind functioned now only in
brief snatches, something within me still drove me
westward. Still drove me on until I recovered consciousness sufficiently to realize that the sun was setting
and that I had wandered into a swamp.

Everywhere was gloom and mist and great fantastic
shadows that seemed neither of this world nor of any
other. The setting sun sliced opaque, diagonal passages
through the gloom and mist. The stagnant water which
lay in lifeless patches all around assumed the appearance of blood spreading in silent pools across the trackless waste.

Then the swamp was stretching all around me, like a
gigantic web. No longer was there any track, nor path
nor any sign of where to go nor whence I had come.
Only the redness of the sinking sun to give me any
sense of direction at all. The evil, gleaming, mud
sucked at my feet as I squelched between the dwarfed
trees and dense patches of bamboo. Everything and
everywhere smelt evil and was enveloped in sullen
mist. No bird sang nor did any animal move. There
was not a breath of air. I slumped down on my knees
in a wave of weakness and nausea and tried to pull
myself up by clutching at a jagged stunted tree nearby.
The bough I caught, rotten right through, came away
in my hand. The splash it made seemed to shatter the
silence, and the decayed splinters of the rotten wood
settled malevolently to float on the surface of the
water.

The whole mist-shrouded waste of mud, water and rotting vegetation seemed trackless. Here and there, avenues appeared to open out and lead on towards some vague trace of hope, in the same way that stray gleams from a street lamp pierce fog and beckon to lost strangers. But every beckoning avenue in this stagnated swamp was identical. Frantically, I realized that I was inextricably lost, and just did not know which way to go. The gigantic web in which I was ensnared began to revolve around me in my delirium and I grabbed at a tree to steady myself. This one did not disintegrate in my hand. Leaning drunkenly against it, I peered to one side and then to the other. A great shadow came crawling down a ray of sunshine, in my imagination the form of an enormous spider clambering down from the web's centre to claim its struggling victim.

I laughed hysterically as I realized that it was not a spider, but was merely my own shadow magnified by reflections on the water. There was no known way out for me this time. No known way, and yet I could not be very far from salvation.

I broke into a squelching run, as in a nightmare. The mud seemed to suck more and more at my stumbling feet. I do not know how long it was before the pools of stagnant water dropped away and a mudbank rose before me. I flung myself down upon that bank and immediately fell into a dreamless sleep that was part fainting and part a sleep of exhaustion.

When I came to, I realized two things. First, that my boots had been sucked off by the mud as I ran. Second, that I was hungry no longer. I had been underfed and famished for so many weeks, and at times the gnawing pains had been sheer agony, but now all hunger had gone. I must have been very near my end.

In the place of hunger had risen a strange longing. I longed for a swiss roll! Why it should have manifested itself in the form it did has always been quite incomprehensible to me, for I had never liked swiss rolls, nor have I liked them since. But now I dreamed of them; rows of them danced before my eyes as I staggered on. I could feel the sugar on my lips and taste cream which was not artificial but was real and quite delicious. I came to imagining that my stomach was full. Full of swiss roll—but oh, how I longed for yet another!

I struggled on. The haunted trees and moribund clumps of vegetation trapped like me in this swamp, seemed to rear up in the mist as gigantic things. My world was now a blue-grey haze, scattered with dancing pinpoints of light and with anything that stood up in it and from it elongated and drawn up in jagged black verticals to disappear through the roof of mist above.

Then I collapsed unconscious on a mudbank. When I recovered consciousness again it was to find myself completely clear-headed and without any fear. I felt very confident that I was going to win through. I was hardly aware of my gaunt and shrunken body with all its marks of pain and suffering. I felt clear and spiritual and capable of travelling vast distances unhindered by my body. And miraculously, the mist had lifted from the swamp.

Without moving, I turned my eyes to the left. At once I came face to face with a pale-green lizard. The lizard rolled one eye to study me critically while the other looked back the other way, apparently seeking the safest line of retreat. My mind appreciated that it was food. I drew my knife. At its glint the lizard scampered away along the mudbank, stumbling in its haste as it went into a depression. But it recovered and continued. I did not see it disappear, because my eyes had left the lizard and were riveted in absolute amazement upon the depression that had caused it to stumble. Slowly I rose to my feet and, with my eyes still fixed upon that depression, I stumbled as fast as I could towards it. When I reached it I went down on my hands and knees and stared at it unbelievingly. My fingers traced its outline. It was something the presence of which in this place, completely astounded me. But I did not attempt to reason how or why it got there. There, before me, was the undeniable imprint of a British Army boot!

From tracing my finger around its outline, I pushed it into each of the stud marks across the sole. Yes, there were thirteen studs in that boot. Without the faintest shadow of a doubt, it was the footprint left by a British Army standard issue ammunition boot. As the joy of my discovery welled up within me I looked up and onwards in the direction towards which the toe of the boot was pointing. Yes. There, clearly discernable as they stretched away before me, were more boot-prints. They led away from where I knelt in a direction cutting diagonally across the wide mudbank. As straight as a ruled line they went, but becoming almost invisible after the first few. I blessed that lizard which had led me to them. Quite unquestioning, I set out to follow the bootprints.

On and on they led me. Unhesitatingly, and filled with the confidence that at last I was being led back to safety, I followed them. I did not look to left or right, neither did I fear that if I followed this clearly marked track I might step onto treacherous ground that would suck me down to die in the black and stinking mud. In complete and utter faith, I followed the boot-prints onwards, and always they led me across the swamp on ground which bore my weight and took me from one firm mudbank to another. The mud was hardening beneath my feet: before long I was on firm dry earth. I was through the swamp! Those blessed prints made by a British soldier's boots had led me safely through!

I could see that the trail continued straight and true across the dry earth from where I now stood; on to where the forest towered up again and a track was discernible disappearing into it. I had to rest for a short while, for I was very weak, so I slumped down on the earth where I was. Again I examined closely the nearest boot-mark. This British soldier, whoever he was, could not be very far in advance of me. The prints were undeniably recent. Minute piles of earth stood behind each of the marks made by each one of the regulation thirteen studs. The hot sun had not yet crumbled and broken them down. The man I was following must be very close. I stood up and I called after the British soldier, hoping to attract his attention. I shouted for him. I shouted again. A lonely man calling for the companionship he knew to be only a few minutes in front of him. But I called in vain. I sank to the ground again, then leaned back wearily against a tree trunk and took a long drink from my water bottle.

Revived somewhat, I corked the bottle and put it down beside the nearest bootprint. I looked back at the trail that had been my salvation and as I did so I was overwhelmed with a sense of the unearthly. My scalp crawled and my heart palpitated with a great fear of the unknown. Behind me, and back into the swamp as far as I could see, were only the prints of my own naked feet. There was absolutely no trace at all of any booted feet having come that same way!

Unbelievably, I got to my feet and slowly walked back along the trail left by my own bare feet. But although I retraced my steps for more than a hundred yards, and well back into the swamp, I could not find even the slightest trace of the booted feet of a British soldier having passed that way. There was only the imprint of my own naked feet! My spine prickled at the uncanniness of it all. I turned and stumbled back to where I had left my water-bottle. Would I find the bootmarks still where I had seen them before, leading off towards the jungle track? Yes, they were there, those prints I had yet to follow. At regular intervals, firmly pressed into the ground, were the bootmarks, each with its thirteen stud holes. I made no attempt to solve the mystery, if indeed I could ever have found an explanation for it. I was quite content to follow my guide who had brought me thus far, as far as he chose to lead me. Wherever those bootmarks went, I would go unquestioningly. I was too weak and too tired to want to try to find any reason why I should do otherwise.

In any case, now I had recovered from the shock of their mysterious appearance and disappearance behind me, I found the presence of those bootmarks always ahead of me strangely comforting. The aching gap of loneliness was filled and I had a companion again. I had nothing to fear.

Westwards those boot-marks led me. Up hills they went and down into rocky chaungs; through jungle and out again; across dusty, paddy fields. On and on we went, my mysterious footprint guide and I. As we marched we discussed the relative beauties of the gentle jungle orchids and the gaudy flame of the forest. We kept no secrets from one another. Those boot-marks understood my innermost fears and we were content in each other's company. In my delicious light-headedness, as I lurched and struggled on, I was conscious that I was talking and singing and shouting—talking garrulously and happily to my companion who left only boot-marks but wasn't there, and whose boot-prints themselves vanished once they were behind me!

Abruptly, at the edge of a stream, the footprints ceased. I was alone. For a few moments I stood there in utter bewilderment. What did I do now? Which way did I go? Before the despair which had begun to mount within me could develop I heard the unmistakable clamour of a large river through the forest just ahead of me. The swish of its waters drew me inevitably, and I surged forward in a new wave of eagerness.

Thorns tore me and creepers tugged at me. I crashed through undergrowth and against trees as I fought through the last hundred yards of jungle towards the sound of that river. I staggered out on to a beach of silver sand, and the wave of heat it flung up at me hit me like the blast of an opened furnace. I recoiled before it and collapsed into the shallows of the river which lapped that silver beach. Even as I did so, my heart rejoiced. I knew that this must be the Yu. Unless the Japanese surrender notices were true, the British base of Tamu could not be many days away upstream.

*   *   *

The flash of steel in bright sunlight is impossible to confuse with anything else. Now I saw just such a flash from the jungle on the far side of the river. As if the incident was something outside my real life, and could not affect me one way or the other, I watched as the sun played on steel again and yet again. Then men in green uniforms detached themselves from the jungle wall and moved down into the opposite shallows with rifles at the ready. They fanned out into extended order and dipped their rifles so that the sun played again along their bayonets in a series of falling and rising arcs of silver light.

Men in green uniforms! So those notices the enemy had posted on trees east of the Chindwin had been true! The Japs *had* advanced beyond the Chindwin! British troops did not wear green uniforms or soft-peaked caps like those men now advancing on me behind glittering bayonets. They could only be Japs.

And now, at last, all my will to win and to get back to the British lines drained from me. I had crossed the Chindwin. I had done absolutely everything I should have done to achieve success. Yet here, now, on the banks of the Yu river, was the inevitable end. There was just no point in going on any more, for my obsession that there was safety across the Chindwin must have been false all the time. Tamu must have fallen, and Imphal, all those miles beyond. The Japs must even now be in India, thrusting out towards the mighty Bramaputrah and the great sub-continent beyond. I could not face the hardships and mortal dangers of hundreds more miles of dense jungle-covered mountains in my present state. My spirit died within me, there just was no point in going on.

I decided to make no attempt to run, for it would have been both futile and fatal. Weak and wavering I rose up from where I had lain in the shallows, the water running from my body and pattering down on to the damp sand. I drew the Sikh's knife from the cord around my waist and let it fall to the sand. I raised my hands and stared weakly, caring no longer, at the men who would be my captors.

Against the blaze of the sunlight I could see their eyes glinting in the shadows thrown by their caps. One

of the men halted out there in the river and brought his
rifle up to the aim, the sun silvering the narrow ring of
the muzzle in a sudden menacing gleam. Any second
now I knew I would see the flash and with it would be
hurled backwards by the impact of the bullet to sprawl
on the sand staring at the darkening sky. And then the
end—the absolute and ultimate end—would come as a
red-black fog of oblivion engulfed me.

But there was no flash. There was no impact. No
crack of rifle nor whine of bullet. In amazement I
watched the river and the jungle beyond swing from
the horizontal to the vertical and then back again to
the horizontal. The sun, blinding in its intensity, suddenly cavorted about the sky. With a vast roaring in
my ears, all was blackness.

*   *   *

It was quite dark when next I was sensible of anything at all. I realized I must be lying on my back for I
could see stars twinkling between the ragged silhouettes
of tree branches high up above me. Armed soldiers
were sitting around a crackling fire in the clearing in
which I lay.

"Oh, so you've come round then! Have a mug of
char, chum!" The English voice shocked me even more
than a Jap voice would have done. I turned my head in
bewilderment to see a young British officer, two stars
above the words Mahrattas on the epaulette of his dark
green shirt.

"You gave us quite a start, you know, rising out of
the water like that!" he said. "If you hadn't looked just
like the wild man of the woods, we might have taken
you for a Jap and shot you!"

Gave them quite a start! Oh, my God! Gave *them*
quite a start! So it was a British patrol. Oh, dear God!

Suddenly I was laughing raucously and uncontrol-
lably. My toneless mirth pierced the silence of the
night, brittle and discordant, as it rang through the
forest. As it rose to a crescendo, it was suddenly cut
short by the sobering violence of a slap with an open

palm. "Just you drink this char, then you'll be all right!" The British officer, in his Jap-style jungle green which was a new issue to the British Army of Burma since the Chindits had set out, was kneeling beside me with a steaming tin mug in his hand. I drank it eagerly, delighting in its sickly sweetness and warmth. Then I slept the most wonderful sleep of my life.

The next I knew was that I was in a motor-boat, chugging up the Yu river. The metal of its hull was hot to the touch. The British officer smiled at me and said: "You'll soon be home, don't you worry, old boy!" The Mahratta naik beside him grinned.

Next, I was lying on a stretcher in the shade of a tree. I was at the advanced British headquarters at Tamu. An extremely tall, gaunt man, wearing a bush hat and one of the recently-issued green uniforms, stood at my side. He was speaking. I concentrated hard, for I felt somehow I owed it to him to listen.

He was saying: "You've been very lucky, my boy. Very lucky indeed. That Mahratta patrol got you back just in time. You were just about at your last gasp. You know, it was by pure chance that they happened to cross the Yu river at the spot where they found you. That patrol was the only one around for about a hundred square miles in that area, and there haven't been any British east of the Yu there for many weeks. We thought all you chaps who were coming back alive were out long ago, you know."

"There are still some more on the far side of the Chindwin," I said weakly. "They can't swim."

"We'll get them out," he replied. "Don't you worry any more, son. You put up a damn good show, but it's all over now. Now you're going to have a really good rest."

He knelt and patted my shoulder comfortingly. As he did so, I saw that he was a major-general.

Terribly weak both mentally and physically, I sat quite still and silent in the front of the ambulance that drove me from Tamu back to Imphal. The newly constructed road sped past as we drove towards the British advanced headquarters. As we ground through the village of Palel, the first spots of the long overdue monsoon blotted the dust-covered windscreen. Dramatically, the monsoon burst upon us in all its fury. If it had not been these few days late I should never have crossed the Chindwin or the Yu!

"What's the date?" I asked the driver.

"It's the sixteenth of May, sir," he replied. The sixteenth of May. So a hundred days had passed since I had last seen Imphal!

The pouring rain drummed loudly on the roof of the ambulance as we drew up before a sign board bearing the legend: "Number 19 Casualty Clearing Station." We drove in after the sentry had raised the red and white barrier boom. We stopped once more.

"This is it. You get off here, sir!" said the driver.

Obediently I allowed myself to be helped down by the driver. I clutched my water-bottle, my Sikh's knife, and a stick of brown native sugar that someone had given me.

I looked around me. The long bamboo plaited bashas stood in rows. The beds, I could see through the wide open doorways, were empty. This was the end of the road, this brand new hospital. This was the finishing point of a 1,200 mile race, and I had come in last. But I had stayed the course, and got there in the end, despite everything the handicappers could do!

"Come away in, this is the officers' ward." A feminine voice with the soft inflection of Scotland caressed my tired brain into consciousness. I turned sharply, expecting to see my mother, for it was her voice which had spoken.

"You seem startled," she said. "Dinna fret yourself, laddie, it's all over now."

I closed my eyes. When I reopened them it was to see that a small, smiling young woman in khaki and red stood before me. She touched my arm. I followed her towards the basha in silence. A mist rose before my eyes, a mist which gave place one after the other to faces I knew well. They were faces which I had seen once, but they had disappeared during that long nightmare out beyond the Chindwin. There was the face of

Arthur Best and Kulbahadur. There were Doc Lusk and Doc Stocks and the brave Sergeant Hayes and, lastly, Harold James. All the old familiar faces which had disappeared during those harrowing weeks which now stretched out behind me.

The face of Harold James seemed clearer than all the others through the mist. It was coming nearer and nearer to me. There was no mistaking the dry smile and I could see his lips were moving. In the distance I heard his voice. "Well, well, Ian, so you finally made it. Welcome home!" he said.

With a start I realized that someone had caught my right hand and was shaking it enthusiastically.

"We have been waiting a long time for you, you know. We thought you were never coming out."

I blinked and the mist cleared. It really was Harold James. He stood there in front of me grinning his welcome. The clean new purple-and-white ribbon of the Military Cross stood out brightly and bravely against the drab background of his green shirt.

They put me to bed in that almost deserted hospital, and the Scottish matron, Agnes McGeary, came to my bedside and said, with an inviting smile: "Is there anything you would like?"

"Yes, please," I answered faintly. "A swiss roll."

She smiled an understanding smile and went out. The following morning, when I awoke, a cream-filled swiss roll lay on my bedside locker. One slice sufficed to satisfy my shrunken stomach, and then the craving had passed.

They nursed me back to health in that hospital on the great plain of Imphal, and then I was fit enough to be allowed to go on leave. I travelled by truck to Dimapur, and from there by train to the depot of the 2nd Gurkhas at Dehra Dun.

The monsoon rains were still lashing down in torrents as the truck drove up to collect me from the station at Dehra Dun. It splashed through innumerable rivulets running across the muddy ground as it delivered me to the marquee which was the unit reception office. Orders had been that all survivors of the 3rd

Battalion had to report there before going on six weeks leave.

"This is the reception office. You'll get your railway warrants here!" shouted the young officer above the thunder of the rain on the canvas roof of the truck.

"Thanks!" I shouted back, and carefully lowered myself over the tailboard. I squelched through the mud to the sideless marquee, my voluminous monsoon cape wrapped tightly around me. The rain ran down the stiff flat brim of my new Gurkha hat. The truck skidded away to the main road and was gone.

Inside the marquee the booted and spurred young major behind the table, snapped: "Name, rank and number!"

I told him. He did not even look up.

"You will proceed on leave within the next day or so. You were wounded, weren't you?" he asked dispassionately.

"Yes," I replied. He looked up, giving me my first glimpse of his face. His cold, blue eyes fixed on mine.

"Sorry," I said, aware of the reproof in his gaze. "Yes, sir!"

"You will be notified of your disposal while you are on leave," he said. His voice crackled above the drumming of the rain. He was very much the regimental officer!

I screwed up my courage. "I . . . I . . ." I began. "I wondered if I might look at your list of survivors, sir?"

"Over there on the table," he replied shortly.

The interview was obviously at an end. It was up to me to find my own way from now on. I crossed to the table he had indicated and eagerly thumbed through the typewritten pages labelled: "Nominal Roll—3/2 G.R.: Gurkha Other Ranks.

I had reached the "K's" and there I found:

"Rifleman Kharaksing Thapa 78:
Naik Khembahadur Pun:
Rifleman Kulbahadur Thapa 48"

I searched my memory for Kulbahadur's Army number. For Kulbahadur Thapa was a common Gurkha name and only those last two digits would identify him definitely. But it was useless. I could not remember. I turned away disappointed.

"Are you looking for me, Sahib?" said a soft voice. I spun round. Kulbahadur stood just inside the tent, the rain streaming from his hat and groundsheet. His face beneath the shadow of the brim was one wide smile.

"I heard you were arriving by train today, Sahib," he said.

"Well met, Kulbahadur!" I said, stepping forward.

Our hands clasped and held in a long, firm grip that testified in silence to the great depth of friendship formed, tried, and proved in battle.

"Jemedar Sahib!" shouted the booted and spurred major in Gurkhali. "This tent is overcrowded. Clear it!"

Kulbahadur touched my arm and grinned sideways towards the table. "Sahib," he said. "We are soldiers again now!"

Side by side we went out into the rain, our laughter lost in a peal of thunder as the monsoon storm rose to a new height.

BANTAM WAR BOOKS

Now there is a great new series of carefully selected books that together cover the full dramatic sweep of World War II heroism— viewed from all sides and representing all branches of armed service, whether on land, sea or in the air. All of the books are true stories of brave men and women. Most volumes are eyewitness accounts by those who fought in the conflict. Many of the books are already famous bestsellers.

Each book in this series contains a powerful fold-out full-color painting typifying the subject of the books; many have been specially commissioned. There are also specially commissioned identification illustrations of aircraft, weapons, vehicles, and other equipment, which accompany the text for greater understanding, plus specially commissioned maps and charts to explain unusual terrain, fighter plane tactics, and step-by-step progress of battles. Also included are carefully compiled indexes and bibliographies as an aid to further reading.

BANTAM WAR BOOKS

These action-packed books recount the most important events of World War II. They take you into battle and present portraits of brave men and true stories of gallantry in action. All books have special maps, diagrams, and illustrations.

☐	12657	**AS EAGLES SCREAMED** Burgett	$2.25
☐	12658	**THE BIG SHOW** Clostermann	$2.25
☐	11812	**BRAZEN CHARIOTS** Crisp	$1.95
☐	12666	**THE COAST WATCHERS** Feldt	$2.25
☐	*12664	**COCKLESHELL HEROES** Lucas-Phillips	$2.25
☐	12141	**COMPANY COMMANDER** MacDonald	$1.95
☐	12578	**THE DIVINE WIND** Pineau & Inoguchi	$2.25
☐	*12669	**ENEMY COAST AHEAD** Gibson	$2.25
☐	*12667	**ESCORT COMMANDER** Robertson	$2.25
☐	*11709	**THE FIRST AND THE LAST** Galland	$1.95
☐	*11642	**FLY FOR YOUR LIFE** Forrester	$1.95
☐	12665	**HELMET FOR MY PILLOW** Leckie	$2.25
☐	12663	**HORRIDO!** Toliver & Constable	$2.25
☐	12670	**THE HUNDRED DAYS OF LT. MACHORTON** Machorton	$2.25
☐	*12668	**I FLEW FOR THE FURHER** Knoke	$2.25
☐	12290	**IRON COFFINS** Werner	$2.25
☐	12671	**QUEEN OF THE FLAT-TOPS** Johnston	$2.25
☐	*11822	**REACH FOR THE SKY** Brickhill	$1.95
☐	12662	**THE ROAD PAST MANDALAY** Masters	$2.25
☐	12523	**SAMURAI** Sakai with Caidin & Saito	$2.25
☐	12659	**U-BOAT KILLER** Macintyre	$2.25
☐	12660	**V-2** Dornberger	$2.25
☐	*12661	**THE WHITE RABBIT** Marshall	$2.25
☐	*12150	**WE DIE ALONE** Howarth	$1.95

*Cannot be sold to Canadian Residents.

Buy them at your local bookstore or use this handy coupon:

Bantam Book Catalog

Here's your up-to-the-minute listing of over 1,400 titles by your favorite authors.

This illustrated, large format catalog gives a description of each title. For your convenience, it is divided into categories in fiction and non-fiction——gothics, science fiction, westerns, mysteries, cookbooks, mysticism and occult, biographies, history, family living, health, psychology, art.

So don't delay——take advantage of this special opportunity to increase your reading pleasure.

Just send us your name and address and 50¢ (to help defray postage and handling costs).

BANTAM BOOKS, INC.
Dept. FC, 414 East Golf Road, Des Plaines, Ill. 60016

Mr./Mrs./Miss_____
(please print)

Address_____

City_____State_____Zip_____

Do you know someone who enjoys books? Just give us their names and addresses and we'll send them a catalog too!

_____

Mr./Mrs./Miss_____

Address_____

City_____State_____Zip_____

_____

Mr./Mrs./Miss_____

Address_____

City_____State_____Zip_____

FC—9/78